The City Lament

The City Lament

Jerusalem across the Medieval Mediterranean

Tamar M. Boyadjian

Cornell University Press
Ithaca and London

First published 2018 by Cornell University Press

Printed in the United States of America

Library of Congress Cataloging-in-Publication Data

Names: Boyadjian, Tamar M., author.
Title: The city lament : Jerusalem across the medieval Mediterranean / Tamar M. Boyadjian.
Description: 1st edition. | Ithaca [New York] : Cornell University Press, 2018. | Includes bibliographical references and index.
Identifiers: LCCN 2018017270 (print) | LCCN 2018028968 (ebook) | ISBN 9781501730856 (epub/mobi) | ISBN 9781501730863 (pdf) | ISBN 9781501730535 (cloth : alk. paper)
Subjects: LCSH: Laments—Mediterranean Region—History and criticism. | Jerusalem—In literature. | Crusades—First, 1096–1099—In literature. | Crusades in literature. | Cities and towns in literature.
Classification: LCC PN1389 (ebook) | LCC PN1389 .B69 2018 (print) | DDC 809.1/9358569442—dc23
LC record available at https://lccn.loc.gov/2018017270

To my family

Contents

Illustrations

Acknowledgments

For over a decade, the subject of medieval lamentation has been on my mind. The idea for this book came from the desire to understand how other cultures translated the loss of their land, and spaces deemed sacred to them. As someone whose grandparents and parents were deported from their home and could no longer claim a "homeland," I started to examine more closely what it meant in the medieval Mediterranean world to mourn the loss of fallen cities. I came to find that despite differences, many ethnoreligious groups reflected on this matter similarly in their literary traditions. They had to find ways to understand the circumstances of their displacement, to outline a history and connection to a particular land, and to think about a future that did not exclude this space in their literary imaginations.

I am indebted to the continuous support and encouragement of my family, friends, and colleagues without whom this book would not be possible. Among these I would like to especially thank those for more than a decade let me continuously expound upon my ideas about the project: Myrna

Douzjian, Lilit Keshishyan, Talar Chahinian, Heitor Loureiro, Bedross Der Matossian, and Tsolin Nalbandian. I am further appreciative of Ani Nahapetian, Ani Kasparian, Rita Hajjar, Lena Buchakjian, Adam Goeman, Dzovinar Derderian, and Roger Kupelian for their supportive friendship. Thank you also to those who read and commented on portions of the manuscript. I appreciated the input of Suzanne Akbari, Awad Awad, Karla Mallette, Kathryn Babayan, Michael Companeou, Cameron Cross, Carole Hillenbrand, Adnan Husain, Gerard Libaridian, Peggy McCracken, Ann Suter, Karla Taylor, and Michael Pifer. To Marc Nichanian, I am grateful for your mentorship, your friendship, and for always challenging me to be the best writer and scholar I can be.

I have also many institutions to thank for their support, encouragement, and generosity during the process of writing this book. As a graduate student at UCLA, I benefited greatly from the questions and comments of Rosie Aroush, Ali Behdad, David Bennett, Chris Chism, Mossimo Ciavollela, Micheal Cooperson, Matthew Fisher, Richard Hovannisian, Shushan Karapetian, Katherine McCloone, Yona Sabar, Ara Soghomonian, Zrinka Stahuljak, Sara Torres, and to others whom I apologize not including here. Thank you also to my former supervisor Theo Maarten van Lint of Oxford University. I also wish to thank my Michigan State University colleagues and friends. I am indebted greatly to the support of my former and current chairs Patrick O'Donnell, David Stowe, and Cara Cilano, as well as that of Stephen Arch, David Bering-Porter, Tamara Butler, Steve Deng, Yomaira Figueroa, Juliette Guzzetta, Kenneth Harrow, Salah Hassan, Gary Hoppenstand, Mohammad Khalil, Sandra Logan, Ellen McCallum, Scott Michaelson, Ruth Mowry, Justus Nieland, Natalie Phillips, Robin Silbergleid, Eswaran Pillai Swarnavel, Judith Stoddart, and Josh Yumibe. To my medieval partner in crime in the department, Morgot Valles, thank you for your continous advice and friendship. I also especially thank Zarena Aslami and Jyotsna Singh for their mentorship, guidance, and support throughout my career at MSU.

Thanks to all individuals and audiences that heard presentations of partial versions and sections from this book at academic conferences. I appreciated all your feedback and questions, which helped to clarify and refine my ideas. I especially would like to acknowledge Sharon Kinoshita and Brian Catlos and their organized Mediterranean seminars, which benefited me greatly as both a presenter and an auditor. Thank you also the Armenian

Studies Program at the University of Michigan and their affiliated faculty for their support, especially to Kathryn Babayan for organizing a roundtable to workshop this book. The financial support of the Comparative Literature department at UCLA and the English department at MSU have also been an integral part of bringing this book to fruition. I also wish to thank Mahinder Kingra at Cornell University Press, along with all the others who contributed their time and expertise to this project.

Thank you to my parents, Ani and Vartkes Boyadjian, for instilling the love of art, music, and literature in my heart; to my grandmother Hripsime, for her smile, for French and etiquette lessons, and for her love; to my grandfather Guiragos for his stories, songs, and mandolin; to my brother Zohrab, for his guidance and encouragement of my dreams; to my sister Maral, who is an inspiration; and to Patricia Doer for her continuous love and reassuring support.

I would like to dedicate this book to Raffi and Daniel, who inspire me, and have always loved and supported me through all my personal and academic endeavors, including the journey of writing this book; to the beautiful Ayana and Giles for their motivating vivacity and splendor; and to my partner, Grag, whose immaculate artistry forever moves me, and whose contagious laugh, positivity, and encouragement constantly remind me of why I continue to engage in my passion for art and literature.

This book is in memory of Tamar Abkarian and Garo Madenlian.

Abbreviations

CCSL	Corpus Christianorum Series Latina. 176 vols. Turnhout, Belgium: Brepols, 1954–65.
NPNF	Nicene and Post-Nicene Fathers. Edited by Phillip Schaff. Series 1, 14 vols.; series 2, 14 vols. Edinburgh: T. & T. Clark, 1886–1900.
PG	Patrologia Graeca. Edited by J.-P. Migne. 161 vols. Paris: Apud Garnier Fratres and J.-P. Migne Successores, 1857–1866.
PL	Patrologia Latina. Edited by J.-P. Migne. 221 vols. Paris: Apud Garnier Fratres and J.-P. Migne Successores, 1841–65.
PPTS	Palestine Pilgrims' Text Society. 13 vols. London: London Committee of the Palestine Exploration Fund, 1896–97.
RHC Doc. Arm.	Recueil des Historiens des Croisades: Documents Arméniens. Edited by Académie des Inscriptions et

	Belles-Lettres. 2 vols. Paris: Imprimerie Nationale, 1869, 1906.
RHC Occ.	Recueil des Historiens des Croisades: Historiens Occidentaux. Edited by Académie des Inscriptions et Belles-Lettres. 5 vols. Paris: Imprimerie Nationale, 1844–95.
RHC Or.	Recueil des Historiens des Croisades: Historiens Orientaux. Edited by Académie des Inscriptions et Belles-Lettres. 5 vols. Paris: Imprimerie Nationale, 1872–1906.

Note on Translation and Transliteration

All translations of primary sources in this book are indicated as either my own or from editions referenced in the chapters.

I have provided the original language when referencing primary sources, but have transliterated all other terms.

Arabic letters have been romanized according to the *International Journal of Middle East Studies* system of transliteration; Armenian letters have been romanized according to the Hübschmann-Meillet system of transliteration.

For citations of secondary sources, the transliteration system used by the works' translators has been retained.

The City Lament

Introduction

A Wasteland Translated

What is that sound high in the air
Murmur of maternal lamentation
Who are those hooded hordes swarming
Over endless plains, stumbling in cracked earth
Ringed by the flat horizon only
What is the city over the mountains
Cracks and reforms and bursts in the violet air
Falling towers
Jerusalem Athens Alexandria
Vienna London
Unreal

—T. S. Eliot, *The Waste Land*[1]

The "Murmur of maternal lamentation," the lament for the "city over the mountains," the "Falling towers" of places that once were: these carry the memories of a cultural past now transformed. That which once was and may never be again—Jerusalem, the wasteland.

T. S. Eliot's poem *The Waste Land* embarks on the journey that loosely follows the medieval legend of the Holy Grail and its wounded guardian, the Fisher King—whose impotence and illness metaphorically reflect the infertility and suffering of his own kingdom, which has turned into a barren

1. T. S. Eliot, *The Waste Land*, ed. Michael North, Norton Critical Editions (New York: Norton 2001), lines 366–76.

wasteland.[2] The poem's theme of life and death are symbolically channeled through the contrast between desolated space and the space of the city, both functioning as wastelands to those who attempt to inhabit them. And when the poem speaks of the "nightingale / Filled all the desert with inviolable voice / And still she cried and still the world pursues,"[3] it references Philomēlē—the raped "princess of Athens" who becomes transformed through suffering into the nightingale, and whose violation becomes the "inviolable voice" that laments the physical and metaphorical death of land and cities.[4]

Eliot's *The Waste Land* incorporates in its narrative many elements similar to the ritual of laments—and specifically those composed and devoted to the loss and destruction of a particular city or space. The wasteland, comparable to ruined and barren cities after war and destruction, stands as a symbolic emblem for infertile lands, thirsty for the vivacious water of healing, for the renewal that can arrive through translating that space into literature, in lamentation.[5] The afflicted land is connected to an overlord—here, the Fisher King—whose curse of impotence can only be lifted through the ap-

2. The figure of the Fisher King appears for the first time in Chrétien de Troyes's unfinished twelfth-century romance, *Perceval le Gallois*, though it is originally believed to be borrowed from Celtic tradition as part of the motif of a barren land whose curse must be lifted by a hero. In the legend, Perceval's silence in inquiring about the nature of\the Holy Grail\ and the bleeding lance during a feast at the disabled Fisher King's castle subsequently results in the Fisher King's wound remaining unhealed and Perceval embarking on the quest for the grail. The legend develops through the Middle Ages in Wolfram von Eschenbach's *Parzival,* Marie de France's *Lanval*, Robert de Boron's *Joseph d'Arimanthie*, Thomas Malory's *Le Morte d'Arthur*, and other works. Though the significance of the grail is not specified in Chrétien's *Perceval*, the *graal* (Old French, "cup" or "vessel") later came to be interpreted in continuations of the text by other authors as the chalice used by Jesus during the Last Supper. Note also that the grail legend in its archetypal pattern does not belong solely to a Christian or European tradition but develops from Celtic, Greek, and Persian origins—in the latter case, the Cup of Jamshīd, which we find in the epic poem *Shāhnāmeh*, among other places.

3. Eliot, *The Waste Land*, lines 100–103.

4. Φιλομήλη (Philomēlē) is a figure in Greek mythology who is transformed into a nightingale after being raped and mutilated by her sister's husband Tereus. In his notes to *The Waste Land* Eliot refers to the story of Tereus and Philomela, as told in Ovid's *Metamorphoses*, book 6. Eliot, *The Waste Land*, 22.

5. Eliot's notes open with the following: "Not only the title, but the plan and a good deal of the incidental symbolism of the poem were suggested by Miss Jessie L. Weston's book on the Grail Legend: *From Ritual to Romance* (Cambridge)." See Eliot, *The Waste Land*, 21. In her study Weston traces the roots of Arthurian legends from pagan to Christian rituals, and attempts to connect the grail legend to pagan fertility rituals. See Jessie L. Weston, *From Ritual to Romance* (Cambridge: Cambridge University Press, 1920).

pearance of a knight expected to decipher those symbols presented to him. But the knight fails. And the "no-thing" of the wasteland becomes filled with memory and desire, inscribed through textual, ritualistic, and cultural references in the poem—from traditions of both the East and West. Life and meaning are engraved upon the dead sculpture of the city, chiseled into it with words and poetic sorrow. But a poem that is to engage in lamentation cannot simply construct itself on ancient myth; that tradition must also reinvent that myth.

This book will explore how various ethnoreligious cultures across the medieval Mediterranean world lamented the loss of the city of Jerusalem, and in what ways these lamentations are informed by reinscribing models of ancient city laments. This book argues that as a result of the contested nature of the city during the battles more commonly (and problematically) referred to as the Crusades, medieval laments over Jerusalem were produced across a number of literary traditions—Arabo-Islamic, Cilician Armenian, and the Latin West—that posited their own contemporary social and political circumstances within an established exemplum of the city lament. This book demonstrates how these lamentations are modeled specifically on Jewish conceptions of lamenting Jerusalem in the Tanakh, or Hebrew Bible, as well as through the poetic traditions respective to each individual ethnoreligious culture. In producing these city laments, each culture furthers its political objectives of reconquering the city by envisaging its own Jerusalem through a textually surrogate geography also informed by the theological and spiritual tradition of the significance of the city for that particular faith. The form and content of these lamentations also informs us of how different cultures imagined Jerusalem. Since these laments appear during moments where the city is contested, they further enable each tradition to allow its own Jerusalem to live anew—through the very paradoxical discussion of its loss and destruction in lamentation.

City laments date back to the ancient Mediterranean world. Dirges formulated over the fall of cities place the voice of lamentation in a city's tutelary goddess—the same goddess who upon abandoning the city and its population brings about the fall and destruction of that city. Some of the most well-recognized city lamentations come from ancient Mesopotamia—one of which is the Sumerian "Lament for Ur" composed as a result of the fall of the city-state Ur to the ancient pre-Iranic Elamites around 2000 BCE.[6] The Akkadian epic poem *Gilgameš* also includes references to the lamenting people of Uruk in tablet 8, who together with the hero Gilgameš wail over the death of Enkidu—a wild man created by the protecting gods to stop Gilgameš from oppressing the people of the city.[7] Homer's ancient Greek epic, the *Iliad*, could even be considered a tale whose overarching frame narrative circles around the destruction of Troy, a city that has been abandoned by its gods. Homer's *Odyssey* is also in some ways a reflective lamentation of Troy, as Odysseus journeys to return home to his "fallen" city. In book 8, Odysseus is described as melting into tears after the bard, Demodocus, sings of how "Troy was fated to perish," and the "death and slaughter bearing down on Troy."[8] Further examples from the ancient world include Euripides's tragedy *Trojan Women*; the Roman epic poem by Lucan, *Pharsalia* (also known as *Bellum Civile*); Aelius Aristides's oration delivered in Rhodes after a devastating earthquake that raged the city in 142 CE; and Aeschylus's tragedy *The Persians*. These are, of course, only a handful of examples of

6. Four other Sumerian city lamentations also survive from the same period, preserved in ancient Babylonian copies: the "Lament for Eridu"; the "Lament for Nippur"; the "Lament for Sumer and Ur"; and the "Lament for Uruk." For a detailed outline and discussion of the structural and thematic characteristics of Mesopotamian city laments, see Paul Wayne Ferris Jr., *The Genre of the Communal Lament in the Bible and the Ancient Near East* (Atlanta: Scholars Press, 1992), 17–62; Stephen Langdon, *Sumerian and Babylonian Psalms* (Paris: Geuthner, 1909); Stephen Langdon, *Babylonian Liturgies* (Paris: Geuthner, 1913); and Heinrich Zimmern, *Babylonische hymnen und gebete, zweite auswähle* (Leipzig: Hinrichs, 1911).

7. At the end of the epic, when a violent storm arrives in tablet 11, and the tutelary goddess Ištar and the other gods depart, the inhabitants engage in lamentation over Uruk, along with Gilgameš, who "sat down and wept, / down his cheek his tears were coursing." See *The Epic of Gilgamesh*, trans. Andrew George (London: Penguin, 1999), 62–69; 99 (tablet 11, lines 309–10). This translation includes the Old Babylonian tablets, which have been used to construct the standard version of the epic, as well as the translation of fragments later discovered from archeological digs dating to 2000 BCE.

8. Homer, *Odyssey*, trans. Robert Fagles (London: Penguin, 1996), 207–8 (book 8, lines 573, 576). Homer differentiates two ancient Indo-European terms for lament, according to the manner of performance and relationship to the deceased. A lament performed by a female member of kin or close friend, and spontaneous in nature, is γόος (*góos*); see for example, *Iliad*, 18.51. Θρηνωδία (*threnodia*) is the Greek term for a song of mourning composed for the dead by those who are not members of kin or are hired mourners. The major source for discussing the lament tradition in ancient Greek and Roman society is Margaret Alexiou, *The Ritual Lament in the Greek Tradition* (Cambridge: Cambridge University Press, 1974), esp. 102–28; see also Richard A. Hughes, *Lament, Death, and Destiny*, Studies in Biblical Literature 68 (New York: Lang, 2004), 11–26.

many city lamentations that appear across different ethnoreligious cultures in the ancient Mediterranean world.[9]

The focus of this book, however, is those city laments composed over the loss of Jerusalem in the medieval Mediterranean world. The extant works discussed in this book pivot around two focal points in the history of the city during the period that most scholars refer to as the First Crusade—the capture of Jerusalem by the Franks in 1099 CE, and the Third Crusade, or Kings' Crusade—initiated as a reaction to the capture of the city of Jerusalem by Ṣalāḥ al-Dīn in 1187 CE. These crusades advanced conflict and contact between various ethnoreligious groups across the medieval Mediterranean; they also produced a number of laments over the loss of cities and principalities that became spaces of contestation between the invading western powers, various Muslim groups of the region, and the Armenians, Greeks, and Jews who were already living there. Isaac bar Shalom's "There Is No One Like You among the Dumb" records in 1147 CE the destruction of a Jewish community during the Second Crusade who refused the crusaders' demands of converting to Christianity.[10] The sack of Constantinople by the Franks in 1204 CE during the Fourth Crusade also produced an elaborate and rhetorical lament by Niketas Choniates, a Byzantine Greek government official and historian who was present during the fall of the city.[11] Niketas's brother, Michael Choniates, the archbishop of Athens in the last quarter of the twelfth century, composes a city lament in the same year on the conquest of Athens by the Franks.[12] An interesting city lamentation also appeared shortly

9. For an extensive study of city laments in the ancient world, see Ann Suter, ed., *Lament: Studies in the Ancient Mediterranean and Beyond* (Oxford: Oxford University Press, 2008); and Mary R. Bachvarova, Dorota Dutsch, and Ann Suter, eds., *The Fall of Cities in the Mediterranean: Commemoration in Literature, Folk-Song, and Liturgy* (Cambridge: Cambridge University Press, 2016).

10. William Morrow, "The Revival of Lament in Medieval *Piyyuṭîm*," in *Lamentations in Ancient and Contemporary Contexts*, ed. Nancy C. Lee and Carleen Mandolfo (Atlanta: Society of Biblical Literature, 2008), 139–50, which includes the original Hebrew text and an English translation by Morrow (146–50). See also William Morrow, *Protest against God: The Eclipse of a Biblical Tradition*, Hebrew Bible Monographs 4 (Sheffield, England: Sheffield Phoenix, 2006); and Jakob J. Petuchowski, *Theology and Poetry: Studies in the Medieval Piyyut* (London: Routledge and Kegan Paul, 1978).

11. [Niketas Choniates,] *Nicetae Choniatae Historia*, ed. Immanuel B. Bekker (Bonn: Weber, 1835), 763–67.

12. S. Lambros, *Μιχαήλ Ακομινάτου τοῦ Χωνιάτου τά σωζόμενα*, vol. 2 (1879–80); repr. Groningen, Netherlands: Verlag Bouma's Boekhuis N.V., 1968.

after the invasion of Hungary by the Tatars of Batu Xan. A monk in service of King Béla IV composed a lament in 1242 CE for the destruction of Hungary; his *Planctus destructionis regni Hungariae per Tartaros* builds on the common theme of ancient Mesopotamian city laments, such as attributing the fall of Hungary to the sins of the inhabiting population.[13]

A limited number of surviving lamentations over Jerusalem exist from this period and center around these two moments in early crusading history where the status of Jerusalem changed hands between various ethnoreligious groups. Though Byzantine Jerusalem was conquered and ruled by different Arabo-Islamic powers from the early seventh century onward, early Latin chronicles of Pope Urban II's famous call to crusade present the city as a lamented space for the Christian believer, imagining a future Latin Christian Jerusalem. The resulting conquest in 1099 CE by the crusading powers produced a lamentation over the city by the Arabic poet Ibn al-Abīwardī, who called for Muslim unity in recapturing Jerusalem. And in the anticipation of the Kings' Crusade after the loss of the city to Ṣalāḥ al-Dīn in 1187 CE, the Armenian high patriarch Grigor Tłay wrote his lamentation over the capture of Jerusalem. The inability of the Kings' Crusade to secure Jerusalem into Latin Christian hands also resulted, however, in narratives of lament, such as that of Richard I of England, or Richard the Lionheart, upon his departure of the city in the anonymous chronicle the *Itinerarium Peregrinorum*.

The medieval Mediterranean world was consumed with wars over territories, principalities, and cities. Mediterranean cities changed hands among rulers, cultures, and sometimes even within the same ethnoreligious group, despite the historical representation of the Crusades by a majority of Western scholars as battles purely between Christianity and Islam. The term *crusade* generally conjures up the image of devout medieval Christian knights marching on Jerusalem to fight for their faith against a forcefully unified Muslim

---

13. The poem has been preserved in a single fourteenth-century manuscript at the Royal State Archives in Wrocław, Poland. See "Planctus destructionis regni Hungariae per Tartaros," ed. Juhász Lászlo, in *Scriptores Rerum Hungaricarum*, vol. 2, ed. Imre Szentpétery (Budapest: Academia Litter. Hungarica, 1937), 589–98. Two historiographic works lamenting the loss of Hungary to the Mongols also appear around this time. The first is included in the *Gesta Hungarorum*, the oldest extant account of the history of the Hungarians by the anonymous notary of King Béla. The second is *Carmen Miserabile super Destructione Regni Hungariae per Tartaro* by the Italian prelate Roger of Torre Maggiore, or Master Roger; see Rogerius, *Carmen Miserabile super Destructione Regni Hungariae per Tartaro, in* Szentpétery, ed., *Scriptores Rerum Hungaricarum*, 11:543–88.

unit. The historical reality was, of course, far more complex than this. In fact, scholars attribute the success of the capture of Jerusalem in 1099 CE by the European Franks to the very disunity of the Arabo-Islamic world. European participants and authors of the period did not generally refer to these events as crusades. The term did not exist in Europe until the thirteenth century, and in the English language as a borrowing from the French.[14] These wars were often referred to by the Latin *bellum dei* (war of God), *negotium dei* (business of God), *passagium* (passage), *iter* (journey), and *peregrinatio* (pilgrimage).[15] What these terms reveal to us is that the focus of crusading was the journey, a movement for the salvation of the believer, a pilgrimage armed by the faith of its soldiers. However, crusading was not universal throughout western Europe. The idea encompasses geographic and ethnic diversity among the many groups of pilgrims who undertook the journey. The term *crusading* presents itself through theological contradictions as the simultaneous embodiment of secular and religious activity, the political through ritualistic movement.

This range of medieval crusading activity came to be simplified through rigid definitions of what constituted a crusade—all of which moves us further away from the cultural and linguistic interconnectiveness of the period. The term *crusade*, from the French *croisade* (literally, the "one bearing the cross"), has come to represent an understanding of campaigns of western Europeans conducted roughly between the late eleventh and the fourteenth centuries due to religious, political, and economic motivations.[16] The application of

14. James A. Brundage, "'Cruce Signari': The Rite for Taking the Cross in England," *Traditio* 22 (1966): 289–310; Kenneth Pennington, "The Rite for Taking the Cross in the Twelfth Century," *Traditio* 30 (1974): 429–35; Michael Markowski, "*Crucesignatus*: Its Origins and Early Usage," *Journal of Medieval History* 10 (1984): 157–65.

15. See, for example, Jonathan Riley-Smith, *What Were the Crusades?* (San Francisco: Ignatius, 2009), 1–8; and Christopher Tyerman, *The Invention of the Crusades* (Basingstoke, Hampshire : Macmillan Press, 1998), 49–55.

16. Whether Jerusalem was the central goal of the Crusades is a point of contestation among historians of the Crusades even today. The German historian Carl Erdmann, noted particularly for his study of the origins of the Crusades in western Europe, argues in his *Die Entstehung des Kreuzzugsgedankens* (Stuttgart: Kohlhammer, 1955) that Jerusalem was a secondary goal, a lure to appeal to all aspects of medieval society—the layperson and the religious person alike—as part of a growing "papal militarism" prior to the First Crusade, which, according to Erdmann, established an ideology that supported the crusading movement toward the Orient. Crusading scholars either agree or argue against Erdmann's claim. See for example, H. E. J. Cowdrey, "Pope Urban II's Preaching of the First Crusade," *History* 55 (1970): 177–88; and E. O. Blake, "The Formation of the 'Crusade Idea,'" *Journal of Ecclesiastical History* 21 (1970): 11–31.

the term *crusade*, and of crusading history and literature, also represents a limited scope in that it confines our understanding of the wars over Jerusalem (in the late eleventh to late twelfth centuries) to western Europe and the views of a European, Latin Christian Occident toward and in conflict with an Islamic Orient. These types of partial, hierarchical, and preferential approaches have contributed to the understanding of this period traditionally as solely antagonistic: Occident versus Orient, Christian versus Muslim, European versus non-European. The Crusades have been presented by a large number of scholars as battles purely between Christianity and Islam—an approach often reflective of the current political climate and used as symbols for national identities.

This strictly dualistic approach is one that views cultures and their textual narratives in continual conflict rather than exploring these ethnoreligious interactions as collaborative and interdependent. Many of the texts from this period have also generally been read against one another rather than as literary works informed from some of the same cultural, geographic, and linguistic realities. This book challenges these types of limited and anachronistic approaches to the period by considering sources in their original languages as analogous creations that contribute to a larger study of the genre of lament in the medieval Mediterranean world. Rather than framing its analyses within the context of individually defined hegemonic and national discourses (i.e., that of France, the Islamic Empire, Latin Christendom, etc.), the book considers lamentations composed over the loss of the city of Jerusalem within the larger trajectory of the city lament tradition and the imagination of Jerusalem across the medieval Mediterranean.

In their watershed study, Peregrine Horden and Nicholas Purcell paradoxically argue for the unity of the Mediterranean precisely in its inherent fragmentation: principalities and polities that were diverse in ethnicity and religion but integrated culturally and politically.[17] The process of acculturation

17. Peregrine Horden and Nicholas Purcell, *The Corrupting Sea: The Study of Mediterranean History* (Malden, MA: Blackwell, 2000). See also Peregrine Horden and Sharon Kinoshita, eds., *A Companion to Mediterranean History*, Wiley Blackwell Companions to World History (Malden, MA: Wiley Blackwell, 2014); Adnan A. Husain and K. E. Fleming, *A Faithful Sea: The Religious Cultures of the Mediterranean, 1200–1700* (Oxford: Oneworld, 2007); Stephen O'Shea, *Sea of Faith: Islam and Christianity in the Medieval Mediterranean World* (New York: Walker, 2006); Brian A. Catlos, *Muslims of Medieval Latin Christendom, c. 1050–1614* (Cambridge: Cambridge University Press, 2015).

and exchange operates within antagonistic but also collaborative enterprises in this period, and it is this very framework that allows us to look at individual representations of Jerusalem, which collectively amalgamate to form a larger understanding of the recursive image of the city across the medieval Mediterranean world. Using the Mediterranean, rather than the Crusades, as a framework for analysis encourages readings that move beyond European realities; such readings recognize reciprocal exchanges and commonalities across cultures in the period and acknowledge the significance of the impact of Mediterranean networks on literary works that have only been considered within national frameworks in the past.[18]

This book also builds on scholarship in the field of medieval literature and Mediterranean studies that attempts to bridge the gaps between confined readings of the Crusades and their relationship to the eastern world.[19] The scale and scope of this book attempts to shift those discourses in a field, which primarily center their discussions on representations of Jerusalem in crusading narratives between the East and the West. Most of these works contextualize their arguments as reactions to larger orientalist discourses of the nineteenth century that focused solely on a western European frame for discussing the battles over Jerusalem (and in the area of the Levant in the late eleventh to twelfth centuries). By focusing on lyrical and poetic lamentations

18. For more on the framework of the Mediterranean for the medieval scholar, see Sharon Kinoshita, "Medieval Mediterranean Literature," *PMLA* 124, no. 2 (2009): 602. For her work on the Mediterranean and French romances, see Sharon Kinoshita, *Medieval Boundaries: Rethinking Difference in Old French Literature* (Philadelphia: University of Pennsylvania Press, 2013).

19. Western historians of the Crusades such as Norman Housley, Thomas Madden, Helen Nicholson, Jonathan Riley-Smith, and Christopher Tyerman have produced a large body of scholarship that interrogates the question of crusading and its relationship with the East. Some recent Scholarship in the field that advances intercultural studies in the Mediterranean world includes Suzanne Conklin Akbari, *Idols in the East: European Representations of Islam and the Orient, 1100–1450* (Ithaca, NY: Cornell University Press, 2009); Suzanne Yeager, *Jerusalem in Medieval Narrative* (Cambridge: Cambridge University Press, 2008); Lee Manion, *Narrating the Crusades: Loss and Recovery in Medieval and Early Modern English Literature* (Cambridge: Cambridge University Press, 2014); and Suzanne Conklin Akbari and Karla Mallette, eds., *A Sea of Languages: Rethinking the Arabic Role in Medieval Literary History* (Toronto: University of Toronto Press, 2013). For Mallette's work on the literary traditions of the medieval Mediterranean, see Karla Mallette, *The Kingdom of Sicily, 1100–1250: A Literary History* (Philadelphia: University of Pennsylvania Press, 2005); and Karla Mallette, *European Modernity and the Arab Mediterranean* (Philadelphia: University of Pennsylvania Press, 2010). Geraldine Heng, *Empire of Magic: Medieval Romance and the Politics of Cultural Fantasy* (New York: Columbia University Press, 2003); Geraldine Heng, *The Invention of Race in the European Middle Ages* (Cambridge: Cambridge University Press, 2018).

over Jerusalem from across the wider Mediterranean region, I pluralize medieval European narratives and reframe antagonistic readings of the past into ones that enable textual and cultural dialogue among literary traditions that are often treated in insular and isolated fashions. The book is also interested in bringing Armenian and Arabic poetry to those who would otherwise not be exposed to it because of linguistic or archival restrictions.

In its exploration into the ways in which the genre of lament works transculturally, this book reflects on a particular historical moment at which the contested nature of the city of Jerusalem becomes the object of lamentation. The goal here is not to purely trace a genealogy of the genre of the city lament but instead to investigate what happens to the rhetoric of lament when the object of lamentation is the city. The center of my book is Jerusalem: how the city is represented, how cultures mourn the loss of the city, and how lamenting Jerusalem becomes a mirror for perceiving political and religious authority. Most scholarship on city laments tends to draw linguistic or cultural boundaries, and lamentations over cities as part of larger historiographical works are often not considered. Throughout this book, I read city laments as part of the larger literary history of each individual tradition. At the same time, I move beyond the realm of individual and nationalized literatures by considering the ways in which these compositions reframe an already established exemplum of lamenting the loss of Jerusalem in the Hebrew Bible. By reading these different traditions alongside one another (Arabo-Islamic, Latin Christendom, and Armenian), this book hopes to expand on our understandings of the ways in which various ethnoreligious cultures across the medieval Mediterranean lamented cities—specifically Jerusalem.

Chapter 1

Lamenting Jerusalem

How doth the city sit solitary, that was full of people! How is she become as a widow! She that was great among the nations, and princess among the provinces, how is she become tributary! She weepeth sore in the night, and her tears are on her cheeks; she hath none to comfort her among all her lovers; all her friends have dealt treacherously with her, they have become her enemies.

—Lamentation 1:1–2

O Jerusalem, Jerusalem, let us speak of Jerusalem,
let us lament Jerusalem.

The language of lament is universal. The ritual of lament is ancient. Performative laments evoke power in their communal mourning. They allow a community to negotiate their fate with the gods or their own god. As the work of Margaret Alexiou argues, the ancient world not only lamented heroes, gods, and the dead, but fallen cities as well. For Alexiou, the city lament is set apart structurally and thematically from ritual laments devoted to the dead—elements that also find themselves in medieval city lamentations.[1] The lyrical and poetic qualities of lamenting a city become shared over time across many cultures in the Mediterranean world. Common tropes in the form and content of ancient ritual lamentation resurface in the medieval world across multiple ethnoreligious cultures, who in their imagination

1. See Margaret Alexiou, *The Ritual Lament in the Greek Tradition* (Cambridge: Cambridge University Press, 1974), esp. 83–101. Roman ritual lamentations (if studied at all) have been contextualized under the larger umbrella of lamentations in the ancient world, relying on Greek sources as representations of Latin literary realities.

of Jerusalem also rely on their own established traditions of expressing loss and mourning for fallen cities. This book is interested in how medieval cultures across the Mediterranean world lamented the fall of the city of Jerusalem. In order to further examine the commonalities and differences of these city laments for Jerusalem, this chapter sets the framework for discussing lamentation across monotheistic cultures by outlining the qualities of lamenting Jerusalem for eastern and western Christianity, Islam, and Judaism. This chapter further demonstrates how medieval lamentations over Jerusalem draw from structural and thematic tropes of lamenting fallen cities in the Hebrew Bible, which become posited into the contemporary sociopolitical moments of each individual ethnoreligious tradition.

Lamenting Jerusalem in the Hebrew Bible

The medieval lamentations over the loss of Jerusalem discussed in this book have been influenced by thematic, structural, and metaphorical tropes present in city laments of the ancient world, specifically those found in the Hebrew Bible. Though the scholarship on city laments is not extensive, studies of the genre focus on three specific areas of ancient culture: premodern Greece and Rome; Mesopotamian city laments; and lamentations in the Hebrew Bible. A majority of studies on Mesopotamian city laments has also argued for Akkadian and Sumerian texts as precursors to those found in the Hebrew Bible—specifically Ezekiel, Lamentations, and Psalm 137.[2] These explorations have generally been concerned with the structure, language, word patterning, and formal properties of these laments as they compare to earlier Mesopotamian prototypes.[3] I gesture here to ancient city lamentations as both a way of acknowledging the far-reaching history of the genre and of

2. See Donna Lee Petter, *The Book of Ezekiel and Mesopotamian City Laments*, Orbis Biblicus et Orientalis 246 (Göttingen: Vandenhoeck und Ruprecht, 2011); Paul Wayne Ferris Jr., *The Genre of the Communal Lament in the Bible and the Ancient Near East* (Atlanta: Scholars Press, 1992); Randall Heskett, *Reading the Book of Isaiah: Destruction and Lament in the Holy Cities* (New York: Palgrave Macmillan, 2011); Jennie Barbour, *The Story of Israel in the Book of Qohelet: Ecclesiastes as Cultural Memory* (Oxford: Oxford University Press, 2012); and Xuan Huong Thi Pham, *Mourning in the Ancient Near East and the Hebrew Bible* (Sheffield, England: Sheffield Academic, 1999).

3. These lamentations are studied within anthropological, linguistic, or religious contexts and alongside interlinear dialectal Sumerian, Sumero-Akkadian, and Akkadian translations.

demonstrating how early examples of lamenting Jerusalem set a foundation through which the medieval world attempted to comprehend and reflect on the loss of the city. Across many traditions, the rhetorical stance of the city lament reverberate political, theological, and cultural circumstances. Though these qualities are individualized based on the culture producing the lament, there are also a number of shared characteristics when the theme is the city of Jerusalem. The goal of this section is to briefly outline these tropes, as they set a number of foundations for the ways in which the medieval Mediterranean world reconceptualizes its own laments over the loss of Jerusalem. The major themes that are discussed here are the structural qualities of lamenting the loss of a city, the justification for that destruction and possible reconquest, and the feminized city.

F. W. Dobbs-Allsopp's work sets the foundation for the study of lament in the Hebrew Bible by outlining the resemblances and differences (from the perspective of genre analysis) between the city lament form in the Mesopotamian world and that of the book of Lamentations, commonly attributed to a poet or poets in Judah lamenting the destruction of Jerusalem by Nebuchadnezzar II of Babylon in 586 BCE.[4] Dobbs-Allsopp proposes nine common motifs present in the ancient Mesopotamian genre that have influenced lamentations in the Hebrew Bible: (1) subject and mood; (2) structure and poetic technique; (3) divine abandonment; (4) assignment of responsibility; (5) the divine agent of destruction; (6) destruction of the city; (7) the weeping goddess; (8) lamentation; and (9) restoration of the city and the return of the gods.[5] A majority of these categories appear across a number of city laments in the ancient world, which also later maintain themselves in the medieval lamentations over the loss of Jerusalem discussed in this book.

---

4. In the Hebrew Bible, Lamentations appears in the Ketuvim, while in the Christian Old Testament it appears after the book of Jeremiah, with the prophet Jeremiah argued to be its author mostly on the grounds of the reference in 2 Chronicles 35:25 to the prophet composing a lament on the death of King Josiah.

5. F. W. Dobbs-Allsopp, *Weep, O Daughter of Zion: A Study of the City-Lament Genre in the Hebrew Bible* (Rome: Editrice Pontificio Istituto Biblico, 1993), 30–93. Allsopp's study is largely dependent on the genre analysis performed in Alistair Fowler, *Kinds of Literature: Introduction to the Theory of Genre and Mode* (Cambridge, MA: Harvard University Press, 1982). See also Samuel Noah Kramer, "The Weeping Goddess: Sumerian Prototypes of the *Mater Dolorosa*," *Biblical Archaeologist* 46, no. 2 (1983): 69–80; and F. W. Dobbs-Allsopp, "Lamentations from Sundry Angles: A Retrospective," in *Lamentations in Ancient and Contemporary Cultural Contexts*, ed. Nancy C. Lee and Carleen Mandolfo (Atlanta: Society of Biblical Literature, 2008), 14–25.

In ancient Mesopotamian city laments, the loss of a city is attributed to the communal sins of the inhabitants and the subsequent movement of the protecting god or goddess from that city. The Hebrew book of Lamentations, which consists of five separate poems mourning the loss of Jerusalem, similarly attributes the destruction of the city to its sinful population and the movement away from God's law.[6] The relationship between YHWH and the Israelites is understood within the context of a Deuteronomic covenant, where YHWH is the divine suzerain and the Israelites his chosen vassals, who are required to live according to YHWH's commandments (Deut. 28:2–20). This covenant exhibits reciprocity, as YHWH provides protection in exchange for obedience.[7] Breaking the treaty of this covenant is punishable (Exod. 20–23; Lev. 26), as exhibited in Lamentations, where God's wrath has already been carried out. In the first chapter, Jerusalem sits in a state of desolation, contemplating its own disobedience and destruction. In the second chapter, which takes the reader back to the moment of physical destruction, YHWH is described as a divine avenger in connection with the sin and punishment of the people. The third chapter begins with the repercussions (affliction and anguish) on the city and its population as a result of God's wrath, and speaks of hope for the future in the process of exile. The fourth chapter returns to descriptions of the destruction of the city and its people, tracing it once again to their sins. The fifth and final chapter calls for repentance, a plea to not abandon the population forever and to return the city to its people.

Fallen cities in the Hebrew Bible reflect the understanding that exile and destruction are the punishment for disobeying the law. The divine retribution on Sodom and Gomorrah (Gen. 18–19) is an example frequently used in Abrahamic religions to demonstrate the consequences of shameless

---

6. The first four poems of Lamentations are written as acrostics, with twenty-two verses corresponding to the twenty-two letters of the Hebrew alphabet. The third poem consists of sixty-six lines, with each letter beginning every third line. The fifth poem is not written as an acrostic, but also has twenty-two lines.

7. For more on the context of the Deuteronomic covenant, see Adele Berlin, "On Writing a Commentary," in Lee and Mandolfo, eds., *Lamentations in Ancient and Contemporary Cultural Contexts*, 8–10; Adele Berlin, *Lamentations: A Commentary* (Louisville: Westminister John Knox, 2002), 21–22; and Robert Williamson Jr., "Lament and the Arts of Resistance: Public and Hidden Transcripts in Lamentations 5," in Lee and Mandolfo, eds., *Lamentations in Ancient and Contemporary Cultural Contexts*, 67–80.

sinning.[8] Throughout Lamentations there is a plea for attention, a desire to renew one's commitment to the temple and thus to regain access to YHWH's presence, where the mourner hopes to be able to praise God in the future. Lamentations is the mourning that happens when the punishment by God is carried out through what Adele Berlin calls the "paradigm of purity": Israel rejects its inhabitants because their moral impurity has defiled the land.[9]

The symptom of immoral behavior is the fall of the city, the mourning of which also becomes expressed figuratively through the personification of Jerusalem as a morally impure female. This prominent trope—which exists across many ancient city laments—emerges from the tradition in western Semitic cultures of the ancient Near East that considers major cities to be female, divine consorts of the male gods whose sanctuaries they protected.[10] Ezekiel, for example, utilizes the female persona of Jerusalem as YHWH's wife to describe the defilement of the city and the temple through the metaphor of a woman's unfavorable behavior: her infidelity, uncleanness, and idolatry. The defilement of the land also becomes paralleled with the city as a menstruating woman (Ezek. 36:17). The husband's vengeance on the unfaithful wife metaphorically reflects YHWH's instigation of the destruction of Jerusalem to Nebuchadnezzar of Babylon.[11] As Hosea emphasizes, her marriage with Gomer is a metaphor for YHWH and the lamenting people, who as his wife, are lifting up their grieving mother (the city) to her husband (Hosea 2:14–20). Other prominent metaphors include the image of Jerusalem as a widow, a betrayed lover, and a mother bereaved of her children. In Ezra, Jerusalem—the mother of all believers—is presented as a persecuted and barren woman (2 Ezr. 9:38–10:54). And throughout Lamentations, the now desolate Jerusalem is a widow (Lam. 1:1, 5:3), whose sins have left her in filth and uncleanliness: "All that honored her despise her, because they have seen her nakedness" (Lam. 1:8). The female city carries the burden of

---

8. Cf. Ezekiel 16:48–50; Isaiah 1:9–10, 3:9, 13:19–22; Jeremiah 23:14, 49:17–18, 50:39–40; and Lamentation 4:6.

9. Berlin, "On Writing a Commentary," 6. Other moral impurities include, for example, the impure leper (Lam. 4:15), which symbolizes a morally impure leader.

10. Ferris, *The Genre of the Communal Lament*, 35.

11. See Julie Galambush, *Jerusalem in the Book of Ezekiel: The City as Yahweh's Wife* (Atlanta: Scholars Press, 1992); and Laurel Lanner, *Who Will Lament Her? The Feminine and the Fantastic in the Book of Nahum* (New York: Clark, 2006), esp. 58–60.

shame (Lam. 2:13), punished for the sins of her people and only able to express her sorrow through a voice that exists in continuous lamentation.

Jerusalem as a personified female could also arguably be influenced by the prominent role of women in ritual lamentation who negotiated the fate of the city and their community with the ruling deity. Examples include specialized female wailers such as the *taptara*-women who performed the funeral ritual called the *sallis wastais* in the ancient Hittite Kingdom that dominated Anatolia during the second millennium BCE.[12] Roman *praeficae* were also professional women mourners, usually hired by affluent families, who conducted the rituals for the dead, chanting the *nenia* dirge to accompanying pipe music.[13] A study by Mary Bachvarova examines how, in ancient Mesopotamia, male *gala* priests cross-dressed as women to perform lamentations in the Sumerian dialect of *emesal*, or the "tongue of a woman." Eventually women's public performance in lamentation was deemed a threat to the male political hierarchies, which resulted in efforts to control, suppress, and co-opt this mediating power ascribed to women. These efforts also reflect the attempt of men to take over an already established tradition of female practice and a relationship with the gods ascribed solely to the art of women performers.[14]

Nancy R. Bowen examines the phrase used by Ezekiel, "daughters of your people," claiming the reference is an allusion to female prophets in the period.[15] Building on the work of Bowen, Nancy Lee argues for the striking theological and rhetorical impact of an unidentified woman singer's voice—whom she calls the "Jerusalem poet"—in dialogue with the male voice, "Jeremiah."[16] Bachvorova's study also demonstrates how two extant city

---

12. See Ian Rutherford, "'When You Go to the Meadow . . .': The Lament of the *Taptara*-Women in the Hittite *Sallis Wastais* Ritual," in *Lament: Studies in the Ancient Mediterranean and Beyond*, ed. Ann Suter (Cambridge: Cambridge University Press, 2008), 53–69.

13. See Dorota Dutsch, "*Nenia*: Gender, Genre, and Lament in Ancient Rome," in Suter, ed., *Lament*, 258–79.

14. See Mary R. Bachvarova, "Sumerian *Gala* Priests and Eastern Mediterranean Returning Gods: Tragic Lamentation in Cross-Cultural Perspective," in Suter, ed., *Lament*, 18–52.

15. Nancy R. Bowen, "The Daughters of Your People: Female Prophets in Ezekiel 13:17–23," *Journal of Biblical Literature* 118 (1999): 417–33.

16. Nancy C. Lee, *The Singers of Lamentations: Cities under Siege, from Ur to Jerusalem to Sarajevo* (Leiden: Brill, 2002); and Nancy C. Lee, "The Singers of Lamentations: (A)Scribing (De) Claiming Poets and Prophets," in Lee and Mandolfo, eds., *Lamentations in Ancient and Contemporary Cultural Contexts*, 33–46. On the female voice in ancient Israel, see Athalya Brener-Idan, ed., *A Feminist Companion to Exodus to Deuteronomy* (Sheffield, England: Sheffield Aca-

laments from ancient Mesopotamia—the Lament over Ur, and the Lament over Nippur—include passages in the female dialect of *emesal* or "the tongue of women," further attesting to the prominent role of women in the ritual of ancient city lamentations.[17] Examples of men lamenting are also present, such as in Jeremiah 41:5, which narrates the story of eighty men from Shechem, Shiloh, and Samaria who tore their garments, shaved their beards, and lacerated their skin as they made an offering at the house of YHWH in Jerusalem. I bring in these few examples as a way of acknowledging the influence of the ritual practice of lamentations, performed primarily by women, on constructions of city laments and the conceptualization of the laments over Jerusalem in the Hebrew Bible.

Lamentations in the Hebrew Bible also seem to work in a cycle of sin and redemption, a form that also sets a model for later city laments. There are many parallels between Ezekiel's message and that of Jeremiah. Both attribute the failure of the people in their worship of YHWH, predicting the anger and calamity of the city and exile in Babylon. They emphasize individual responsibility and foretell the return from Babylonian captivity. Jerusalem is presented as an abandoned and weeping widow overcome with the miseries of her community, and the misfortunes brought about by their sins. But there is hope for the people through God's response and in the subsequent offerings of vows and public praise for recovery.[18] As David Stowe notes in his study of Psalm 137, the trauma of the Babylonian exile to which the psalm refers "served as a crucible, forcing the Israelites to rethink their relationship

---

demic Press, 1994). Richard A. Hughes, *Lament, Death, and Destiny*, Studies in Biblical Literature 68 (New York: Lang, 2004), 43, also argues that Lamentations was compiled "on the basis of the dirge, city lament, and communal lament traditions, for liturgical uses in public memorial services."

17. Laments and hymns composed in *emesal* by cross-dressed male *gala* priests are attested to in material dating from the ancient Babylonian period (1900–500 BCE). Bachvarova claims the three types of *emesal* laments existed from the Old Babylonian period up until the Neo-Assyrian period: *balags*, *ershemmas*, and *ershahungas*. *Balags*, named after the accompanying *balag* lyre, were lengthy and repetitive compositions contemplating the destructive power inflicted by gods on cities. The *ershemmas* were similar to *balags*, but shorter and more compact in nature. The "wail that pacifies the heart"—the *ershahunga*—had apotropaic functions, personally appealing to the gods through the medium of a priest. See Bachvarova, "Sumerian *Gala* Priests," in Suter, ed., *Lament*, 18–52.

18. Derived from Canaanite and Mesopotamian mythic stories of the struggle of gods against chaos, such as Baal and Marduk, the poetic hymn in Exodus 15:1–21 identifies God as a divine warrior whose conquest against the Egyptians leads to the salvation of the people from chaos. The hymn also sets the foundation for the future establishment of the temple from which God rules his people. See also Isaiah 9:15b–19, and esp. 63:1–6.

to Yahweh, revise their understanding of the covenant, reassess their standing as a chosen people, and rewrite their history."[19]

City laments are spaces of mourning, memory, and reflection. They mirror the people's relationship with themselves and their ruling deity. They are poetic, but also formulaic in a sense. Their temporality works in the realm of past memories that attempt to politically and spiritually shape the future of the city and community. Ancient Mesopotamian city laments and those of the Hebrew Bible include several qualities that maintain themselves in medieval laments over Jerusalem; these include the attribution of the fall of the city due to the sins of the inhabitants; intense and graphic descriptions of the destruction and desolation of the city; and the desire for forgiveness, the return of God, and the eventual reconquest of the city. These categories then become shaped by individual traditions informed by their own respective spiritual, social, and political relationships to Jerusalem.

Jerusalem, the Latin Church, and the Old Testament Book of Lamentations

What are the ways in which the lamenting the city of Jerusalem in the Hebrew Bible came to be interpreted in Christian thought? Christianity's relationship to Jerusalem (and lamentation) was defined throughout the medieval European world through concepts of Jewish identity. As Jeremy Cohen argues, the discourse of Christian theology and their interpretations of scripture were constructed in accordance to a "hermeneutically and doctrinally crafted Jew."[20] Christianity's assertions relied primarily on its polemic confrontation with Judaism and the negation of Jewish belief, through what Daniel Boyarin claims is a "hermeneutics of supersession."[21] Christian super-

19. David W. Stowe, "History, Memory, and Forgetting in Psalm 137," in *The Bible in the Public Square: Its Enduring Influence in American Life*, ed. Mark A. Chancey, Carol Meyers, and Eric M. Meyers, Society of Biblical Literature 27 (Atlanta: SBL Press, 2014), 137–58.

20. See Jeremy Cohen, *Living Letters of the Law: Ideas of the Jew in Medieval Christianity* (Berkeley: University of California Press, 1999), esp. 1–7, 158–65; and Jeremy Cohen, "The Muslim Connection, or, On the Changing Role of the Jew in High Medieval Theology," in *From Witness to Witchcraft: Jews and Judaism in Medieval Christian Thought*, ed. Jeremy Cohen (Wiesbaden: Harrasowitz, 1996), 141–62.

21. See Daniel Boyarin, *A Radical Jew: Paul and the Politics of Identity* (Berkeley: University of California Press, 1997); Daniel Boyarin, *Carnal Israel: Reading Sex in Talmudic Culture* (Berkeley:

sessionism, primarily embedded in an Augustinian and Pauline theology, argued that the new covenant of the Christian church had superseded the Israelites and the Mosaic covenant in the Old Testament. This *Adversus Iudaeos* polemic, which formulated some of the vital theological doctrines of Christianity, also established Christian attitudes toward the city of Jerusalem and Lamentations up until the medieval period. I provide here a brief summary of the conceptualization of Jerusalem in the period leading up to the capture of Jerusalem in 1099 CE by the invading European powers (the First Crusade), whereas the reclassification of the Jew, along with other enemies of the Latin church, promoted discourses of alterity against Muslims and heretics—a thesis developed in the work of Suzanne Akbari.[22] This survey is a necessary context to understanding what I argue are theological shifts in Christian perceptions of Jerusalem following the First Crusade, where the earthly Jerusalem received a higher status than it had in the past and thus became an object of lamentation.

Christianity's connection to Jerusalem in the period leading up to the First Crusade was far from uniform. The foundations of Christian thought had a clear position in regard to the earthly Jerusalem and were based on the Hebrew prophets and apocryphal writing. Christianity's confrontation with Judaism further manifested itself in the ways in which the early Church Fathers constructed their relationship to the city, and in turn the ways in which Jerusalem was represented in western European narratives. Historical circumstances, theological debates, and ecclesiastical policies molded the position toward Jerusalem in the Latin church. As Joshua Prawer notes, "the concept of Jerusalem became part of the transcendentalist theological or philosophical trends in Christian European religion and culture . . . only the name Jerusalem remained, burdened by myriad fantasies and hyperbolic allegories."[23] The status of Jerusalem as a city to be lamented is evident in

---

University of California Press, 1993); and Daniel Boyarin, "'This We Know to Be the Carnal Israel': Circumcision and the Erotic Life of God and Israel," *Critical Inquiry* 18 (1992): 474–505.

22. The work of Suzanne Conklin Akbari builds on that of Cohen; see Suzanne Conklin Akbari, *Idols in the East: European Representations of Islam and the Orient, 1100–1450* (Ithaca, NY: Cornell University Press, 2009), esp. 112–54.

23. Joshua Prawer, "Christian Attitudes towards Jerusalem in the Early Middle Ages," in *The History of Jerusalem: The Early Muslim Period, 638–1099*, ed. Joshua Prawer and Haggai Ben-Shammai (New York: New York University Press, 1996), 312. See also Sylvia Schein, *Gateway to the Heavenly City: Crusader Jerusalem and the Catholic West* (Aldershot, England: Ashgate, 2005), esp. 1–8.

Paul's Epistle to the Hebrews: "For we have here no remaining city, but [that which] we seek to come" (Heb. 13:14).[24]

In Hebrews 12:22–24, the place of the believer in relation to the heavenly city was also clarified. The earthly city was built by humans and therefore had no meaning; in contrast, the Promised Land, or the heavenly Jerusalem, was established by God and therefore was superior. Since the physical Jerusalem housed the tribes of old Israel (Ps. 122:3–4), in Christian thought it had to be replaced by the heavenly or new Israel (Rev. 14:1). Christian exegesis further endeavored to disassociate itself from the centrality of the temple in Judaism and in turn attempted to eliminate the foremost role of the physical Jerusalem, as evident in the two synoptic Gospels of Luke (19:42–44) and Matthew (24:1–2). This elevated status of the heavenly city over the earthly placed a wedge between Jerusalem and its Jewish past and served as a basis for a new understanding of moral and theological concepts pertaining to life, death, and the road to salvation—an attitude prevalent in the book of Revelation.

This antithetical relationship between the heavenly and the earthly city of Jerusalem reveals Christianity's attempts to move away and deny the earthly, Jewish Jerusalem. In Paul's letter to the Galatians, for example (Gal. 4:24–26), the earthly Jerusalem is presented as being in slavery with its children, whereas the heavenly Jerusalem is a mother who is free.[25] The ethereal city represents the Christian realization of Isaiah's prophecy (Isa. 65:17–18) of the new heaven and the new earth, God's dwelling place (Rev. 21:1, 22:3–4), and the locus for the future Jerusalem (Bar. 32:2–6; Rev. 21:9–21; Zech. 8:3).[26]

The adoption of the Pauline doctrine, which relegated the earthly city of Jerusalem to an almost nonexistent entity in Christian thought, led to the belief that the earthly city was solely the city of the Jews. This position, however, held an internal contradiction since Christianity attempted to both inherit the Old Testament (and the essential position of Jerusalem) and reject

24. "Non enim habemus hic manentem civitatem sed futuram inquirimus." The quotation is taken from the Latin Vulgate; my translation.

25. Schein, *Heavenly City*, 3.

26. For a detailed discussion see Schein, *Heavenly City*, 3–4; and Prawer, "Christian Attitudes," 312–14.

it at the same time.[27] This paradox did not allow for the earthly Jerusalem to be completely ignored, and the city eventually reasserted its position in the secular sphere as a destination of pilgrimage and the means through which absolution could be achieved.[28] The presence of buildings and other edifices in the city became symbolically manifested as tangible monuments of a once divine presence because they also represented places connected to the life of Jesus. The physical edifices were translated as proofs of the triumphs of Christianity, and were argued by early theologians as emblems that moved the city from a Jewish past into a Christian-Roman one.

The works of the early Church Fathers and their biblical exegesis further molded and reflected the Christian position toward Jerusalem. Jerome, in fact, defends the status of the earthly Jerusalem and recognizes the city as a significant space where the triumphs of Christianity become visible. He writes how as a result of misunderstandings the earthly city of Jerusalem has been replaced by the heavenly. He criticizes the view that the resurrection of the saints took place in the heavenly Jerusalem (Heb. 12:22). In the preface to his translation of the *Chronicle*, Jerome also advocates pilgrimage to the Holy Land, claiming that those "who have seen Judea with their eyes" will gain clearer insight into the scriptures.[29] However, despite Jerome's opinions about visiting the Holy City, he upholds the attitude that there is no particular

---

27. See Prawer, "Christian Attitudes," 316; Robert Konrad, "Das himmlische und das irdische Jerusalem in mittelalterlichen Denken: Mystische Vorstellungen und geschichtliche Wirkung," in *Speculum historiale, Festschrift J. Spörl*, ed. C. Bauer (Munich, 1965), 523–40; and Adriaan H. Bredero, "Jerusalem in the West," in *Christendom and Christianity in the Middle Ages: The Relations between Religion, Church, and Society*, trans. Reinder Bruinsma (Grand Rapids, MI: Eerdmans, 1994), 259–71.

28. E. D. Hunt, *Holy Land Pilgrimage in the Later Roman Empire* (Oxford: Oxford University Press, 1982); Bernhard Kötting, *Peregrinatio religiosa: Wallfahrten in der Antike und das Pilgerwesen in der alten Kirche* (Münster, West Germany: Regensberg, 1950); John Wilkinson, *Jerusalem Pilgrims: Before the Crusades* (Jerusalem: Ariel, 1977); Steven Runciman, "The Pilgrimages to Palestine before 1095," in *History of the Crusades*, vol. 1, *The First Hundred Years*, ed. Marshall W. Baldwin (Philadelphia: University of Pennsylvania Press, 1955), 68–78. See also the discussion on Christian pilgrimage as a liminal phenomenon in Victor Turner and Edith Turner, *Image and Pilgrimage in Christian Culture* (New York: Columbia University Press, 1978), 1–39, 172–202.

29. "Quomodo Graecorum historias magis intelligunt, qui Athenas viderint . . . ita sanctam Scripturam lucidius intuebitur, qui Judaeam oculis contemplatus est, et antiquarum urbium memorias locorumque vel eadem vocabula, vel mutata cognoverit." *Praefatio Hieronymi in librum Paralipomenon juxta LXX interpretes*, in PL 29, col. 401A. All translations of Jerome's works are my own.

reason to live or pray in Jerusalem since God is everywhere and believers hold the temple within them.[30]

The rejection of pilgrimage to Jerusalem by the church was, however, a belief not supported by the layperson. Pilgrimage was understood as an expression of popular piety, and the Jerusalem of the Jewish past had now become holy again through a Christian supersessionist hermeneutic. As Cyril of Jerusalem argues in his *Catechesis*, it was not the prophecy of Jesus that brought about the temple's destruction, but rather the offenses of the Jews.[31] The destruction of the first Jerusalem became further molded into a symbolic moment foreshadowing the days of the Last Judgment. Jewish traditions pertaining to the Temple Mount were then applied to the Church of the Holy Sepulcher.[32] In his *De vita Constantini*, Eusebius claims that "the monument of salvation itself [the Church of the Holy Sepulcher] was the new Jerusalem built, over again the one so famous of old, after the pollution caused by the murder of the Lord."[33] Pilgrims' accounts of the Holy Land, such as that of Egeria, also reveal both a typological interpretation of Christian sites in Jerusalem and a transfer of meaning from Jewish to Christian ones.[34] Jerusalem came to be recognized as a sacred city in the Christian world

30. "Et de Hierosolymis et de Britannia aequaliter patet aula coelestis; regnum enim intra nos est" (The doors of heaven open equally both in Jerusalem and in Britain; for the kingdom is within us). Hieronymous [Jerome], Epistula 58, in *S. Eusebii Hieronymi Epistulae*, ed. Isidorus Hilberg, Corpus Scriptorum Ecclesiastocorum Latinorum 54 (Leipzig: Akademische Verlagsgesellschaft, 1910), sec. 3. See also Prawer, "Christian Attitudes," 322; and P. W. L. Walker, *Holy City, Holy Places? Christian Attitudes to Jerusalem and the Holy Land in the Fourth Century* (Oxford: Oxford University Press, 1990).

31. [Cyril of Jerusalem,] *S. Cyrilli Hierosolymitani archiepiscopi Catechesis*, in PG 33, bk. 7, chap. 6; bk. 10, chap. 11; bk. 15, chap. 15; Prawer, "Christian Attitudes," 323.

32. See Prawer, "Christian Attitudes," 326–31; and Joshua Prawer, "Jerusalem in Christian and Jewish Perspectives of the Early Middle Ages," in *Settimane di studio del centro Italiano di studi sull'alto medioevo XXVI. Gli Ebrei nell' Alto Medioevo* (Spoleto: Centro italiano di studi sull'alto medioevo, 1980), esp. 740–41. See also Sabine MacCormack, "*Loca Sancta:* The Organization of Sacred Topography in Late Antiquity," in *The Blessings of Pilgrimage*, ed. Robert Ousterhout (Urbana: University of Illinois Press, 1990), 7–40; John Wilkinson, "Jewish Holy Places and the Origins of the Christian Pilgrimage," in Ousterhout, ed., in *The Blessings of Pilgrimage*, 41–53; Sylvia Schein, "Between Mount Moriah and the Holy Sepulchre: The Changing Traditions of the Temple Mount in the Central Middle Ages," *Traditio* 40 (1985): 175–95.

33. [Eusebius], *De vita Constantini*, in PG 20, col. 1094, trans. J. H. Bernard in PPTS 1, 6–7.

34. [Egeria,] *Itinerarium Egeriae*, trans. John Wilkinson as *Egeria's Travels* (London: SPCK, 1971). See also *Breviarius de Hierosolyma*, ed. R. Weber, in *Itineraria et alia Geographica*, CCSL 175; Athanasius [Bishop of Alexandria], *Oratio de Incarnatione verbi*, in PG 25, col. 165.

through a process of reconsecration.[35] With the Muslim conquest of the city in the early seventh century, the Pauline doctrine—which argued for the superiority of the heavenly Jerusalem—asserted itself further.[36] Under Muslim control, Jerusalem became connected to a greater extent to the eschaton and the Apocalypse. Oracles and Christian apocalyptic works began to rise, such as the Syriac apocalypse of Pseudo-Methodius, which speaks of the conquest of the physical city by the Antichrist, and the eventual appearance of a Christian emperor who will transfer the rule of the city to [a Christian] God:

> And afterward [the king of Rome] will come to Jerusalem, and there he will remove from his head the diadem and all his regal clothes, relinquishing the kingdom of Christians to God the father and his son Jesus Christ. And when the empire of the Romans comes to an end, then the Antichrist will reveal himself and will sit in the house of the Lord in Jerusalem.
>
> Et postea veniet [rex Romanorum] Ierusalem, et ibi deposito capitis diademate et omni habitu regali relinquet regnum christianorum Deo patri et Iesu Christo filio eius. Et cum cessaverit imperium Romanum tunc revelabitur manifeste Antichristus et sedebit in domo Domini in Ierusalem.[37]

Christian attitudes toward the city of Jerusalem in the period following the fifth century up to the First Crusade can therefore be summarized as follows: the city, with its many new churches and monuments, became a locus for pilgrimage and marked the presence of a Christian Jerusalem based on a rejection of Jewish practice. As a result of pilgrimage, the city of Jerusalem also became recognized as a sacred city for the European Christian world, and the concept of the eschaton and the Apocalypse became linked to Jerusalem. After the conquest of the city in 638 CE by Caliph ‘Umar ibn al-khaṭṭāb, the considerations of Jerusalem as an earthly city were made even more inferior to its status as heavenly.[38]

Jerusalem's position in Christian thought leading up to the medieval period paralleled the views of the Latin Church toward lamentation. From the

35. Prawer, "Christian Attitudes," 328.

36. See [Rabanus Maurus,] *Rabani Mauri De Universo*, in PL 111, col. 379; Paschasius Radbertus, *Expositio in Matthaeum*, in PL 120; Walafrid Strabo, *De subversione Jerusalem*, in PL 114.

37. [Pseudo-Methodius,] "Die Tiburtinische Sibyllae," in *Sybillinische Texte und Forschungen*, ed. Ernst Sackur (Halle an der Salle, West Germany: Niemeyer, 1963), 186.

38. Prawer, "Christian Attitudes," 323–35.

early patristic period onward, the Catholic Church persisted in associating lamentation with non-Christian behavior. Lamenting a city, and laments in general, were translated by the church as a genre associated with pagan and especially Jewish custom. To lament a city such as Jerusalem was to establish a preference for the physical city over the ethereal. Public lament in sermons and funeral orations was therefore rejected by the early Church Fathers, arguing that true grief should be measured and moderate because believers would reunite in the heavenly afterlife. Lament was, of course, not a practice completely dissolved in the secular realm, as is evident in the Mater Dolorosa (Our Lady of Sorrows), which is depicted in Christian iconography as an anguished Virgin Mary lamenting, or sometimes with seven swords in her heart as indicative of the Seven Sorrows.[39] Mary's silent lamentation is interpreted as a Christian message of penitence and hope.[40]

Christian practices attempted to shift the meaning of death as not an end of life but a deliverance to God. The practice of lamentation—though continued in the secular realm—was believed to act against the understanding that the separation between the living and the dead was temporary.[41] For this reason, Greco-Roman dirges performed by women were considered a form of idolatry. Saint Ambrose publicly repudiates lamentation practices, arguing for their excessively feminine and sexual nature when he describes women tearing open their garments, disheveling their hair with filth, and public displaying their anguish.[42] In his homilies, John Chrysostom describes the performative dirges of women in public lamentation—their wailing, the tearing of their hair, and the intense movement of their arms—as shame-

39. The swords are a reference to the prophecy of Simeon the Righteous (Luke 2:35) at the presentation of Jesus at the temple. The Seven Sorrows of the Virgin Mary (as well as the feast devoted to the same) grew in popularity in the twelfth century. Across the Mediterranean, images of the Mater Dolorosa are carried in the processions preceding Good Friday.

40. See, for example, James S. Amelang, "Mourning becomes Eclectic: Ritual Lament and the Problem of Continuity," *Past and Present* 187 (2005): 3–31.

41. Damien Sicard argues that the Roman order for the dead (including the practice of lamentation) evolved in six stages from the second to the fourth centuries CE. See Damien Sicard, *La liturgie de la mort dans l'église Latine: des origines à la Réforme Carolingienne* (Münster, West Germany: Aschendorff, 1978). See also Hughes, *Lament, Death, and Destiny*, 67–79.

42. Saint Ambrose, "On His Brother Satyrus II," in *Funeral Orations by Saint Gregory Nazianzen and Saint Ambrose*, trans. Roy J. Defarrari, The Fathers of the Church (Washington, DC: Catholic University of America Press, 1968), 202.

ful.[43] In contrast he urges for the rejoicing of death and the honoring of the dead through the singing of the psalms.[44] The orations and scripts of the Cappadocian Fathers, such as Gregory of Nyssa, also supported this critique of lamentation.[45] The Church Fathers, therefore, formulated doctrines that substituted practices of lament (and the negotiation of faith with the gods); they promoted the repressing of the natural practice of grieving. For example, in his *Confessions*, Augustine accepts the difficulty of his mother's death but decides to repress the desire to lament, and instead rejoices through singing the psalms.[46] In his *Life of Solon*, Plutarch claims, "Solon attempted to curb women's disorderly and unbridled expressions of grief by restraining breast-beating and lamentation, and prohibiting them from lacerating their bodies."[47]

Rejection of the practice of lamentation as it pertained to pagan and Jewish origins was further reflected in Christian doctrine through the lack of commentaries and translations of the book of Lamentations. Jewish doctrine read Lamentations not only as a reminder of the original Babylonian destruction of Jerusalem but also as reflective of other catastrophes in Jewish history. Though debated among scholars, the book is predominantly positioned as part of the larger understanding of Jewish suffering and both public and private Jewish devotion.[48] For the Latin church, the book of Lamentations

---

43. St. John Chrysostom, "Homily 62 on the Gospel of John," in *St. Chrysostom: Homilies on the Gospel According to St. John, Hebrews*, NPNF, ser. 1, vol. 14, 230. See also Plato's *Republic*, 3.395d, where he speaks of imitating acts that suppress liberty, such as lamentation, as shameful.

44. For example, "I fear no evil; for you are with me; your rod and your staff—they comfort me" (Ps. 23:4). See also St. John Chrysostom, "Homily 4 on the Epistle of the Hebrews," in *St. Chrysostom: Homilies on the Gospel According to St. John, Hebrews*, NPNF, ser. 1, vol. 14, 382–87; St. John Chrysostom, "Homily 62 on the Gospel of John," 231; and St. John Chrysostom, "Homily 31 on the Gospel of Matthew," in *St. Chrysostom: Homilies on the Gospel According to St. John*, NPNF, ser. 1, vol. 10, 208.

45. See, for example, Gregory of Nyssa, "The Life of Saint Macrina," in *Ascetical Works*, trans. Virginia Woods Callahan, The Fathers of the Church (Washington, DC: Catholic University of America Press, 1999), 170.

46. Augustine, *Confessions*, vol. 2, *Books 9–13*, trans. William Watts, Loeb Classical Library (Cambridge, MA: Harvard University Press, 1979), 9.12.

47. Plutarch, *Lives*, vol. 1, *Theseus and Romulus, Lycurgus and Numa, Solon and Publicola*, trans. Bernadotte Perrin, Loeb Classical Library 46 (Cambridge, MA: Harvard University Press, 1914), 21.5.

48. Robin A. Perry, "Wrestling with Lamentations in Christian Worship," in *Great Is Thy Faithfulness? Reading Lamentations as Sacred Scripture*, ed. Robin A. Parry and Heath A. Thomas (Eugene, OR: Wipf and Stock, 2011), 175–97.

ascribed to Jeremiah was reflective of practices of penitence and asceticism in the face of sin. As Heath Thomas summarizes, Lamentations "fit within the overall approach of patristic interpretation of the [Old Testament]: Christological, prophetic, and oriented toward the life of the church."[49] The tenets of medieval interpretation did not differ greatly in this regard from those of the early patristic period. The book was not central to Christian identity, but was still used for didactic purposes to provide moral guidance for the believer on the themes of penitence, fasting, and mourning. Lamentation 4:20 also served as an important prophetic witness to the coming of Christ. Luke likens Jesus to the prophet Jeremiah, whose rejection by the people had resulted in the fallen fate of the city (Luke 19:41–44). Christ is further compared to Lady Zion (Lam. 1, 2), the destroyed temple (Lam. 2), and the valiant man (Lam. 3).[50] Biblical scholars also translate the lament of Jesus over Jerusalem as the attempt to transfer divine wrath into compassion and deliverance (Matt. 23:37–39). Dating back to the Carolingian period, Lamentations was also used in the office of matins as part of the liturgy of the Holy Week.[51]

As Thomas's study outlines, early patristic commentaries of the Old Testament book of Lamentations were rooted in Greek translations—interpretations of which were primarily influenced by Jerome's translation of the Vulgate, and the readings of Origen, Jerome, and later Gregory the Great.[52] The earliest Christian commentary of Lamentations was that of Origen—a work now lost but reconstructed in part from the translations of Aquila and Symmachus and the Byzantine catenae. In his discussion of

49. Heath A. Thomas, "Lamentations in the Patristic Period," in Parry and Thomas, eds., *Great Is Thy Faithfulness?*, 113.

50. A number of early Church Fathers used Lamentations to speak of repentance over sin when reflecting on the work of Christ, such as Augustine, John Cassian, Eusebius, Gregory the Great, and others.

51. Lamentation 1:1–4 was read on Maundy Thursday, Lamentations 2:8–10 and 3:1–9 on Good Friday, and Lamentations 3:22–30, 4:1–6, and 5:1–11 on Holy Saturday. For more on Lamentations in the medieval church see Edmund Bishop, *Liturgica Historica: Papers on the Liturgy and Religious Life of the Western Church* (Oxford: Clarendon, 1962); John Walton Tyrer, *Historical Survey of Holy Weeks, Its Services and Ceremonial* (Oxford: Oxford University Press, 1932); and Thomas J. Heffernan and E. Ann Matter, eds., *The Liturgy of the Medieval Church*, 2nd ed. (Kalamazoo, MI: Medieval Institute Publications, 2005).

52. Thomas argues that an old Latin text preceded the translation of Jerome and this was the version that Tertullian was dependent on. See Thomas, "Lamentations in the Patristic Period," 114.

Lamentation 1:10, Origen metaphorically reads Jerusalem's captivity to Babylon as the entrapment of the soul, or the church, by demonic power. For Origen, Lamentations becomes instructive for the believer, since God's sanctuary is condemned and corrupted through the invasion of a spiritual sanctuary, Jerusalem. Origen's hermeneutical approach is grounded on the meaning of the text as it relates to the spiritual, and as instructive for the heart of the believer.[53]

Perhaps the most influential interpretation of Lamentations is that of Jerome, and one that dominates the reading of Lamentations among Christian theologians and the Latin church through the medieval period.[54] Jerome completed his translation of the Vulgate between 393 and 406 CE. As part of his translation, he also included significant commentaries and interpretation of the Old Testament. In his preface to the translation of Lamentations, Jerome links the book with the prophet Jeremiah and the fall of the city of Jerusalem—elements absent from the Hebrew tradition. He relies, however, on the acrostic inherent in the original Hebrew to claim that each letter (alef, bet, gimel, dalet, hey, etc.) is a larger symbol for deeper spiritual meaning, governed by a deeper understanding that can direct the reader toward a more intimate spiritual path.[55] As he outlines the seven major spiritual teachings, his work also includes claims that the book of Lamentations reveals the coming of Christ and the spiritual direction of Christian living under God's word. For example, Jerome follows the Greek pattern of translating the word *messiah* as *christos* in Lamentation 4:20 as a reflection

53. For a discussion of the Greek versions of Lamentations, see Kevin J. Youngblood, "The Character and Significance of LXX Lamentations," in Parry and Thomas, eds., *Great Is Thy Faithfulness?*, 64–69. See also Dominique Barthélemey, *Les davancirs d'Aquila*, Vetus Testamentum Supplements 10 (Leiden: Brill, 1963). For an English translation of Origen's commentary, see Joseph W. Trigg, *Origen* (London: Routledge, 1998), 73–85. For a critical edition, see Erich Klosterman, *Die griechischen christlichen Schriftsteller der ersten Jahrhunderte*, vol. 6. (Leipzig: Heinriche, 1901).

54. Jerome's reading of Lamentations can be seen in the medieval commentaries of figures such as Hrabanus Maurus, Paschasius Radbertus, Thomas Aquinas, and Gilbert of Auxerre.

55. Jerome also includes this interpretation in his Letter to Paula (Epistle 30). For both the original Latin and an English translation, see Jerome, "A Letter from Jerome (384)," Columbia Center for New Media Teaching and Learning, http://epistolae.ccnmtl.columbia.edu/letter/278.html. See also Andrew Cain, *The Letters of Jerome: Asceticism, Biblical Exegesis, and the Construction of Christian Authority in Late Antiquity* (Oxford: Oxford University Press, 2009), 81–82.

of the book's Christological and prophetic quality—a general hermeneutic for reading the Old Testament as a whole by the early Church Fathers.[56]

In the medieval period, Gregory the Great also follows the allegorical reading of Lamentations in his *Moralia in Job* as one that reflects spiritual teachings for the Christian believer.[57] Gregory's work is the first extensive treatment of Lamentations in the medieval period.[58] He claims that the book directs the believer to let go of the earthly and await God's kingdom in the heavenly. The suffering of the people who mourn the loss of Jerusalem is linked with the experience of Christ in the Passion. The book is therefore recognized as a prophetic witness to the coming of Christ and the suffering he will endure for the believer—particularly Lamentation 4:20, which speaks of the capture of the Lord's anointed.[59]

For the Christian church, Lamentations also served the function of spiritual formation. The book was reflective of practices of sin and repentance, mourning, and confession. Tertullian reads Lamentation 3:40–41 as an instructive practice for fasting; Augustine reads Lamentation 3:48 in his *Confessions* as an invitation for confession and repentance; John Cassian argues for Lamentation 2:18 as being ruminative of the kind of repentance and sadness that emerges from the sin of humanity. Weeping is seen as an act of penitence to God and a reflection of the state of the sinner. John Chrysostom's "Homily 15" uses Lamentation 3:27 to examine God's ways of shaping spiritual discipline. For Eusebius, Lamentation 2:1–2 shows the reversal of the honorable believer, where God's wrath is a result of the sins of the inhabitants—a common trope in reading Lamentations in both Christian and Hebrew hermeneutics.

The *Gloss Ordinaria* contained what would be the most prominent interpretation of Lamentations in the medieval European world. Informed by the

56. This hermeneutic can be seen in the works of Ambrose, Augustine, Eusebius, Irenaeus, and Rufinus, among others.

57. See, for example, Gregory's interpretation of Lamentation 3:1, in *S. Gregoroii Magni, Moralia in Iob*, ed. Marci Adriaen, CCSL 143–143A; and Gregory the Great, *Morals on the Book of Job*, vols. 1–3, Library of Fathers of the Holy Catholic Church (Oxford: Parker, 1844–50).

58. For interpretations of Lamentations in the medieval period, see David S. Hogg, "Christian Interpretation of Lamentations in the Middle Ages," in Parry and Thomas, eds., *Great Is Thy Faithfulness?*, 120–24.

59. Bertil Albrektson, *Studies in Text and Theology of the Book of Lamentations*, Studia Theologica Lundensia 21 (Lund, Sweden: Gleerup, 1963), 193; Philip S. Alexander, *The Targum of Lamentations*, The Aramaic Bible 17B (Collegeville, MN: Liturgical Press, 2007), 48–49.

work of the Carolingian theologian Paschasius Radbertus, Gilbert the Universal maintained the same hermeneutics of the classic period in the Middle Ages. These included the allegorical and prophetic interpretation the city of Jerusalem as the church, and the coming of Christ and the heavenly kingdom.[60] Gilbert's reading aligns with medieval Christian exegesis, which saw Christ as the center of the Old Testament. Christianity's confrontation with Judaism was to understand the past as a divine precept for the present and future Christian believer. The readings of Tenebrae reflect how Jesus is understood to represent the Jewish people and embodies their stories in himself as a way of redeeming them. This theological belief then links the five books of Lamentations with the figure of Christ, where Jerusalem is read as an allegory for the church. As in Lamentations, the female Jerusalem endures affliction, suffering, nakedness, and public humiliation. Like the city, Jesus was mocked, despised, attacked by a pagan occupying force, and reduced from a noble status to one of loss and desolation (Lam. 1, 2). The temple of the earthly Jerusalem was also seen as the embodiment of Christ, whose death and resurrection were read as reflective of the rebuilding of the temple (Lam. 2 is often compared to John 2:19–22). Lamentations is also read in Augustine's *City of God* as the coming judgment of God upon sinners and those who disobey the faith, such as Mathew 23:35, which is often read as alluding to Lamentation 4:13.

The reading of Lamentations by the Latin church in many ways parallels the significance of Jerusalem for Christianity outlined above. The Latin church saw the earthly Jerusalem as a means toward the heavenly, just as Lamentations is read as a prophetic reflection of the coming of Christ and his Passion. After the conquest of Jerusalem in 1099 CE, a shift occurred in Christian theology in which the earthly Jerusalem received a higher status than it had in the past. This theological perspective also promoted the movement toward the representation of Jerusalem through the model of lamentations. The narratives that outline the victories of the First Crusade demonstrate not only an advancement toward finding the earthly Jerusalem as a significant part of Christian belief but one where believers had to begin by lamenting Jerusalem.

60. Alexander Andrée, *Gilbertus Universalis Glossa Ordinaria in Lamentationes Ieremie Prophete, Prothemata et Liber I*, Acta Universitatis Stockholmiensis Studia Latina Stockholmiensia 52 (Stockholm: Almquist och Wiksell, 2005).

Jerusalem, City Laments, and the Arabo-Islamic Tradition

The relationship of the Arabo-Islamic world to lamentation and the city of Jerusalem has a far-reaching history. Elegies devoted to fallen cities, the *rithāʾ al-mudun*, were influenced primarily by established traditions of the pre-Islamic world—the era termed the Jāhilīyya (often translated as the "age of ignorance"), the time before the advent of Islam. Since most of the pre-Islamic world was examined through an Islamic reconstruction of its past history, evidence of lamentation is difficult to trace in the written tradition.[61] Furthermore, the *rithāʾ al-mudun* has seen very little scholarly attention.[62] Most explorations into city elegies in Arabic are generally part of larger studies on nostalgia in the Arabic poetic tradition, focusing also on tracing the trajectory of the pre-Islamic poetic form, the *qaṣīda*, from the age of Jāhilīyya to the contemporary world.[63]

In its efforts to distinguish itself from its pagan and Jewish neighbors, lamentation was also a practice rejected early on by Islam.[64] The identity of the *umma* (Islamic community) was to set itself up against the pre-Islamic Jāhilīyya society, and this included the realignment of rituals devoted to the dead. Lamenting, or *niyāḥa*, was considered incompatible with the Islamic belief of salvation; to negotiate one's faith was seen as a rebellious act against God's judgment. Death was only the end of a period of testing, a transition necessary to reach the afterlife. According to Leor Halevi, lament manifested

61. Suzanne Pinckney Stetkevych, "Archetype and Attribution in Early Arabic Poetry: Al-Shanfara and the Lamiyyat al-Arab," *International Journal of Middle East Studies* 18, no. 3 (1986): 363.

62. See ʿAbd al-Raḥmān Ḥusayn Muḥammad, *Rithāʾ al-mudun wa-al-mamālik al-zāʾila* (Cairo: Maṭbaʿat al-Jabalāwī, 1983); and Ibrahim al-Sinjilawi, "The Lament for Fallen Cities: A Study of the Development of the Elegiac Genre in Classical Arabic Poetry" (PhD diss., University of Chicago, 1983).

63. Muḥammad Ibrāhīm Ḥuwwar, *Al-Ḥanīn ilā al-waṭan fī-al-adab al-ʿarabī ḥattā nihāyat al-ʿaṣr al-umawī* (Cairo: Dār nahḍat Miṣr lit-ṭabʿ wa-l-nashr, 1973); Jaroslav Stetkevych, *The Zephyrs of Najd: The Poetics of Nostalgia in Classical Arabic* Nasib (Chicago: University of Chicago Press, 1993); Suzanne Pinckney Stetkevych, *The Mute Immortals Speak: Pre-Islamic Poetry and the Poetics of Ritual* (Ithaca, NY: Cornell University Press, 2010); Stetkevych, "Archetype and Attribution," 363.

64. See, for example, Fred Astren, "Depaganizing Death: Aspects of Mourning in Rabbinic Judaism and Early Islam," in *Bible and Qurʾan: Essays in Scriptural Intertextuality*, ed. John C. Reeves (Leiden: Brill, 2004), 183–99.

a conflict between two religious modes: the *jāhilī*, which constituted "spontaneous, emotional, and violent rituals," and what Halevi calls an "Islamic mode" characterized by "conformity to dogmatic beliefs and by an emphasis on routinization."[65]

The practice, primarily undertaken by women, was also forbidden by Muḥammad at an early stage of Islam—not only the display of grief but also the actions of tearing one's hair and clothes, striking and scratching the face and body, and shaving the head. Muslim exegesis and the Islamic *ḥadīth* tradition—the sayings attributed to the prophet Muḥammad—reflect a negative attitude toward female lamentation and its practices. Commentators interpret the phrase "nor disobey me in any just matter" in sura 60:12 of the Qur'an, for example, as a direct condemnation of *niyāḥa*.[66] Ibn Sa'd recounts in his *Kitāb al-ṭabaqāt* several instances where the interpretation of this verse is that women are forbidden by the Prophet to lament.[67] Muḥammad is also believed to have explicitly condemned the work of the *nawā'iḥ* (professional mourners), claiming that the deceased would be punished if they were present. Lamenting the dead (*al-niyāḥa 'alā al-mayyit*) was singled out by Muḥammad as one of the pre-Islamic customs that all Muslims had to abandon (also including the attacking of ancestral lineage and summoning the planets for rain). As Nadia Maria El Cheikh notes, the emerging Muslim community replaced the private and unofficial modes of mourning attributed to women with official, institutionalized spheres where male poets were allotted the task of expressing the community's reaction to loss.[68]

---

65. Leor Halevi, "Wailing for the Dead: The Role of Women in Early Islamic Funerals," *Past and Present* 183 (2004): 32.

66. "O Prophet! When believing women come unto thee, pledging unto thee that they will not ascribe any as partners unto God, nor steal, nor fornicate, nor slay their children, nor bring a slanderous lie that they have fabricated between their hands and feet, nor disobey thee in anything honorable, then accept their pledge and seek God's forgiveness for them Truly God is Forgiving, Merciful." Seyyed Hossein Nasr, ed., *The Study Quran: A New Translation and Commentary* (New York: HarperCollins, 2017). All quotations herein from the Qur'an are taken from this edition.

67. Ibn Sa'd, *Kitāb al-ṭabaqāt al-ḳabīr*, ed. 'Alī Muḥammad 'Umar (Cairo: Maktabat al-Khānjī, 2001), 8:7–9.

68. For studies on female lament tradition and Islam, see Nadia Maria El Cheikh, *Women, Islam, and Abbasid Identity* (Cambridge, MA: Harvard University Press, 2015), esp. 38–58; Nadia Maria El Cheikh, "The Gendering of Death in *Kitab al-'Iqd al-Farid*," *Al-Qantara* 31 (2010): 411–36; and Nadia Maria El Cheikh, "Women's Lamentations and Death Rituals in Early Islam" (video), https://www.youtube.com/watch?v=adMv1H-zzNc. See also Olga M. Davidson, "Women's

Despite these types of rejections, the Arabo-Islamic world saw a number of laments devoted to cities, the surviving majority of which came from Muslim Spain. Laments devoted to the fall of Cordova, Granada, Seville, Valencia and other cities help us better understand the poetics of loss and nostalgia in al-Andalus and the way in which constructed textual spaces feed and satisfy symbolic cultural and political imaginations.[69] The thirteenth-century poet Ibn ʿUmayra al-Makhzūmī writes in his lament for Valencia that he "yearns for Najd [*yaḥinnu ilā Najdin*], but all in vain."[70] Abū al-Baqāʾ al-Rundī composed a lamentation for the fall of Seville in which he addresses how Seville and other places were "capitals which were the pillars of the land, yet when the pillars are gone, it may no longer endure!"[71] Ibn Ḥazm's elegy

---

Lamentations as Protest in the Ṣhāhnāmaʾ," in *Women in the Medieval Islamic World*, ed. Gavin R. G. Hambly (New York: St. Martin's, 1999), 131–46; and David Pinault, "Shia Lamentation Rituals and Reinterpretations of the Doctrine of Intercession: Two Cases from Modern India," *History of Religions* 38, no. 3 (1999): 285–305.

69. ʿAbd Allāh Muḥammad al-Zayyāt, *Rithāʾ al-mudun fī al-shiʿr al-Andalusī* (Benghazi: Jāmiʿat Qāryūnus, 1990); Alexander E. Elinson, *Looking Back at al-Andalus: The Poetics of Loss and Nostalgia in Medieval Arabic and Hebrew Literature*, Brill Studies in Middle Eastern Literatures 34 (Leiden: Brill, 2009); Alexander E. Elinson, "Loss Written in Stone: Ibn Shuhayd's *Rithaʾ* for Cordoba and Its Place in the Arabic Elegiac Tradition," in *Transforming Loss into Beauty: Essays on Arabic Literature and Culture in Honor of Magsa al-Nowaihi*, ed. Marlé Hammond and Dana Sajdi (Cairo: American University of Cairo Press, 2008), 79–114; Alexander E. Elinson, "Tears Shed over the Poetic Past: The Prosification of the *Rithāʾ al-Mudun* in al-Saraqusṭī's *Maqāma Qayrawāniyya*," *Journal of Arabic Literature* 36, no. 1 (2005): 1–27; Julie Scott Meisami, "Between Arabia and al-Andalus: Nostalgia as an Arabic Poetic Genre," in *Poetica medieval tra Oriente e Occidente* (Rome: Carroci editore, 2003); Teresa Garulo, "La nostalgia de al-Andalus. Génesis de un tema literario," *Qurtuba* 3 (1998): 47–63; Gustave E. von Grunebaum, "Aspects of Arabic Urban Literature Mostly in the Ninth and Tenth Centuries," in *Al-Andalus* 20 (1955): 259–81.

70. A partial English translation can be found in Stetkevych, *The Zephyrs of Najd*, 106–7. This reference is not to the modern-day area of Najd in Saudi Arabia. The term *najd* refers to a raised geographic area, and has been noted as being between the borders of modern-day Iraq and Saudi Arabia, with any of thirteen possible locations in the region. Beginning with the ʿUdhrī poets, who composed elegiac verses on unrequited love, scholars have argued that the *najd* (perhaps also like the *bilad al-shām*) metonymically functioned as a "lost paradise," a mythical region that manifested the nostalgia for lost territories.

71. James T. Monroe, *Hispano-Arabic Poetry* (Berkeley: University of California Press, 1974), 332–34. See also Abū al-Baqāʾ al-Rundī, "Lament for the Fall of Seville," trans. James T. Monroe, in *Medieval Iberia: Readings from Christian, Muslim, and Jewish Sources*, ed. Olivie Remie Constable (Philadelphia: University of Pennsylvania Press, 1997), 220–22; [Abū al-Baqāʾ al-Rundī,] "A Lament for the Loss of Seville (646/1248)," in *Christians and Moors in Spain*, vol. 3, *Arabic Sources (711–1501)*, ed. Charles Melville and Ahmad Ubaydli (Warminster, England: Aris and Phillips, 1992), 145. For the original Arabic with English translation, see "The Fall of Seville—A

for the ruins of Cordova in 1013 CE draws from its pre-Islamic form when it calls, "O abode, it was not our choice that you were deserted by us, / for if we could have our way, you would be our burial place."[72]

These city elegies are informed by the pre-Islamic *qaṣīda,* the structure of which dominated Arabo-Islamic poetry for centuries. The initial section, the *nasīb*, reflects on the abandonment and movement away from the campsite. With the founding of Baghdad as the imperial capital of the Abbasids, the city became the new landscape that replaced the aesthetic of the desert in the pre-Islamic *rithā' al-mudun*. The urbanization of Arab culture then marked a shift in lamentation from the ruined campsite or abode (the *aṭlāl*) to the city, where the language and tone of the *qaṣīda* was infused with a comparably evocative and symbolic urban space, drawing from past memories. One of the earliest elegies over the city of Baghdad was composed following the civil war between the two sons of Hārūn al-Rashīd, al-Amīn and al-Ma'mūn. In the elegy by Abū Ya'qūb Isḥāq al-Khuraymī the nostalgia of a past city is recalled as the narrator stands among the debased ruins, mourning its present destruction: "They said, when Time had not yet had the chance to play with Baghdad, / when her ill luck had not yet caused her to topple." Baghdad was also a topic of city lamentation after its destruction by the Mongols in 1258 CE. The *rithā' al-mudun* of Shams al-Dīn al-Kūfī mourns the destruction of Baghdad by the Mongols utilizing common tropes of ancient city lamentations, such as the fall of the city based on the sins of the population and their movement away from the faith; the description of the events of war and destruction in the city; the city as the female lover who has often also departed; the call for the believers to recapture the city; and the evocation of (a once glorious) past as a means of reflecting on the current lamentable state of the city.[73]

Poem by Abu al-Baqa' al-Rundi," Lost Islamic History, http://lostislamichistory.com/the-fall-of-seville-a-poem-by-abu-al-baqa-al-rundi/.

72. Elinson, *Looking Back at al-Andalus*, 27. See also Lisān al-Dīn Ibn al-Khaṭīb, *A'māl al-a'lām*, 2nd ed., ed. E. Lévi Provençal (Beirut: Dār al-makshūf, 1956), 107–8; and al-Zayyāt, Rithā' al-mudun fī al-shi'r al-Andalusī, 658.

73. Abū Ya'qūb Isḥāq al-Khuraymī, *Dīwān al-Khuraymī*, ed. 'Alī Jawād al-Ṭāhir and Muḥammad Jabbār al-Mu'aybid (Beirut: Dār al-Kitāb al-Jadīd, 1971), 27. For an English translation, see "Details and Results of the Siege of Baghdad," in *The History of al-Ṭabarī*, vol. 31, *The War between Brothers*, trans. Michael Fishbein (Albany: State University of New York Press, 1985), 139. Ed Naẓīm Rashīd, *Dīwan Shams al-Dīn al-Kūfī* ('Ammān, Dār al-Diyā', 2006).

These tropes resemble those found in ancient Mesopotamian city laments and the Hebrew Bible, and they reflect Islam's supersession of both Christianity and Judaism. The term *taḥrīf*, meaning "distortion or alteration," is used to express the belief that Islam supersedes Christian and Jewish scripture as the final and most authentic expression of Abrahamic monotheism. Sandra Toenis Keiting argues that in its desire to "replace the corrupted scriptures possessed by other communities," Islam was supersessionist from its inception.[74] Irmiyā (Jeremiah) is present in Islamic literature and exegesis, and his stories closely resemble the accounts of the Hebrew Bible. Muslim literature also provides accounts of the destruction of Jerusalem that resemble those of the book of Lamentations.[75]

The early Islamic period therefore defined its relationship not only to lamentation but also to the city of Jerusalem. The Islamic sanctity of the city dates back to the time of Muḥammad; sacred cities were categorized through levels of religious significance, stemming from the presence of the prophet Muḥammad and his descendants, as well as the city's role in soteriology and cosmology.[76] Adopting the concept of Jerusalem as the navel of the earth from Hebrew lore, Islam did not deprive Jerusalem of this function, though it did also transfer the concept to Mecca. The navel of the earth had five functions, as A. J. Wesnick notes: "it is exalted over the territories surrounding it; it is the origin of the earth; it is the center of the earth; it is the place of communication of the upper and the nether worlds; it is the medium through which food is distributed over the earth."[77]

This specific sanctity of the city of Jerusalem for the Islamic faith is reflected both in the Qur'an and within the traditions attributed to Muḥammad, known as the *ḥadīth Qudsī*—a special category of *ḥadīth* that involve

---

74. Sandra Toenis Keiting, "Revisiting the Charge of Taḥrīf: The Question of Supersessionism in Early Islam and the Qur'ān," in *Nicholas of Cusa and Islam: Polemic and Dialogue in the Late Middle Ages*, ed. Ian Christopher Levy, Rita George-Tvrtković, and Donald Duclow (Leiden: Brill, 2014), 202–17.

75. G. Vajda, "Irmiyā," in *Encyclopaedia of Islam*, 2nd ed., ed. Th. Bianquis, C. E. Bosworth, E. van Donzel, P. Bearman, and W. P. Heinrichs (Leiden: Brill, 2002), http://dx.doi.org/10.1163/1573-3912_islam_SIM_3594.

76. Gustave E. von Grunebaum, "The Sacred Character of Islamic Cities," in *Islam and Medieval Hellenism: Social and Cultural Perspectives*, ed. Dunning S. Wilson (London, 1976), 26–27.

77. A. J. Wensinck, "The Ideas of the Western Semites concerning the Navel of the Earth," in *Verhandelingen der Koninklijke Akademie van Wetenschappen te Amsterdam: Afdeeling Letterkunde*, n.s., 17, no. 1 (Amsterdam: Müller, 1916): 11–12.

Muḥammad's report of what God said. Sura 17:1 of the Qur'an describes Muḥammad's nocturnal journey (*al-Isrā'*) as follows: "Glory be to Him who carried His servant by night from the Sacred Mosque to the Farthest Mosque, whose precincts We have blessed, that We might show him some of Our signs. Truly He is the Hearer, the Seer." A majority of Islamic religious scholars have recognized the *masjid al-aqṣā* (the farthest mosque), which is connected to the nocturnal journey of Muḥammad, as a reference to Jerusalem. One interpretation was that the *al-aqṣā*, where Muḥammad was carried at night, was the heavenly temple or the heavenly Jerusalem, where he conversed with God and then returned to Mecca. Another opinion was that the *al-aqṣā* represented the physical city of Jerusalem, since other suras in the Qur'an (e.g., 17:7, 21:71) call the temple by the name al-Masjid (the mosque), which later was interpreted as a reference to the al-Masjid al-Aqṣā, the mosque near the Dome of the Rock. The Islamic *ḥadīth* tradition and the commentaries on the Qur'an came to understand the reference in sura 17 to mean the terrestrial Jerusalem, which connected the city to certain events in the life of the Prophet. This interpretation is strengthened through the verses following sura 17:1, which make references to both the temple and its destruction as a result of the Israelites and their movement away from the faith (17:2–8)—a theme also prominent in the Hebrew Bible. The subsequent verses therefore tell the believer to turn to the bounties of the Lord (17:12, 17:20), to ask him for forgiveness and for him to bestow mercy upon the believer.

This story of Muḥammad's night journey developed further into various forms, one of which was how Muḥammad was awakened one night by the Angel Gabriel and led to the winged animal called Burāq, who carried Muḥammad to the farthest mosque, *al-aqṣā*—that is, to Jerusalem, where he landed and left his footprint on the rock where Abraham had prepared to sacrifice Ismā'īl (or Isaac, in the Judeo-Christian tradition). From there he ascended beyond the seventh heaven, where he conversed with God, Moses, and other prophets. There he set down the five prayers, which the Muslims are required to recite daily, and then he returned to Mecca.[78] Jerusalem

78. For discussions on the various interpretations of this verse, see Izhak Hasson, "The Muslim View of Jerusalem in the Qur'ān and the Ḥadīth," in Prawer and Ben-Shammai, eds., *The History of Jerusalem*, 353–59; Hava Lazarus-Yafeh, "The Sanctity of Jerusalem in Islam," in *Jerusalem*, ed. John M. Oesterreicher and Anne Sinai (New York: Day, 1974), 216–18; and S. D. Goitein, *Studies in Islamic History and Institutions* (Leiden: Brill, 1968), 135–48.

as the scene of Muḥammad's two-part journey *al-isrāʾ wa-al miʿrāj* is also mentioned in Saladin's letter to Richard the Lionheart and reflects part of the dialectic of negotiations during the Third Crusade.[79]

The significance of the city of Jerusalem in the early days of Islam was further apparent since it was the first direction of prayer, or the *qibla*, also known as *ʿūlā al-qiblaṭayn* (the first of the two *qiblas*).[80] It is reported that during Muḥammad's residence in Mecca he and his disciples would face Jerusalem while praying. Yet it has also been argued that even while facing Jerusalem, Muḥammad situated himself toward the Kaʿba (the Cube) in Mecca, to ensure a positioning during prayer to both Mecca and the temple in Jerusalem. Muḥammad's continuous struggle with the Quraysh tribe, the established leader of Mecca and guardians of the Kaʿba (suras 8:35, 106:1), to which he also belonged, resulted in his being forced to flee to Medina in 622 CE with his followers, who were members of his own tribe as well as others. Numerous sources provide varying reports of how after sixteen months in Medina, Muḥammad was instructed by God to turn the direction of the *qibla* southward toward the Kaʿba in Mecca: "The fools among the people will say: 'What has turned them from the *qiblah* they had been following?' Say, 'To God belong the East and the West. He guides whomsoever He will unto a straight path.'"[81]

---

79. C. P. Melville and M. C. Lyons, "Saladin's Ḥaṭṭīn's Letter," in *The Horns of Hattin*, ed. Benjamin Z. Kedar (Jerusalem: Yad Izhak Ben Zvi Institute, 1992), 208–12. For a larger discussion of this letter as part of the dialogue of interactions during the Third Crusade, see Adnan Husain and Margaret Aziza Pappano, "The One Kingdom Solution?: Diplomacy, Marriage, and Sovereignty in the Third Crusade," in *Cosmopolitanism and the Middle Ages*, ed. John M. Ganim and Shayne Aaron Legassie (New York: Palgrave Macmillan, 2013), 121–40.

80. See Maurice Borrmans, "Jerusalem dans la tradition Religieuse musulmane," *Islamochristiana* 7 (1981): 4.

81. Sura 2:142–46; See also Muḥammad Ibn Isḥāq, *Sīrat Rasūl Allāh* (Cairo, 1972; reprint, Beirut, 1995), 550–606. See also *The Life of Muhammad: A Translation of Ishaq's "Sirat Rasul Allah,"* trans. A. Guillaume (Oxford: Oxford University Press, 1955), 258–59; *The Commentary on the Quʾrān, by Abū Jaʿfar Muḥammad b. Jarir al-Ṭabarī; Being an Abridged Translation of Jāmiʿ al-bayān ʿan taʾwīl āy al-Qurʾān*, vol. 1, trans. J. Cooper, ed. W. F. Madelung and A. Jones (Oxford: Oxford University Press, 1987); Mālik Ibn Anas, *Muwaṭṭaʾ al-Imām Mālik* (1962), trans. Aisha Abdurrahman Bewley as *Al-Muwatta of Imam Malik ibn Anas: The First Formulation of Islamic Law* (London: Kegan Paul, 1989); For secondary material, see also W. M. Watt, *Muhammad at Medina* (Oxford: Clarendon, 1956); Patricia Crone and Michael Crook, *Hagarism: The Making of the Islamic World* (Cambridge: Cambridge University Press, 1977); and Moshe Gil, "The Political History of Jerusalem during the Early Muslim Period," in Prawer and Ben-Shammai, eds., *The History of Jerusalem*, 1–37. For a literary biography, see *Arabic Literary Culture 500–925*, ed. Michael Cooperson and Shawkat M. Toorawa (Detroit: Gale, 2005).

Under the Umayyads, the status of the city of Jerusalem was further emphasized as a holy place in Islam. The war between the Persians and the Byzantine Empire during the first quarter of the seventh century resulted in the eventual surrender of the city of Jerusalem by the patriarch Sophronicus to the Caliph ʿUmar ibn al-Khaṭṭāb in 638 CE. Upon their negotiations the churches and worship of the Christians were to remain unaltered, and peaceful negotiations resulted in Muslim domination over the city. ʿUmar, in his efforts to both seek a place for Muslim prayer and avoid defying the conditions of the treaty, decided on the temple area and built a temporary meeting hall of wood against the eastern wall of the public walkway.[82]

In 691 CE, the fifth Caliph of the Umayyad dynasty, ʿAbd al-Malik, constructed the octagon shaped Dome of the Rock (Qubbat al-Ṣakhra) over the highest point of the temple esplanade, presumably the rock of the Holy of Holies in the Jewish temple.[83] Although ʿAbd al-Malik is principally known for the construction of the Dome of the Rock, his name is also connected to the construction of the al-Aqṣā mosque, as well as two gates in Jerusalem.[84] The edifices erected within the city of Jerusalem under the initiatives of the Umayyad caliphs were part of the efforts to not only make Jerusalem a religious and political center but also to promote traditions in praise and glorification of Jerusalem.[85] Amikam Elad conveniently provides us with a list in his study of the Umayyad building projects that includes not just Qubbat al-Ṣakhra and al-Masjid al-Aqṣā but also "the Ḥaram (Qubbat al-Silsila, Qubbat al-Nabī, Qubbat al-Miʿrāj); the Ḥaram wall with its holy gates, which have combined Jewish and Islamic resonances (Bāb al-Nabī, Bāb al-Sakīna); the six large structures, outside the Ḥaram, including the large two-storeyed palace, from the second floor of which a bridge led apparently to the al-Aqṣā;

82. Adrian J. Boas, *Jerusalem in the Time of the Crusades* (London: Routledge, 2001), 8–13; Amikam Elad, *Medieval Jerusalem and Islamic Worship: Holy Places, Ceremonies, Pilgrimage* (Leiden: Brill, 1995), 29–33.

83. For an interesting discussion of the connections, see Heribert Busse, "Jerusalem and Mecca, the Temple and the Kaaba: An Account of Their Interrelation in Islamic Times," in *The Holy Land in History and Thought*, ed. Moshe Sharon (Leiden: Brill, 1988), 236–46.

84. Ibn Kathīr, *Al-Bidāya wa-al-Nihāya fī al-Tāʾrīkh*, vol. 10 (Cairo: Maṭbaʿat al-Saʿāda, 1935), 226; Al-Muqaddasī, *Aḥsan al-Taqāsīm fī Maʿrifat al-Aqālīm*, vol. 3 (Leiden: Brill, 1906), 166–68; Ibn al-Biṭrīq, *Al- Taʾrīkh al-Majmūʿ ʿalā al-Taḥqīq wa-al Taṣdīq*, vol. 2 (Beirut, 1909), 35–40.

85. See Chase Robinson, *ʿAbd al-Malik* (Oxford: Oneworld, 2005); and Chase Robinson, *Islamic Historiography* (Cambridge: Cambridge University Press, 2003), esp. 76–80.

and finally, the roads to and from Jerusalem built and repaired by ʿAbd al-Malik."[86]

The extensive building projects of the Umayyads therefore promoted the sanctification of Jerusalem and particularly the *ḥaram*, the area enclosing the holy sites. Over time the significance of the city produced an abundance of the *faḍāʾil al-Quds* (traditions in praise of Jerusalem), exegeses of passages of the Qurʾan devoted to the city of Jerusalem, and traditions concerning the conquest of the city.[87] The scholarship surrounding this corpus as well as the significance of the city of Jerusalem for the Islamic faith is indeed extensive, and what is provided here is only a brief summary. Other factors, such as the presence of *zuhhād* (ascetics), *quṣṣāṣ* (storytellers), legends about the Prophet, and the graves of prophets and righteous people within the city of Jerusalem further contributed to its status as a holy place, particularly because Islam both recognizes the prophets of Christianity and Judaism and elevates certain biblical kings, such as David and Solomon, to the status of prophets.[88]

City Laments and the Cilician Armenian Element

The rising control of Byzantium in the eleventh century, and the Byzantines' eventual seizure of the city of Ani in 1045 CE, ended the last major Armenian kingdom in Greater Armenia, the Bagratid dynasty, and resulted in disintegration of Armenian rule over its own territory. As noted in many contemporary sources, including the highly esteemed *Patmutʿiwn* (History) of the eleventh-century Armenian figure Aristakes Lastivertcʿi, in 1064 CE the expanding Seljuq powers captured the city of Ani from Byzantium, and on August 26, 1071 CE, on the plains of Manzikert, the Seljuq Army under

86. Elad, *Medieval Jerusalem and Islamic Worship*, 159–60. For the Dome of the Rock, see Oleg Grabar, "The Umayyad Dome of the Rock in Jerusalem," *Ars Orientalis* 3 (1959): 33–62.

87. Emmanuel Sivan, "The Beginnings of the Faḍāʾil al-Quds literature," *Israel Oriental Studies* 1 (1971): 263–71; Hartmut Bobzin, "Jerusalem aus muslimischer Perspektive während der Kreuzfahrerzeit," in *Jerusalem in Hoch und Spätmittelalter*, ed. Dieter Bauer, Klaus Herbers, and Nikolas Jaspert (Frankfurt: Campus Verlag, 2001), 215–17; Hasson, "The Muslim View of Jerusalem," 365–77.

88. For an interesting discussion of the role of biblical figures in Islamic exegesis, see Brannon M. Wheeler, "'The Land in Which You Have Lived': Inheritance of the Promised Land in Classical Islamic Exegesis," in *Studies in Jewish Civilization* 11 (2001): 49–83.

the leadership of Arp Aslan defeated the Byzantine Army, ultimately weakening its authority of Anatolia and Armenia. A majority of scholars trace the beginning of the Armenian kingdom of Cilicia to this pivotal Battle of Manzikert, after which a number of Armenian lords and princes led their people across the Taurus Mountains and settled north of the Mediterranean in the region of Cilicia, where there had been an Armenian presence for many centuries, as well as those of Arabs, Greeks, and Jews. Here they were ruled by two rival dynasties, the Rubenids and the pro-Roman Het'umids (later Lusignans), finally establishing their own independent kingdom of Armenian Cilicia in 1198 CE with Prince Leo II or Levon II (later King Levon I) as its first ruler, lasting until 1375 CE.

Around the middle of the seventh century, Arab invaders had encountered strong resistance from local Armenian militia. In the tenth century, after Byzantium eventually succeeded in driving the Arabs out of Cilicia, a large number of Armenians settled there and a number of bishoprics were established. In 1021–22 CE, the Byzantine emperor Basil II settled some of the fourteen to fifteen thousand Armenians who abandoned Vaspurakan into the plains of Cilicia, and a number of Armenian princes were appointed governors in various regions. Although these regions were nominally under Byzantine rule, Armenians occupied key positions.

The advancement of the Franks from western Europe in the late eleventh century had a huge impact on the Armenians in Cilicia. As a strong Christian presence in the region, the crusaders sought out Armenians to serve as soldiers or guides and to provide supplies. Cilician Armenian lords aided these crusaders, considering them valuable allies, but also sometimes also became targets of crusading advancements. One prime example is the crusader capture of Edessa. The Greek Orthodox Armenian prince T'oros, who had recently secured Edessa from the Seljuqs, requested the assistance of Baldwin of Boulogne to maintain control of his territory. Baldwin agreed, but only if Toros would make him heir by adopting him as his son. During one of Baldwin's raids against the Seljuqs, the Armenian Orthodox population of Edessa attempted to overthrow its pro-Byzantine ruler. Baldwin neglected to aid his "father," resulting in T'oros's death and Baldwin's title as the Count of Edessa.

This example reflects one of many intercultural exchanges between the Armenians of Cilicia and the Latin West, alongside already existing relations between the Armenians, Byzantium, and the Arabo-Islamic world. Yet, like other material from the East, Armenian sources have also seen little consideration in past scholarship of this period. Cilician Armenians are generally named or hinted at as a presence in the medieval Mediterranean during the crusading period, but few sources actually consider the Armenians as part of larger discussions. This exclusion can partly be due to the fact that many of these Armenian texts have not been translated, or have only been partially and inaccurately translated, into modern European languages. The difficulty to access some of these sources could also be a contributing factor to their absence in scholarship.

Earlier compilations of crusading sources, even in their consideration of the Armenians, seem to hold the general opinion that Armenian material of the period is either lacking in content or includes erroneous or inaccurate information. The Armenian historiographer Matthew of Edessa, for example, is referred to as "a naïve man with hatred for the Greeks," and the information about the crusaders in his *Chronicle* is claimed to be "derived from some ignorant Frankish soldier."[89] Karl F. Neumann, the translator of the chronicle of Vahram Ṙabuni printed for the Oriental Translation Fund in 1831, refers to the text as having "monotonous historical rhymes," being "defective in its brevity," and relating "barren facts."[90] This judgment extends to Armenian literary sources of the period as well. The *Ołb Etesioy* (Lament on Edessa) composed by the Catholicos or Armenian high patriarch Nersēs Šnorhali, and argued by scholars to be one of the greatest literary creations in the Armenian language, is believed to be "somewhat lacking in both poetical and historical interest."[91]

89. Steven Runciman, *A History of the Crusades*, vol. 1, *The First Crusade and the Foundation of the Kingdom of Jerusalem* (Cambridge: Cambridge University Press, 1987), 334–35, makes the following observation about Armenian sources: "There is one invaluable Armenian source covering the period of the First Crusade, the *Chronicle* of Matthew of Edessa. . . . Matthew was a naïve man with hatred for the Greeks and no great love for those of his compatriots who were Orthodox in religion. Much of his information about the Crusades must have been derived from some ignorant Frankish soldier."

90. "The greatest defect of the following Chronicle is its brevity. . . . He [Vahram] relates many barren facts, without stating the circumstances with which they were connected, and he mistakes everywhere the passions of men for the finger of God. The compilers of chronicles were in those days ignorant of the true end, and unacquainted with the proper objects of history. But with all its defects, the chronicle of the Armenian kings of Cilicia . . . is valuable." Karl F. Neumann, *Vahram's Chronicle of the Armenian Kingdom of Cilicia during the time of the Crusades* (London: Oriental Translation Fund, 1831, vii).

91. Runciman, *A History of the Crusades*, 1:483.

These opinions reflect a desire to position eastern sources within an already established history of the period provided through the perspective of western Europe. Furthermore, when Armenian sources are considered, they seem to expand more on knowledge of the crusading efforts from western Europe, since the sections that are included from Armenian texts focus on the presence and history of the European crusaders in Armenian Cilicia. For example, the famous compilation of sources in the Recueil des historiens des croisades dedicates two volumes to Armenian sources entitled Documents Arméniens. The first volume, published in 1896, comprises excerpts only from the medieval Armenian literary and historiographic tradition that pertain to the relationship of Cilician Armenians to the Latin West, functioning mostly as addenda to supplement western Europe presence and victories in the Levant. These excerpts are also not contextualized within the larger framework of Armenian and Cilician history nor Cilician Armenian interactions with other ethnoreligious groups in the region. Armenian accounts fall under rubrics such as "Expeditions [of the crusaders] to Syria and Palestine" and "The First Crusade."

This viewpoint is further reflected in the selection of chronicles that makes up volume 2 of the Documents Arméniens: the volume has no texts in the Armenian language, but contains four Latin and two French chronicles, which are all roughly dated to the fourteenth century. These include the *Chronicle of Armenia* by Jean Dardel, a Franciscan monk who became an adviser and confessor to the Cilician Armenian king Levon, or Leo V, who was imprisoned by the emir of Aleppo and sent to Cairo in 1375. According to his history, Dardel met Levon in Cairo and accepted his invitation to act as his adviser and secretary. Other chronicles in the series include Het'um (or Hayton) of Korikos's *La Flor des Estoires de la terre d'Orient* (The flower of the history of the Orient), a history dictated in French and later translated to Latin for the purpose of convincing Pope Clement V for a new crusade in alliance with the Mongols; Pseudo-Brocardus's *Directorium ad passagium faciendum* (Initiative for making the passage), a history addressed to King Phillip VI of France and aimed at reviving the crusading energies of western Europe against the Byzantine Empire and the eastern church; Guillaume (William) Adam's *De modo saracenos extirpandi* (Regarding the extirpation of Saracens); Daniel of Thaurisio's *Responsio ad errores impositos Hermenis* (Response to the wrongdoings imposed by the Armenians), which reprimands Armenian doctrinal differences with the Church of Rome; and the

Old French *Les gestes des Chiprios* (The deeds of the Cypriots), attributed to the Templar of Tyre, which provides a detailed account of Christian's activities in the Holy Land in the thirteenth century and their disagreements with the Egyptian Mamluks.

Whereas the literary and historiographic texts in Armenian included in volume 1 of the Documents Arméniens were only excerpts, the chronicles in volume 2 are included in their entirety. In addition, except for the figure Hayton of Korikos, an Armenian constable who converted to Roman Catholicism in 1305 CE, all authors in volume 2 are of European origin. Among the selections are also testimonies to the failures of the East and attempts to propagate a new crusade in Western Europe against such groups as the eastern Christians. This second volume therefore seems to not entirely reflect Documents Arméniens, as its title suggests, but European perspectives on the Armenians—or the interaction of the Armenians and other eastern cultures with the Franks—from the viewpoint of European authors.

The desire of European orientalists to supplement their perspectives of the Crusades through eastern sources is not unique to the works of the Armenians, and can be seen across editions and volumes of literary and historiographic works of other eastern (i.e., Arabo-Islamic, Byzantine, and Jewish) sources of the period. By acknowledging and considering Armenian material as part of the larger question of how the medieval Mediterranean world lamented the loss of Jerusalem, this book invites Armenian texts to be part of larger conversations around Arabo-Islamic and Latin sources of the period, further complicating the belief that the medieval Mediterranean world was dominated purely by conflicts between Christianity and Islam—an opinion that has for the most part ruled the framework of this period in the past. As eastern Christians, Cilician Armenians had relations with both the Latin West and the Arabo-Islamic world, further attesting to the intricate interchange of contact and conflict in the medieval Mediterranean world. By including an examination of the rhetoric of lament over cities composed in Armenian in this period, *The City Lament* further advances our knowledge of the interpenetration of ethnoreligious cultures of the medieval Mediterranean and exposes the significant presence of Armenians in the period—a presence that was for the most part overlooked in the past.

The period of Armenian Cilician culture is, despite the opinion of orientalist scholars, praised by Armenians for its great production of historical and literary works, its extensive translation projects (into various languages, including Arabic, French, and Latin), and its revival of learning and contact with the Latin West. This "silver age" of Armenian literature produced a wide variety of religious and secular material that serves as valuable resources for the study of the Byzantine world, the Caucasus, the Levant, and Syria, as well for other ethnoreligious groups such as the Caucasian Albanians, Mamluks, Mongols, Persians, Seljuqs, among others. This period also saw the inception and rise of Armenian poetry, including laments dedicated to the loss of cities and principalities.

As with the other cultures named above, the lament, or *ołb*, became a popular social and political genre in the Armenian tradition, allowing the community to come to terms with many disasters, including the devastation of large cities. Short prose lamentations appear among early Armenian historiographies, as in the historical compilation of Movsēs Xorēnac'i—named the "father" of Armenian history. Davt'ak K'ert'oł's "Lament for the Death of the Great Prince Zevanšen" from the seventh century also includes oratorical expressions and amalgamations that draw from ancient city lamentations. After the pivotal Battle of Manzikert in 1071 CE, Aristakes Lastivertc'i included a thirty-four-line lamentation as a preamble to his history, expressing deep grief over the state of his people. In this lamentation describing the expansionist policy of the Byzantine emperor Basil II and the victory of the Seljuqs over the Greeks at Manzikert, Lastiverc'i expresses the opinion that the Byzantines were wrong in absorbing the Armenians into their empire rather than keeping them as a buffer against Byzantine enemies. His work brings together ancient tropes of lamenting cities found in the Hebrew Bible, including the claim that the loss of Manzikert was a result of the sins of the Christian population.

Whereas early laments in Armenian were either written in prose or included among long historiographies, from the twelfth century onward the dominant form of laments were poetic works, usually composed by upper ecclesiastical figures, that utilized many of the tropes of lamenting cities in the Hebrew Bible. One of the most acclaimed poems in Armenian literature is a city lament from this period produced in the kingdom of Cilicia—a lamentation that also set a number of precedents for the Armenian literary tradition. The *Ołb Edesioy* (Lament on Edessa) was composed by the high patriarch Nersēs Šnorhali (Nersēs the Gracious) after the loss of the crusader principality Edessa to Nūr al-Dīn Zengī in 1144

CE.[92] The poem begins by calling to each of the five major episcopal sees of the Roman Empire to lament for the destruction of Edessa: Jerusalem ("city of the King of Heaven"); Rome ("mother of cities"); Constantinople ("the second Jerusalem and the amazing new Rome"); the "desirable" Alexandria; and Antioch.[93] In its verses of mourning, the poem juxtaposes destruction and chaos with the possible rebirth of the city. The lament also foregrounds the significant role of these cities as a representative of the universal church and the body of Christ on earth, also further contextualizing Edessa into the greater ideological and theological narrative of the poem, which through its didactic and pastoral spirit calls for Christian unity.

The inventory of the numerous influences of Nersēs's *Ołb Edesioy* on Armenian literature also includes the furthering of the trajectory of the Antiochene model of historiography, as argued and outlined by the philologist and historian Jean-Pierre Mahé, through representations of the destruction and conquest of Edessa within the poem's larger didactic message of Christian

92. Nersēs Šnorhali, *Ołb Edesioy* , with text and commentary by Manik Mkrtč'yan (Erevan: Armenian SAH GA, 1973). For an English translation and commentary, see Theo Maarten van Lint, "Seeking Meaning in Catastrophe: Nersēs Šnorhali's *Lament on Edessa*," in *East and West in the Crusader States: Context—Contacts—Confrontations*, ed. Krijnie Ciggaar and Herman Teule (Leuven, Belgium: Peeters, 1999), 49–105. The studies on Nersēs Šnorhali, his life, and works are vast in number; a bibliographical survey of primary and secondary sources can be found in Robert W. Thomson, *A Bibliography of Classical Armenian Literature to 1500 AD*, Corpus Christianorum (Turnhout, Belgium: Brepols, 1995), 178–84; and Robert W. Thomson, "Supplement to the *Bibliography of Classical Armenian Literature to 1500 AD:* Publications 1993–2005," *Le Muséon* 120 (2007): 198–99. According to the colophon, Nersēs claims to have written the lament at the request of his nephew Apirat, who was present in Edessa during the siege by Zengī.

93. Nersēs Šnorhali, *Ołb Edesioy*, lines 174–77. In medieval literature, these Christian centers have differing variants in number, order, and epithets depending on political circumstances and dogmatic debates. The four original patriarchates, which were associated with the four evangelists, were each assigned one of the four beings from Ezekiel's throne vision. For the Armenian tradition, Theo Maarten van Lint, "Grigor Narekac'i's *Tal Yarut'ean*: The Throne Vision of Ezekiel in Armenian Art and Literature," in *Apocryphes arméniens: Transmission, traduction, creation, iconographie. Actes du colloque international sur la literature apocryphe en langue arménienne, Genève, 18–20 septembre 1997*, ed. Valentina Calzolari Bouvier, Jean-Daniel Kaestli, and Bernard Outtier (Lausanne: Éditions du Zèbre, 1999), 105–27. In contrast to the glorifying references made to the first four Christian centers, the schema of Antioch materializes in this lament through an incongruous attitude of respect, discontent, and disillusionment—a position influenced by the lament's own contemporaneous social, historical, and political circumstances. See Tamar M. Boyadjian, "Crusader Antioch: The Sister-City in the Armenian Laments of Nersēs Šnorhali and Grigor Tłay" in *East and West in the Medieval Eastern Mediterranean*, vol. 3, *Antioch from the Byzantine Reconquest until the End of the Crusader Principality*, ed. Krijnie Ciggaar and V. Van Aalst (Leuven, Belgium: Peeters, 2017), 37–50.

unity and salvation.[94] Mahé claims that the historical writing of Armenian literature is largely reflected through the reading of the Christian Bible in conformity with the spirit of its early Armenian translation, which considered the Old and New Testaments as part of the larger history of God's work in the world and in providing salvation for humankind.[95] Nērses's lament furthers the trajectory of adopting the Bible as predecessor and literary archetype through its positioning of the events and repercussions of the fall of the principality of Edessa within the model of the book of Lamentations. His work was also influenced by the monumental lyric poem of Grigor Narekac'i, or Gregory of Narek, a monk, poet, and theologian who composed his *Matean Ołbergut'ean* (Book of lamentations) based on biblical wisdom and the Christian doctrine.

Several medieval city laments in Armenian followed Nersēs's poem on Edessa. Xač'atur Keč'arec'i, a nobleman from the medieval Proshians, mourns the losses endured in Greater Armenia by the invasion of the Mongols in his "Lament over the Loss of the Eastern Lands."[96] According to Peter Cowe, Step'anos Õrbelian's "Elegy over the Holy Cathedral of Ējmiacin," a poem mourning the destruction of the ancient Armenian cathedral Ējmiacin by the Mongols, can also be considered a city lament because of the ways in which it draws on characteristic features of the genre.[97] Finally, a highly

94. Jean-Pierre Mahé, "Entre Moïse et Mahomet: réflexions sur l'historiographie arménienne," *Revue des Etudes Arméniennes* 23 (1992): 121–53.

95. Mahé specifically uses the example of Koriwn in his *Vark' Maštoc'i* (Life of Maštoc'). Koriwn was the pupil of Saint Mesrop Maštoc', the individual believed to be responsible for the invention of the Armenian alphabet in the fifth century. Shortly after the invention of the Armenian alphabet came the translation of the Bible into Armenian. See also Theo Maarten van Lint, "From Reciting to Writing and Interpretation: Tendencies, Themes, and Demarcations of Armenian Historical Writing," in *The Oxford History of Historical Writing*, vol. 2, *400–1400*, ed. Sarah Foot and Chase F. Robinson (Oxford: Oxford University Press, 2012), 182.

96. For Keč'arec'i's lament, see M. T'. Avdalbegyan, *Xač'atur Keč'arec'i* (Erevan: Armenian SAH GA, 1958), 129–33. An English translation, "Lament on the Destruction of the Eastern Realm," can be found in Agop J. Hacikyan, Gabriel Basmajian, Edward S. Franchuk, and Nourhan Ouzounian, eds. and trans., *The Heritage of Armenian Literature*, vol. 2, *From the Sixth to the Eighteenth Century* (Detroit: Wayne State University Press, 2002), 569–71.

97. Peter Cowe, "Medieval Armenian Literary and Cultural Trends (Twelfth–Seventeenth Centuries)," in *The Armenian People from Ancient to Modern Times*, vol. 1, *The Dynastic Periods: From Antiquity to the Fourteenth Century*, ed. Richard G. Hovannisian (New York: St. Martin's, 1977), 313–14. For further study and a critical translation, see Avedis K. Sanjian, "Step'anos Orbelian's 'Elegy on the Holy Cathedral of Etchmiadzin': Critical Text and Translation," in *Armenian and Biblical Studies*, ed. Michael E. Stone (Jerusalem: St. James, 1976), 237–83.

overlooked city lament in Armenian is the "Poem of Lamentation over the Capture of Jerusalem" by the successor and nephew of Nersēs Šnorhali, the high patriarch Grigor Tłay (Grigor the Boy). Grigor's lament reflects a significant moment both in the history of the Crusades and the Armenian kingdom of Cilicia, with its propagation of the Armenian prince and later first king of Cilicia, Levon, as an ally of Rome and the future savior of Jerusalem. At the same time, this source has features that expose intercultural exchange and acculturation between the East and the West in the medieval period, both in its conceptualization of the city of Jerusalem and in its attempts to foreground the position of the Armenians in the lament's contemporary social and political world.

Drawing from the work of Alexiou, Połos Xač'atryan names two distinct categories among medieval Armenian city laments, or what he also names "historical laments."[98] Within these categories he identifies certain structural tropes in the composition of city laments. The first section is a lyrical introduction in which the author or personified hero appeals to the audience and invites it to engage in lamentation. The second section recounts the story the fall of the city, providing details such as the time of year, the invading powers, and extensive descriptions of its destruction. The last section is a reflection from the community, which seeks repentance and expresses a desire to have the city conquered anew. These city laments therefore also rely on the tradition of mourning cities in the ancient world—specifically, lamenting Jerusalem in the Hebrew Bible—to lament the city again in their own contemporary present and future.

Medieval Mediterranean Laments over Jerusalem

To lament is to become a witness to death. Though it seems that death is what calls for lament, female lamentations were historically what attempted to resolve the fact of death. For Jerusalem, our texts suggest that we must

98. Połos Xač'atryan, *Hay mijnadaryan patmakan ołber* (Erevan: Armenian SAH GA, 1972). For a study of laments in the ancient Armenian tradition, see Alessandro Orengo, "Funeral Rites and Ritual Laments of the Ancient Armerians," in *Cultural, Linguistic, and Ethnological Interrelations in and Around Aumenia*, ed. Jasmine Dum-Tragut and Uwe Bläsing (Newcastle: Cambridge Scholar Publishing, 2011), 127–144.

begin with the discourse of loss and mourning. Unveiling Jerusalem means first submitting to the city's death, because the lamentations over Jerusalem in the medieval texts discussed in this book are a recursive representation of a single death—the metaphorical death of cities, such as Jerusalem, in the ancient world. To bear witness to Jerusalem's death, our narratives return to ancient models as precursors for their own present moment of understanding the loss and destruction of cities. Jerusalem's destruction in the Hebrew Bible, for example, establishes the city's position in a state of mourning, an unreturnable sacrifice, that provides the imagery and language to describe its loss—the way cultures could represent its destruction in textual narratives.

To speak of Jerusalem, to represent the city, one must begin with lament. Lamenting Jerusalem involves a genealogy of responsibility to the genre of ritual lament, and to the city itself: in the way that is understood in the past, but now posited within the contemporary social, political, and literary world of each individual tradition. Jerusalem becomes a space that transitions the human and the divine, a mirror through which these ethnoreligious cultures shape the ways in which they envisage their own individual Jerusalem and the Jerusalem of the other. Jerusalem is the fabric, the interplay between the secular and the spiritual, the space where loss and gain become intertwined within modes of lamentation. Those who possess Jerusalem have lost the city; those who do not have it long for it; those who gain the city will lose it. This cycle of loss and return is the framework within which each of these ethnoreligious cultures comes to claim Jerusalem: they negotiate the city's fate through lamentations. Though lament was a ritual oral tradition, the lamentations considered in this book are those composed in writing through poetry or through historiographical prose.

As an envisioned space, Jerusalem inherently contains an awareness of its own death, assembled through three models of representation: the geotopographical, the sacred, and ultimately a space that is (and remains) contested. These narratives of mourning, therefore, translate Jerusalem by remapping the city into their own individual textual and conceptual spaces, informed through the contested nature of the city, and the sacred quality of Jerusalem for their own respective traditions.

For our medieval authors, it is the sacred landmarks within the city that metonymically function as the city of Jerusalem: the Qʿubbat al-Ṣakhra, the Church of the Holy Sepulcher, the Armenian Quarter. For each tradition to produce its own Jerusalem means that each is allowed to lament the city as their own, and since Jerusalem then belongs to the economy of sacrifice, the city's conquest is always presented as a reconquest. This rhetoric of death allows the authors of these lamentations to anticipate and repeat the initial loss of the city through the iteration of ritual lament. Lamentations become the mirror in which each text confronts its own subjectivity—the desire to both physically and textually rule Jerusalem and its history.

In my analysis of the ways in which various ethnoreligious cultures lamented Jerusalem across the medieval Mediterranean world, I begin by examining in chapter 2 nineteen lines of an Arabic lamentation over the loss of Jerusalem to the Franks in 1099 CE by the Abbasid court poet Abū al-Muẓaffar Ibn al-Abīwardī. I provide an overview of the study of the elegy over fallen cities in the Arabic tradition, the *rithāʾ al-mudun*, bringing in examples from the Jāhilīyya to the medieval period. I further trace how this lamentation develops from an established pre-Islamic tradition that incorporates within its verses qualities akin to ancient Mesopotamian city laments. My discussion of this lamentation is framed within the greater context of the Arabo-Islamic tradition of the *rithāʾ al-mudun*, Abbasid court poetry, and the sanctity of Jerusalem for the Islamic faith. I also contextualize the lamentations within the larger historiographical work of Ibn al-Athīr and his account of the battle of 1099 CE.

I then move, in chapter 3, to examining European sources of the same battle over Jerusalem and analyze the ways in which European chronicles and literary works produced after the crusader conquest of Jerusalem in 1099 CE begin their narratives by lamenting Jerusalem, despite the fact that the works are ultimately representing a western European Christian victory over the city. Considering the five accounts of Pope Urban II's speeches at the Council of Clermont—the accounts of Fulcher of Chartres, Baldric of Dol, Robert the Monk, Guibert of Nogent, and William of Malmesbury—I argue that despite Christian beliefs and practices that associate lamentations with a Judaic and pagan past, these sources position their narratives of Pope Urban II's call to crusade in a model that assumes the reconquest of a once Christian city, a Jerusalem already in a state of mourning. This chapter also concludes with the argument that there was a shift in the theological approach to the city of Jerusalem (and also to lamentation) in a brief period after the victory of 1099 CE in which earthly Jerusalem and lamentation achieved a higher status in the Latin West than they had in the past.

Moving forward to the period of a once again contested and lost Jerusalem, I examine in chapter 4 an Armenian poem of lamentation reacting to the capture of Jerusalem in 1187 CE by the great Islamic leader Ṣalāḥ al-Dīn Yūsuf Ibn Ayyūb (better known as Saladin in the West) by Grigor Tłay, the Catholicos, or high patriarch, of all Armenians. The chapter is devoted to the discussion of this Armenian lamentation within the greater context of the genre of city laments produced both in the Armenian literary tradition and the sociopolitical (intermediary) position of the Armenian in the medieval Mediterranean world. Through the point of view of the female city, Jerusalem laments its loss to Ṣalāḥ al-Dīn, and by providing a map of the world (in the T-O model) establishes a genealogical connection between the Armenians and the city of Jerusalem. Grigor Tłay's poem envisions and remaps a Jerusalem that culturally, geographically, and ideologically belongs to a medieval Cilician Armenian world. Connecting the city to the Armenians means the lament can then present the city's hero and savior as the Armenian prince and future king Levon I—the monarch who will save the female city from the hands of the Muslim enemy. The political agenda of the lament is also highlighted through its reliance on common tropes from the Hebrew Bible as a model to plead an Armenian Jerusalem's loyalty to the Roman papacy for the establishment of an Armenian kingdom of Cilicia with Prince Levon II as its monarch.

In chapter 5, I return to Western narratives of the Crusades, this time focusing on the crusade of 1192 CE, more commonly referred to as the Third Crusade, or the Kings' Crusade. I consider here the anonymous English chronicle *Itinerarium Peregrinorum et Gesta Regis Ricardi* (Regarding the itinerary of the pilgrims and the deeds of king Richard) and one of its source texts, the Anglo-Norman verse chronicle by Ambroise entitled *L'estoire de la Guerre Sainte* (The history of the holy war). I argue that with the inability of Richard the Lionheart and the crusaders from western Europe to regain the city of Jerusalem from the hands of Ṣalāḥ al-Dīn comes a regression to earlier modes of considering the position of Jerusalem and lamentation. Here the attitudes toward the city of Jerusalem revert to the understandings of the early patristic fathers, before the victory of 1099 CE, where the heavenly Jerusalem is given preference over the earthly city. The text reflects this belief through its continuous association of the city as the city of the Jews, the pagan past, and the city of Ṣalāḥ al-Dīn. Though Richard and the western crusaders do not regain the city for the Latin West, the text does not present this "loss" as a lamentation. In fact, Richard avoids advancements toward the conquest of Jerusalem on a number of occasions, finally arriving to the city as the text's exemplary pilgrim—a status that reaffirms the Latin church's position toward the city as a place of pilgrimage, a city of Christ, and a place that stands in the realm of the heavenly. I support these claims through my analysis of the end of the chronicle, where Richard seems to "lament" his departure from the city. However, loss is translated not as the inability to physically reconquer Jerusalem, but as the transference of entering physical space only as a means to the heavenly.

The primary sources considered in this study constitute a selective group. They are part of the small extant corpus of lamentations that exist over the loss of Jerusalem in the early medieval period. Though not large in number, this selection does offer us a spectrum through which to consider the development of the genre of the city lament in the medieval Mediterranean world. Collectively these lamentations offer us insight into how various cultures lamented cities in their narratives, enabling us to observe further the interconnectiveness among different ethnoreligious groups through their shared practices of mourning the loss of Jerusalem. The city lament is positioned between the reality of a tangible loss and the memory of the same loss informing that expression of mourning. This interdisciplinary study hopes to set forth further conversations on the theme of city laments, particularly also on the shifting role of women in lamentation practices. But here we embark on a journey with our authors to Jerusalem—to their own Jerusalem, the murmur of maternal lamentations, the city over the mountains, and the fallen wasteland of a city: a Jerusalem translated.

Chapter 2

The Lost City

Ibn al-Abīwardī, Ibn al-Athīr, and the Lament for Jerusalem

When the city undressed herself . . .
I saw in her sad eyes:
The gardens of ashes
Drowned in shadow and stillness.
When the evening covered her nudity
And the silence enveloped her blind houses,
She sighed
And smiled despite the pallor of her sickness.
Her black eyes shone with goodness and purity.

—ʿAbd al-Wahhāb al-Bayātī, "The City"[1]

She was a city dressed in the colored brushstrokes of the "other," but she was our city.

According to the Muslim chronicler Ibn al-Athīr, after the fall of Jerusalem to the Europeans from the west on Shaʿbān 489 (July 1099), Muslim refugees from the Levant arrive in Baghdad and recount the story of the conquest of Jerusalem to the caliph's ministers. On a Friday they make a journey to the main mosque in the city, weeping and begging for military aid from the caliph. There they describe the tribulations of the Muslims in the Holy City as a result of the Frankish invasion of Jerusalem. After this section

1. Abdul Wahab al-Bayati, *Love, Death, and Exile: Poems Translated from Arabic.* Trans. Bassam K. Frangieh (Wasington D.C.: Georgetown University Press, 1990), 17.

dedicated to the description of the capture of Jerusalem in Ibn al-Athīr's *al-Kāmil fī al-Tārīkh* (The complete history), composed in 628 AH /1231 CE and a major source for the history of the Arabo-Islamic communities in the medieval period, comes a poem of lamentation ascribed to Abū al-Muẓaffar Ibn al-Abīwardī, a jurist and poet born in Abīward and living in Baghdad. Though Ibn al-Abīwardī is believed to have composed several poems on this occasion, only one of these poems is extant: twenty-two lines of lamentation over the capture of Jerusalem.[2]

Ibn al-Abīwardī's lament opens with an image of blood and tears, describing the destruction of the city and its grieving population. It urges the community to take arms in protecting itself and the city. Through refrains it repeats that there is war, an attacking army, and suffering of the people. The poem calls out the fear of those who perished at the hands of the enemy and urges Muslims to fight without a fear of death. The image of the shame of the community is also intertwined with a call to regain its honor and respect. Ibn al-Abīwardī's poem draws from ancient tropes of lamenting the loss of cities through its metaphors, personification, attribution of the fall of the city to the sins of the inhabitants, and call for repentance and conquest. The poem also draws on the tradition of composing elegies for lost cities in Arabic, known as the *rithā' al-mudun*, which it positions within the larger understanding of the sanctity of the city of Jerusalem for the Islamic faith.

The existing scholarship around the lamentation over the loss of Jerusalem by Ibn al-Abīwardī, the main focus of this chapter, is limited to historian Carole Hillenbrand's discussion in an article on Muslim sources of the First Crusade and her larger study *Islamic Perspectives*; the loose (and problematic) translation by Francesco Gabrieli as part of his volume *Arab Histo-*

2. ʿIzz al-Dīn Ibn al-Athīr, *al-Kāmil fī al-Tārīkh*, vol. 10, ed. C. J. Tornberg (Beirut: Dār Ṣādir, 1967), 284–85. Another version can be found in ʿAbd al-Bāsiṭ al-Anisī, ed., *Dīwān al-Abīwardī Abī al-Muẓaffar Muḥammad ibn Aḥmad ibn Isḥaq al-Matūfī*, vol. 2 (Damascus: Majmaʿ al-Lughah al-ʿArabīyah bi-Dimashq, 1975), 106–7. An incomplete version of Ibn al-Abīwardī's poem is also printed in Ibn al-Jawzī, *Al-Muntaẓam*, vol. 9 (Hyderabad: Da'irat al-Ma'ārif al-'Uthmāniyya, 1940), 108; sixteen verses have been translated by Francesco Gabrieli in *Arab Historians of the Crusades Arab Historians of the Crusades* (Berkeley: University of California Press, 1969), 12. Because Gabrieli tends to translate both terms and phrases very loosely from the original Arabic, the translations provided in this chapter, unless otherwise noted, are my own, with the assistance of Awad Awad. Line numbers are cited parenthetically in the text.

rians of the Crusades; and a short article by Hadia Dajani-Shakeel.[3] As part of an excerpt from the history of Ibn al-Athīr, and nested under the rubric of "The Franks Conquer Jerusalem," comes a translation of Ibn al-Abīwardī's verses into English in Gabrieli's *Arab Historians*. The translation does not provide any analysis or information on Ibn al-Abīwardī or his lamentation, only referencing in a footnote that he was "an Iraqi poet of the eleventh and twelfth centuries."[4] Gabrieli's translation from the Arabic, later translated from Italian to English by E. J. Costello, has for decades now been quoted continuously as part of discussions on Muslim reactions to the Crusades, without further analysis of the poem in the larger context of Arabic poetry and the contemporary Arabo-Islamic world. These multiple levels of translation have not only moved readers away from the original source text but have also resulted in mistranslations and possible misinterpretations of the lament.

As the extensive study of Hillenbrand demonstrates, Muslim sources dating from the period most commonly referred to as the First Crusade (or shortly afterward) have not seen much scholarly attention. The general opinion of European orientalists has been that the Arab sources are either nonexistent for this period or lacking in content. A majority of these sources also tend to include selections from larger Islamic histories, with the purpose of, as Gabrieli notes in his introduction to *Arab Historians*, "help[ing] the European reader to see the period of the Crusades from 'the other side.'"[5] These volumes become attempts to supplement already antagonistically framed European perspectives on the period rather than reading Arabo-Islamic sources (as well as sources of other groups in the East) as their own cultural productions that partake in textual dialogues with the literary and historiographic sources of other ethnoreligious cultures of the medieval Mediterranean. As Edward Said points out in his seminal study *Orientalism*, "Orientalism is—and does not simply represent—a considerable dimension of modern

3. See Carole Hillenbrand, *Islamic Perspectives* (New York: Routledge, 2000), 31–88; Carole Hillenbrand, "The First Crusade: the Muslim Perspective," in *The First Crusade: Origins and Impact*, ed. Jonathan Phillips (Manchester, England: Manchester University Press, 1997), 130–41; Gabrieli, *Arab Historians*, 12; and Hadia Dajani-Shakeel, "Jihād in Twelfth-Century Arabic Poetry: A Moral and Religious Force to Counter the Crusades," *Muslim World* 66, no. 2 (1976): 96–113.

4. Gabrieli, *Arab Historians*, 12n1.

5. Ibid., xi.

political-intellectual culture, and as such has less to do with the Orient than it does with 'our' world."[6]

Orientalist scholars have based their knowledge of the Muslim reaction to the crusade of 1099 CE by relying heavily on the same sources (often mistranslated) that are themselves excerpts from longer works and often never fully consulted in either their entirety or in the original language. With a majority of attention being directed toward historiographic material as a means for orientalists to strengthen hegemonic claims and European national identities, the poetry of the period has frequently also been overlooked as a significant source for the study of the period and thus remains largely unexplored. When they are considered, literary sources have for the most part been contextualized within larger contemporary and nationalized frameworks. Arabo-Islamic texts are read as precursors to the modern political world, and sometimes posited within the contemporary political climate and notions of jihad. Steven Runciman, the celebrated historian of the Crusades, argues in his famous three-part volume that Arabic sources for the period are few and lacking (for the European reader). This opinion has, however, been refuted by scholars in the field who have consulted Arabo-Islamic sources in larger, noncompartmentalized and overarching frameworks such as the Mediterranean.

Despite the opinion of orientalists in the past that Arab sources of the period (as well as other eastern sources) are lacking in both information and content about the Crusades, scholars such as Brian Catlos, Chris Chism, Niall Christie, Carole Hillenbrand, Adnan Husain, and others have demonstrated that sources such as Ṭāhir al-Sulamī's *Book of Holy War* (among many others) can contribute to our understanding of the intercultural exchange of the medieval Mediterranean.[7] Considering Arabo-Islamic poetry of the period alongside historiographic accounts can further contribute to our understanding of the interaction between Europe and the Middle East in the medieval world. Some of the surviving poetry we have from the period includes lines of an anonymous poet quoted by the Mamluk historian Ibn Taghrībirdī; the

6. Edward Said, *Orientalism* (New York: Random House, 1979), 12.

7. For more on al-Sulamī, see *The Book of the Jihad of 'Ali ibn Tahir al-Sulami*, ed. and trans. Niall Christie (Farnham, England: Ashgate, 2015). An Arabic text with French translation may also be found in Emmanuel Sivan, "Un traité Damasquin du début du XIIe siècle," *Journal Asiatique* 254 (1966): 206–22.

work of Ibn al-Khayyāṭ; and the lamentation of the Ibn al-Abīwardī quoted by Ibn al-Jawzī and appearing in the historical compilation of Ibn al-Athīr.[8]

The critical objective of this chapter is to analyze the lamentation concerning the fall of Jerusalem composed by Ibn al-Abīwardī, a jurist living in Baghdad during the time of the Frankish invasion of Jerusalem in 1099 CE. Rather than expanding the scholarship on this work by reading this lamentation within the historical framework of the Crusades, I am interested in exploring the ways in which Ibn al-Abīwardī's work can be seen as part of the poetic tradition of the *rithā' al-mudun*, or elegies over fallen cities. This chapter traces the ways in which the lament draws from pre-Islamic and medieval poetic forms, and from understandings of the significance of Jerusalem for the Islamic faith, and then places this lament within the larger context of medieval Jerusalem and lamentations composed about the city in the medieval Mediterranean world. Rather than positioning Arabo-Islamic sources as ones that are reactive to or complement already existing dominant European accounts, this chapter seeks to critically analyze this lamentation as part of the larger tradition of the genre in the medieval Mediterranean world, reading it alongside those of other ethnoreligious cultures further explored in this book.

The city elegy finds itself in the reality of a tangible loss of space and a constructed memory of that space for which the loss is both understood and expressed through traditional forms, such as rhetoric, metaphors, tropes, and language. For this reason I am also particularly interested in exploring the ways in which the elegy of Ibn al-Abīwardī functions within the historiographic work of Ibn al-Athīr, utilizing the construction of the city of Jerusalem to move the narrative from the past to the future through the call for liberation and the foreshadowing of the rise in the political and military front of 'Imād al-Dīn, Nūr al-Dīn Zengī, and Ṣalāḥ al-Dīn. In addition, given that the lament appears in Ibn al-Athīr's work, it further becomes an appropriation, which comes to terms with the earlier loss of Jerusalem and reflects on the internal tensions in the Arabo-Islamic world during the Frankish invasions of the late twelfth century. Both the lament of Ibn al-Abīwardī and the

8. Ibn Taghrībirdī, *Nujūm al-ẓāhira*, (Cairo: Maṭba'at dār al-kutub, 1939); Ibn al-Khayyāṭ, *Dīwān* (Damascus: Al-majma' al-'Arabī, 1958), 184–86. The importance of this poetry is also discussed in Emmanuel Sivan, *L'Islam et la Croisade* (Paris: Librairie d'Amérique et d'Orient, 1968); see also Hillenbrand, *Islamic Perspectives*, 69–71.

account of the loss of Jerusalem in Ibn al-Athīr move toward the assertion of Islamic unity as the only means of reconquering the city.

The Elegy for the Fallen City: The *Rithā' al-Mudun* in the Arabic Poetic Tradition

The *rithā' al-mudun*, the study of the elegy for a fallen city in the Arabic tradition, has not seen much scholarly attention. Though studies on Arabic poetry are numerous, specific attention has not been given to the study of city lamentations composed in Arabic in the medieval period. It is therefore beneficial to provide a brief overview of this tradition as a way of exploring how the work of Ibn al-Abīwardī furthers the already established tropes of elegies in Arabic—specifically the genre of the *rithā' al-mudun* and how the lament itself positions its narrative of the loss of Jerusalem within larger Arabo-Islamic and Mediterranean frameworks.

Elegies to fallen cities have a long history in the Arabic tradition. They appear both in poetry and prose, sometimes as individual poems or as part of longer compositions (such as the lament of Ibn al-Abīwardī, which is embedded within the longer narrative of Ibn al-Athīr's historical composition). These panegyrics predate Islam and are highly influenced by the forms and traditions of pre-Islamic poetry in Arabic from an era known as the Jāhilīyya, the age of "ignorance" or "impetuousness," the time before the advent of Islam traditionally dating from the Hegira, when Muḥammad and a small group of Muslims migrated from Mecca to Medina in 1 AH /622 CE. Ibrahim al-Sinjilawi argues that classical Arabic scholars have often classified the elegy, or *rithā'*, as purely a form of panegyric, or *madīḥ*, rather than interrogating specifically the development of the *rithā'* within pre-Islamic and Arabo-Islamic poetry.[9] Arabo-Islamic poetry of the medieval period is highly influenced by forms that existed in the pre-Islamic world and are believed to have been orally composed and transmitted, mostly in Bedouin culture. These works were eventually put into writing during the *tadwīn*

9. Ibrahim al-Sinjilawi, "The Lament for Fallen Cities: A Study of the Development of the Elegiac Genre in Classical Arabic Poetry" (PhD diss., University of Chicago, 1983). See also 'Abd al-Raḥmān Ḥusayn Muḥammad, *Rithā' al-mudun wa-al-mamālik al-zā'ila* (Cairo: Maṭba'at al-Jabalāwī, 1983).

movement (c. 750–800 CE), which was initiated by the Abbasid caliph al-Manṣūr in 761 CE to rewrite or more accurately write and record the history of the pre-Islamic and early Islamic periods from the perspective of the political and social concerns of the Abbasid period.

Among the corpus of pre-Islamic poetry there was a traditional verse form—the pre-Islamic ode, or *qaṣīda*, that dominated Arabo-Islamic poetry from about 500 CE onward. Its foundations lie in the rich oral tradition of pre-Islamic tribal world. The word *qaṣīda* itself means "intention," usually because the genre includes a petition or is directed to a patron. The *qaṣīda*, therefore, is most often a panegyric or *madīḥ*, "praise." The form was practiced by the warrior aristocracy in tribal Arabia, but was later also adopted in the courts of Arab client kings in the Byzantine and Sassanian Empires.[10]

The *qaṣīda,* most broadly defined, is a monometric, polythematic poem, usually of fifteen to eighty lines, in monorhyme; it is an ode of praise, boast, and elegy. The polythematic *qaṣīda* maintains a single meter, where every line rhymes in the same sound throughout. In its traditional form, the *qaṣīda* is comprised of three thematic units.[11] The first is the *nasīb*, or prelude, where the poet, departing from the campsite, recalls the departure of the women, the tribe, and the beloved. In its evocation of the lost campsite or the abode (the *aṭlāl*), this section includes expressions of departure, nostalgia, and desolation.[12] The second section is the *raḥīl*, or desert journey. The poet often describes his disengagement and movement away from his lover, land, and tribe. The final section reflects the *gharaḍ*, or the goal, of the *qaṣīda*. As outlined by Suzanne Pinckney Stetkevych, some of the common themes in this section include the *madīḥ*, praise of a ruler; the *fakhr*, a boast for the tribe; the *hijā'*, a satire or incentive; and the *rithā'* or elegy, which is usually for a

10. On the transition from orality to literacy, see Suzanne Pinckney Stetkevych, "From *Jāhiliyyah* to *Badī'iyyah*: Orality, Literacy, and the Transformation of Rhetoric in Arabic Poetry," *Oral Tradition* 25, no. 1 (2010): 211–30.

11. See 'Abd Allāh Ibn Muslim Ibn Qutaybah, *Kitāb al-Shi'r wa al-Shu'arā'*, ed. M. J. de Goeje (Leiden: Brill, 1904), a translation is available in Reynold A. Nicholson, *A Literary History of the Arabs* (Cambridge: Cambridge University Press, 1956), 77–78. See also Renate Jacobi, *Studien zur Poetik der altarabischen Qaṣide* (Wiesbaden: Steiner, 1971).

12. For a discussion of nostalgia in pre-Islamic and early Islamic poetry, see Muḥammad Ibrāhīm Ḥuwwar, *Al-Ḥanīn ilā al-waṭan fī al-adab al-'arabī ḥattā nihāyat al-'aṣr al-umawī* (Cairo: Dār nahḍat Miṣr lit-ṭab' wa-al-nashr, 1973). For an overview of nostalgia in Andalusī poetry, see Teresa Garulo, "La Nostalgia de al-Andalus: Génesis de un Tema Literario," *Qurtuba* 3 (1998): 47–63.

dead warrior.[13] The Umayyad and early Abbasid eras experienced not only the *qaṣīda* as the genre of the court, but also its derivatives such as the *khamrīyya* (wine poem), the *ṭardīyya* (hunt poem), the *zuhdīyya* (ascetic poem), and the *ghazal* (lyric love poem).[14] The *qaṣīda* form extended beyond the borders of the Arabic language to the literary cultures of the Arabo-Islamic world, as well as neighboring non-Muslim communities. Some scholars argue that the *ghazal*, which many think of as a Persian poetic form, seems to have separated itself off from the *nasīb* section of the *qaṣīda* into a distinctive literary genre in the Umayyad period. The *ghazal* form appears in languages such as Armenian, Persian, Swahili, Turkish, Urdu, and others.[15] The influence of the *qaṣīda* is so extant in the Arabo-Islamic world (and beyond) that Stetkevych regards it as one of the twin foundations of literary culture—the other being the Qur'an.[16]

In addition to influencing Arabo-Islamic poetic forms (as well as poetic forms of many other cultures) the pre-Islamic *qaṣīda* has also had an impact on the *rithāʾ al-mudun*. Scholars argue that the *rithāʾ al-mudun* genre flourished with the urbanization of Arabo-Islamic societies in the eighth and ninth centuries, particularly during the Abbasid period and the founding of Baghdad as the imperial capital in 762 CE. One of the earliest elegies for the city of Baghdad was composed following the civil war (809–13 CE) between

13. For more on the tripartite *qaṣīda* form, see Suzanne Pinckney Stetkevych, "Introduction," in *Early Islamic Poetry and Poetics*, The Formation of the Classical Islamic World 37 (Burlington, VT: Ashgate, 2009), xiii–xxxviii.

14. For a study of the *qaṣīda* in the Abbasid court, see Suzanne Pinckney Stetkevych, "Abbasid Panegyric and the Poetics of Political Allegiance: Two Poems of al-Mutanabbī on Kāfūr," in *Qasida Poetry in Islamic Asia and Africa*, ed. Stefan Sperl and Christopher Shackle (Leiden: Brill, 1996), 35–63. See also Magda al-Nowaihi, "Elegy and the Confrontation of Death in Arabic Poetry," in *Transforming Loss into Beauty: Essays on Arabic Literature and Culture in Honor of Magda al-Nowaihi*, ed. Marlé Hammond and Dana Sajdi (Cairo: American University of Cairo Press, 2008), 3–20.

15. The first arguably medieval Armenian poem, "For Manučʿē," was written by the prominent writer and political figure Grigor Magistros around 1045 CE and was inspired by the challenge made by an Arabic scholar he met in Constantinople in 1045 CE who claimed that the Bible was inferior to the Qur'an because it was not written in verse. See Manuk Abełyan, *Erker*, vol. 4 (Erevan: Armenian SAH GA, 1970), 109. Magistros composed his thousand-line poem of the Old and New Testament in verse, drawing from the Arabo-Islamic *qaṣīda* form. Abraham Terian argues that the name "Manučʿē" is a corruption found only in a single text, and that the original reads "Manazi." See Abraham Terian, *Magnalia Dei: Biblical History in Epic Verse by Grigor Magistros* (Leuven, Belgium: Peeters, 2012).

16. Suzanne Pinckney Stetkevych, *The Mute Immortals Speak: Pre-Islamic Poetry and the Poetics of Ritual* (Ithaca, NY: Cornell University Press, 2010), xi.

Hārūn al-Rashīd's two sons, al-Amīn and al-Ma'mūn regarding their succession. The poet Abū Ya'qūb Isḥāq al-Khuraymī composed a city lament that followed all the tropes inherent to the *qaṣīda* form; the loss of the beloved is the city, which continues to live on in verse.[17]

The urbanization of Arabo-Islamic culture marked a shift in the organization of Islamic society where tribal lands were replaced with communal spaces. Thus the early theme of yearning for one's homeland (*al-ḥanin ilā al-awṭān*) found in pre-Islamic Bedouin poetry began to also be applied to cities. The *rithā'*, or elegy, for the loss of a warrior in the *qaṣīda* also became replaced by the mourning of the loss of a city, along with the conventional use of the abandoned campsite in the *nasīb* section of the pre-Islamic *qaṣīda*.[18] City elegies were composed in Arabic for Mecca and Medina and for Baghdad, Basra, Damascus, and Kufa. With the numerous defeats experienced in al-Andalus beginning in the eleventh century and the eventual fall of the last Muslim bastion in Granada in 1492 CE, the *rithā' al-mudun* became a common genre for the Andalusī poet.

In fact, a majority of scholarship on city lamentations in Arabic has focused on the lamentation of fallen cities in Muslim Spain simply because they make up the most extant examples. As a highly evocative site of nostalgic expression, al-Andalus came to take on a mythical status, and at its peak of power in the tenth and eleventh centuries it was an important military, political, and intellectual center in the Mediterranean world. The loss of cities within Muslim Spain produced a large number of elegies that came to understand these places as a lost paradise of a once growing cultural splendor, translated later as symbols of displacement and exile—spaces that had come embraced in the past and mourned in the present. One of the first elegies composed for an Andalusian city is Ibn Shuhayd's elegy for the city of Cordova. Umayyad claimant Sulaymān Ibn al-Ḥakam attacked the city under the rule of the Umayyad caliph Hishām II al-Ḥakam, eventually sacking the city in 1013 CE—a loss that, scholars claim, led the decline and end of Umayyad rule. The city here stands as an emblem for a lost past. Our poet

---

17. Abū Ya'qūb Isḥāq al-Khuraymī, *Dīwān al-Khuraymī,* ed. 'Alī Jawād al-Ṭāhir and Muḥammad Jabbār al-Mu'aybid (Beirut: Dār al-Kitāb al-Jadīd, 1971), 27. Michael Fishbein has translated this poem in *The History of al-Ṭabarī*, vol. 31, *The War between Brothers* (Albany: State University of New York Press, 1985), 139.

18. Jaroslav Stetkevych, *The Zephyrs of Najd: The Poetics of Nostalgia in Classical Arabic Nasib* (Chicago: University of Chicago Press, 1993), 107.

laments the ruins of the city and appeals to time to restore the city's courtyards. In this elegy for Cordova, the poem becomes a larger reflection of the nostalgia for lost space and an idyllic past, but also calls for the restoration of that place in the lamentable present. Following the tropes present in city elegies, the lamentation serves as a testament to the past and the potential future of the city and the community remaining there.[19] The *rithā' al-mudun* continued to be evoked by many poets following Ibn Shuhayd's elegy—for such cities as Seville, Toledo, and Valencia, among others.[20]

Cities have symbolic resonance; they stand for a memory of the past, but also a reflection of how the past impacts and molds the present. The mourning of the loss of cities in poetry becomes a reflection of an already established culture of mourning, now posited onto a changing and growing nostalgia for the land. The city elegy, therefore, is positioned between the loss of tangible space in the present and the memory of a nostalgic connection of that place as a symbolic reflection of the past. The language used to compose and understand the loss of this space is rooted in a long-standing tradition of both individual and communal mourning. A nostalgic discourse was in place for the Arab poet, and it was one that would influence the later composition of Ibn al-Abīwardī's elegy over the loss of Jerusalem.

Ibn al-Abīwardī and the Jerusalem Lament

Ibn al-Abīwardī's panegyric ode begins with the acknowledgment of the situation of war and desecration in the city of Jerusalem: "we mixed blood with flowing tears / not a courtyard was left for the women" (مَزَجْنا دِماءً بِالْموعِ السَّواجِمِ / فَلَمْ يَبْقَ مِنَّا عَرْصَةٌ لِلمَراحِمِ; line 1).[21] The elegy uses a series of similes that compare a once glorious situation to the current moments of disaster. These

19. Alexander E. Elinson, "Loss Written in Stone: Ibn Shuhayd's *Ritha'* for Cordoba and Its Place in the Arabic Elegiac Tradition," in Hammond and Sajdi, eds., *Transforming Loss into Beauty*, 79–114. See also 'Abd Allāh Muḥammad al-Zayyāt, *Rithā' al-mudun fī al-sh'ir al-Andalusī* (Benghazi: Jāmi'at Qāryūnis, 1990).

20. Samuel the Nagid, a contemporary of Ibn Shuhayd, was the first to use the Hebrew *qaṣīda* in his poem about his flight from Cordova.

21. Gabrieli translates the line as follows: "We have mingled blood with flowing tears, and there is no room left in us for pity(?)." The word *marāḥim* in this line could have multiple meanings, such as "merciless," "women," or "womb." Gabrieli has chosen the first meaning, whereas I have chosen "women," since I believe the sense of the line is an appeal to protect the

juxtapositions at the onset of the lament further elevate the gravity of the conflict and not only heighten the immediacy of the retrieval of the city but also demonstrate its influence on the everyday life of the bereaved population. The poem draws from tropes of ancient city laments and those of the *rithāʾ al-mudun* to lament the loss of Jerusalem; these include the evocation of lament by the people, an attribution of the loss of the city to the sins of its inhabitants, a description of the loss and destruction of the city, and a call for unity and for liberation of the city from the hands of the invading enemy. The "hardship" (خِمارِها; line 11) of war has penetrated the lives of all, including the girls who hide their beauty (line 8); this evokes a picture of them seated and hunched over, with their foreheads on their wrists in shame and disappointment, mourning the loss of the city. Even the children (الوِلْدانُ; line 10) had their hair turn white at the sounds of stabbing and the hammering of swords (10). The thicket or brush (الخَميلَةِ; line 4) is evoked to symbolize a place of shade and safety, which has now been disrupted by the war in Jerusalem. The peaceful one napping in the shade (4) is now one whose eyelids (جُفونِها; line 5) cannot be shut because of the clamor that wakes all who are asleep. All are sacrificing sleep because of war and the invasion of foreigners (line 6). It is this peaceful state of slumber that the poem hopes will be achieved through the reconquest of the city.

The plight of all Muslims, including the women and children, is attributed in the poem to the disunity of the people, their movement away from the faith, and the neglect of their duty to rise up against the enemy. The claim is that the faith of the Muslim people has been resting on "weak pillars" (واهِي الدَّعا ئِم; line 14). The people are described as avoiding the war out of fear of death, and not considering such negligence as a form of dishonor (15). As the poem sees it, Islam has been humiliated, and the lament calls on all Muslims to defend themselves, their faith, and their holy places. The people who have now moved away from their faith and their obligations to defend the city are called to join together as a single unit against the enemy. This sense of unity becomes apparent through several references within Ibn al-Abīwardī's poetic verses. The first appears in line 3, where the poem calls to "sons of Islam" (فَإِيهاً بَني الإسْلامِ) to take up the sword against the enemy. Later the successes of unity are recalled through the conquests of the forefathers and

women whose homes have been destroyed. This translation also fits with the image of the unprotected women in line 8.

their defeat of the Persians (line 16). Under these circumstances, the lament claims how Islam neither suffers nor is shamed by the dishonor of the enemy. The qualities of bravery, generosity, and courage have been lacking in these men, and the verses urge all Muslims to reflect on the qualities of Arab pride that have been handed down from pre-Islamic times.

A significant reference of unity also appears in line 6, which makes an allusion to the "brothers in the *al-shām*," (وَ إِخوانُكُمْ بِالشّامِ), who according to the lamentation have been sacrificing sleep (lines 5–6). Bilād al-Shām or al-shām is the most common medieval Arabic reference to the area of Greater Syria or the Levant, and etymologically means "the left-hand region," since an individual in western or central Arabia was considered to face the rising sun, and thus the *shām* would fall on his or her left side.[22] The geographic region known as al-*s*hām also includes within its boundaries the city of Jerusalem (al-Quds, or "the holy"). According to the Arab geographer Al-Muqaddasī, al-*s*hām, which lies to the left of the Kaʿba (the Cube), is divided into four zones, and the city of Jerusalem is situated in the second zone.[23] The inclusion of al-Quds within the shām is also apparent in the *ḥadīths*, which reveal the shām to be the purest of all lands, the origin and heartland of the abode of Islam, "ʿUqr dār al-Islām al-shām."[24]

The reference to the *shām* within the poetic verses of Ibn al-Abīwardī could well be interpreted as an allusion to the larger geographic context of greater Syria, the term also utilized by Gabrieli in his translation of Abīwardī's verses (line 12). The reference would then be understood to call on and unify as one all the "brothers" or Muslim believers who once occupied the area of modern-day Jordan, Lebanon, and Syria; the contested regions of Israel/Palestine; and certain Turkish provinces in the north, Aīntāb and Diyārbekir.

22. ʿAli al-Masʿūdī, *Murūj al-Dhahab wa-Maʿādin al-Jawhar*, vol. 3 (Beirut: Dār al-Fikr, 1973), 140–42; Al-Muqaddasī, *Aḥsan al-Taqāsīm fī Maʿrifat al-Aqālīm*, ed. M. J. de Goeje (Leiden: Brill, 1906), 151–79. A partial translation is Al-Muqaddasī, *Aḥsan at-Taqāsīm fi Maʿrifat al-Aqālīm: La meilleure repartition pour la connaissance des provinces*, trans. André Miquel (Damascus: Institut français de Damas, 1963), 145–211; Guy Le Strange, *Palestine under the Moslems* (London: Watt, 1890), 14–18; René Dussaud, *Topographie historique de la Syrie antique et médiévale* (Paris: Guenther, 1927); Eugen Wirth, *Syrien: eine geographische Landeskunde* (Darmstadt, West Germany: Wissenschaftliche Buchgesellschaft, 1971).

23. Al-Muqaddasī, *al-Taqāsīm*, 167–72, trans. on 188–97.

24. For a discussion of al-shām in the *ḥadīth* tradition, see Al-Sayyid Muḥammad Ibn ʿAlawī, *The Hadith of Israʾ and Miʿraj/The Immense Merits of Al-Sham*, trans. Gibril Fouad Haddad (Fenton, MI: Islamic Supreme Council of America, 1999), 98–133, and esp. 98–99, 105–6.

This regional reference to al-shām would not, however, include the Abbasid administrative capital city of Baghdad.[25] Therefore, in this geographic reference, Ibn al-Abīwardī's verses not only attempt to transpose the events in the physical city of Jerusalem to Baghdad but also create a linkage between these two cities. This momentous event of the fall of the city of Jerusalem in the *shām* becomes therefore becomes placed in an Abbasid context in order to further the lament's call for unity and defense of the faith. Noting the significance of the city for the Islamic faith, Ibn al-Abīwardi's verses also seem to make an appeal to the Abbasids to join their "brothers in the *shām*" (line 6) and alleviate them from the attacks by the European powers. In this sense, the lament positions the loss of Jerusalem into the poem's own contemporary political, social, and cultural context.

The lament's attempt to connect the events in Jerusalem to the Abbasids is reflected further in the naming of the enemy as the *al-Rūmu al-hawāna* in line 7: "Despicable Byzantines impose themselves on them [people in the shām] while you drag the tail ends of your coats like someone who is at peace" (تَسُومُهُمُ الرُّومُ الهَوانَ وَ أَنْتُمُ / تَجُرُّونَ ذَيْلَ الخَفْضِ فِعْلَ المُسالِمِ). Although Gabrieli chooses to translate these two terms as merely "foreigners," the poem utilizes the usual term for the Byzantines, *al-Rūm*, and not, for example, *franj* (Frank). The assumption could very well have been that these attacks were from the Byzantines, who had been rivals for a century, and that the poet had confused the enemy.[26] Yet considering the poem's premise of Islamic unity, the reference to the enemy as *al-Rūm* becomes a way through which the lament can link the events in the *shām* with those in Baghdad. The Byzantines were the official rivals of the Abbasids, and thus by perhaps presenting the enemy as the usual and familiar one, the poem's appeal for Abbasid intervention becomes further heightened. Furthermore, it was the Greek emperor Alexius I Comnenus who appealed to Pope Urban II for aid against the Seljuqs, so the Fatimid alliance with the Byzantines could also very well be reflected in the naming of the enemy as *al-Rūm*.

---

25. For an interesting study on the city during the Abbasid period, see Gaston Weit, *Baghdad: Metropolis of the Abbasid Caliphate*, trans. Seymour Feiler (Norman: University of Oklahoma Press, 1971).

26. For a discussion of Muslim responses to the crusaders, see by Hillenbrand, *Islamic Perspectives*, 61–74.

The general call for defense within the poem also seems to be one that furthers its desire for unity through an appeal to the Abbasid caliph in Baghdad for whom Ibn al-Abīwardī presumably composed these verses.[27] Ibn al-Abīwardī was born in the Khurāsān province of the Persian Empire, the geographic area that gave birth to the Abbasid Revolution against the Umayyad caliphs.[28] His longtime connection to the Abbasid, and his reputation as a scholar and courtly poet of great celebrity, might also warrant the suggestion that he attempted to champion the caliph as a means of gaining an upper hand over the Fatimids.[29] In Stetkevych's study of the movement of Arabic poetry from the Jāhilīyya era to the postclassical genre of the *badī'iyya*—examining, among other things, a poem to the prophet Muḥammad in which each line utilizes a particular rhetorical device—she argues for the "retooling" of rhetorical devices in the high Abbasid age as correlatives to Islamic hegemony as witnessed in court panegyrics. After arguing for what she calls an "Islamic Manifest Destiny," Stetkevych claims that court panegyric poets had to match the dominion and high standard of their patron: "In other words, just as the caliph exercised a God-given might and dominion far beyond that of the kinglets and tribal lords of the *Jāhiliyya*, so were the court poets required to come up with a poetic idiom that could express this previously unimagined and God-given might."[30]

27. Dajani-Shakeel, "Jihād in Twelfth-Century Arabic Poetry," 101, claims that line 7 is a direct attack on the Abbasid caliph, al-Mustaẓhir billāh, and his sultan, Rukn al-Dīn Birkyārūq, who "was seen to have abandoned his community as well as his religious duties, particularly the jihād." This type of interpretation contradicts the poem's main theme of arguing for the need for Islamic unity, as indicated through the multiple references to "all Muslims" and "sons of Islam." More significantly, it would be difficult for the poet Ibn al-Abīwardī, whose role it was to uphold of the duty of princes and his obligation to praise his patron to display any explicit opposition or disloyalty to the caliph. In a note to line 13, Gabrieli, *Arab Historians*, 12, mentions "the unworthy Caliphs whose opposition to the Crusades is only half-hearted." The basis for the connection of this line to caliphs is unclear.

28. See M. A. Shaban, *The 'Abbāsid Revolution* (Cambridge: Cambridge University Press, 1970), esp. 138–68; and Elton L. Daniel, *The Political and Social History of Khurasan under Abbasid Rule* (Chicago: Bibliotheca Islamica, 1979), esp. 25–72.

29. Aḥmad Ibn Khallikān, *Wafayāt al-A'yān wa-anbā' abnā' al-zamān/Ibn Khalliḳān's Biographical Dictionary*, trans. MacGuckin de Slane, vol. 3 (Paris: Oriental Translation Fund of Great Britain and Ireland, 1868), 144–48; Clément Huart, *A History of Arabic Literature* (New York: Appleton, 1903), 108.

30. Stetkevych, "From *Jāhiliyyah to Badī'iyyah*, 215. For more on court poets in Baghdad, see James L. Kugel, *Poetry and Prophecy: The Beginnings of a Literary Tradition* (Ithaca, NY: Cornell University Press, 1990); Hugh Kennedy, *The Court of the Caliphs: The Rise and Fall of Islam's Greatest Dynasty* (London: Weidenfeld and Nicolson, 2004); and Hugh Kennedy, *When Baghdad*

In line 13, the poem makes an explicit call to the Abbasids, "Oh, sons of Hashim" (يا آل هاشم;). The Abbasids, who were the descendants of al-ʿAbbas ibn ʿAbd al-Muṭṭalib, uncle of the prophet Muḥammad, belonged to the branch of the Banū Hāshim, one of the tribes of the Quraysh in Mecca and the tribe to which Ibn al-Abīwardī is also believed to have belonged.[31] The lament's call to the "sons of Hashim" (line 13) becomes a way in which the poem can both make an appeal to the Abbasid caliphate and call them to defend those in the *shām* who have suffered at the hands of the crusaders. The lament also claims that those who are absent from the hardship of these wars will repent afterwards (line 11). The destruction of Jerusalem therefore becomes the channel through which Ibn al-Abīwardī's lament can make his call to defend the Islamic faith against the enemies not only to the Abbasids but to all Muslims.

Ibn al-Abīwardī's verses of the loss of Jerusalem are a testimony of the wars for the capture of Jerusalem in the late eleventh century, and can be used to analyze the internal relationship in the Arabo-Islamic world and with other ethnoreligious cultures of the Mediterranean. But these verses are also lines of poetry, a lamentation for the city. They represent the long-lasting poetic tradition of the *rithāʾ al-mudun*, extending from pre-Islamic times to the poet's contemporary moment. As has been noted, Ibn al-Abīwardī's elegy contains tropes common to the genre of the city laments found in the pre-Islamic and the Arabo-Islamic traditions. This *rithāʾ* over Jerusalem also seems to follow the three thematic units of the *qaṣīda*. The prelude, or *nasīb*, recalls the destruction of the city, the departure or lament of women and children who have suffered at the hands of enemy invasion. In its evocation of loss for the city emerge metaphors of unsettling peace along with expressions of nostalgia, grief, and suffering. Following this early call for lament comes a disengagement from protecting the city and a movement away from a life of peace. The final section therefore offers a solution to

---

Ruled the Muslim World: The Rise and Fall of Islam's Greatest Dynasty (Cambridge, MA: De Capo, 2006), esp. 112–29, 243–60.

31. E. de Zambaur, *Manuel de Genealogie et de Chronologie pour l'Histoire de l'Islam* (Hanover, Germany: Lafaire, 1927), esp. table G; B. Lewis, "Abbāsids," in *Encyclopaedia of Islam*, 2nd ed., vol. 2, ed. Th. Bianquis, C. E. Bosworth, E. van Donzel, P. Bearman, and W. P. Heinrichs (Leiden: Brill, 2002). See also Claude Cahen, "Points de vue sur la 'Révolution 'abbāside,'" *Revue Historique* 468 (1963): 295–338; and Jacob Lassner, *The Shaping of ʿAbbāsid Rule* (Princeton, NJ: Princeton University Press, 1980).

this desolate state by calling for all believers to strengthen their faith and join together in reconquering the city, taking it back from the enemy.

The lament's evocation of certain metaphors and images also recalls past elegies over cities in Arabo-Islamic literature. The lament frequently draws on the image of water, which perhaps recalls the ancient tradition of asking the supreme deity to send forth rain to water the deceased's grave and thus renew the lives that were lost and, in turn, the life of the city.[32] Other tropes in the lament include the city as the beloved; the fall of the city based on the sins of the inhabitants; the use of the imagery of blood and water (or bodies of water); the rhetorical device of repetition and refrain; the imagery of suffering, including that of women and children; and the evocation of the eyes and the notion of sleeplessness.[33] For example, in his lament over the destruction of Basra in 871 CE during the Zanj Rebellion, a major slave uprising against the Abbasid caliphate from 869 to 883 CE, Ibn al-Rūmī evokes the notion of sleeplessness through a series of rhetorical questions in a refrain that asks, "What sleep [is possible] after the great misfortunes which have befallen Basra / What sleep after the Zanj have violated openly the sacred places of Islam?"[34] And Abū Tammām recalls the destruction of the town Zibaṭra through the metaphor of sleep in his poem celebrating the capture of the Byzantine fortress city ʿAmmūriya (Amorium) in western Asia Minor by al-Muʿtaṣim when he writes, "You replied to a Zibaṭrian voice, for which you poured out the cup of slumber and the sweet saliva of living maidens."[35] For Ibn al-Abīwardī, sleeplessness is equated with a lack of safety, the disregard of believers, and the unsettled condition of both Jerusalem and Islam. The beloved is the city, the poet a seeker in it; and through lament, the poem awakens the sleeper, the believer seeking a place for peace-

32. For a discussion of the symbolic use of liquid flow in the *rithāʾ* and the associated *taḥrīḍ* (provocation to seek vengeance), see Stetkevych, *The Mute Immortal Speaks*, 161–205.

33. Elinson outlines various common tropes among the *rithāʾ al-mudun* form used by Andalusī poets. He attributes these characteristics to tropes present in the pre-Islamic *qaṣīda* form, which include repetition of the city; imagery and style common to Bedouin tribes; and the use of the imagery of water (such as in descriptions of eyes, the sky, gods and their sending of rain). Elinson, "Loss Written in Stone," 79–114. For more on rhetorical tropes and techniques used in city lamentations, see also the introduction in this book.

34. A. J. Arberry, "Ibn al-Rūmī," in *Arabic Poetry: A Primer for Students*, ed. A. J. Arberry (Cambridge: Cambridge University Press, 1965), 62–63.

35. "Abū Tammām," in Arberry, ed., *Arabic Poetry*, 58–59.

ful slumber. Paradoxically, this state is found through lament, an evocation of the past, and the poem's hope for the future.

Remapping Jerusalem: Ibn al-Athīr's Account and Competing Jerusalems

The *rithā*ʾ of Ibn al-Abīwardī becomes embedded within the historiographical account of Ibn al-Athīr's narrative, functioning as an intermediary space—a pause of mourning—after which the chronicle shifts from the past moments of Islamic disunity and weakness to the conquests and glories of the Zengid powers (Nūr al-Dīn, Ṣalāḥ al-Dīn) upon which the narrative will expound in the rest of the chronicle. Yet the image of the city of Jerusalem within the account of Ibn al-Athīr appears not as a single physical locus; rather, competing images of the city surface through allusions to the various powers that dominated the city up until its acquisition by the Franks in 1099 CE. References to the sacred edifices erected during the early rule of Islam in Ibn al-Athīr's chronicle call to mind not only the sanctity of the city for the Islamic faith but also the presence of the previous caliphs and the extensive building projects they undertook within the city of Jerusalem. Ibn al-Athīr's narrative of the conquest of the city also alludes to the presence of the Seljuqs and the Fatimids, their rivalry, and the eventual loss of the city to the Frankish powers of the West.

The section in the *al-Kāmil fī al-Tāʾrīkh* narrating the story of the fall of Jerusalem chronologically presents a succession of conquerors that evoke four periods of domination over the city of Jerusalem: the Umayyads and Abbasids, the Seljuqs, the Fatimids, and finally the crusaders. Therefore, a deeper examination of these alternate images of the city of Jerusalem within the greater context of Ibn al-Athīr's account gives rise to simultaneous multilayered constructions that reveal Jerusalem's position not only as a doubled metaphor for past and present but also as a space that symbolizes and exposes the rising internal conflicts of the Muslim powers prior to the onset of the First Crusade. Within Ibn al-Athīr's account, Jerusalem stands as a symbol that reflects the disunited and fragmented state of Islam prior to the Frankish invasions, calls to mind the various powers that dominated the city both in the past and within the narrative's contemporaneous present, and renders these groups' confrontation with the crusaders.

Figure 1. Medieval Islamic map of the world, which shows "Christian sects and states of Byzantium in the south." Library of Congress, Washington, DC.

Ibn al-Athīr al-Jazarī (1160–1233 CE) was an Arab or Kurdish historian who lived at different times in Aleppo, Damascus, and Mosul. He also traveled for some time with Ṣalāḥ al-Dīn's army, and is best known for his historical compilation *al-Kāmil fī al-Tāʾrīkh* (The complete history). Ibn al-Athīr's account of the capture of the city of Jerusalem by the Franks begins with a brief discussion of Jerusalem under the Seljuq ruler Tāj al-Dawla Tutush. In 1079 CE, Tutush murdered the Turkic emir Atsiz Ibn Uvaq al-Khwārizmī, a general of his brother Malik-Shāh I, who had captured the city of Jerusalem in 1070 or 1071 CE and transferred the rule of the city from the Fatimid caliph at Cairo to the rule of the Abbasids. In 1077 CE, returning to Jerusalem after a fruitless mission to overtake Cairo, Atsiz besieged the city a second time, as a rebellion had occurred during his absence. Tutush, who was fighting his brother Malik for control of greater Syria, murdered Atsiz and established firmer Abbasid rule within the city. Tutush appointed Emir Suqmān Ibn Artuq as the ruler of Jerusalem in 1086 CE. After Artuq's death in 1091, his two sons Suqmān and Īlghāzī, who were bitter rivals, were expelled from the city in 1098 CE by the Fatimid vizier al-Afḍal Ibn Badr al-Jamālī.[36] According to Ibn al-Athīr's brief account of the circumstances in

36. See al-Maqrīzī, *Ittiʿāẓ al-ḥunafāʾ*, ed. J. al-Shayyal (Cairo: Dār al-Fikr al-ʿArabī, 1948); Ibn al-Dawādārī, *Die Chronik des Ibn al-Dawādārī*, vol. 6, ed. S. Munaggid (Cairo: Cairo; Wiesbaden:

Jerusalem before the arrival of the crusaders from the west, Badr al-Jamālī demolished parts of the walls of Jerusalem, and after forty days of fighting the city fell to the Fatimids in Sha'bān 489 AH /July 1096 CE Fatimids.

The general state of the Islamic world in the period leading up to the crusader invasion of Jerusalem was one marked by a succession of political changes and adversities. The Islamic world had been weakened by a series of deaths of great caliphs and commanders, among them the murder of the Seljuk vizier Nizam al-Mulk; the death of the Fatimid caliph al-Mustanṣir billāh and his Armenian Mamluk vizier Badr al-Jamālī; and the death of the great Malik-Shāh. A great religious schism between the Fatimids of Egypt, an Ismaili Sh'ite sect, and the neighboring Sunni Muslim Seljuks both divided and diminished power within Islam. This loss of effective leadership resulted in the dissolving of powers into smaller, dynastic states. The period is thus generally marked as one of disunity and an overall sense of disorganization and disorientation—characteristics that according to Islamic historians mark the success of the crusaders' capture of Jerusalem.[37]

Carole Hillenbrand, in her wide-ranging study, argues based on contemporaneous Muslim sources that it is highly plausible that the Byzantines had warned the Fatimids about the arrival of the crusaders from the west, and the Fatimids saw the Seljuqs as a greater threat than the crusaders, with whom they might have had some prearranged alliances.[38] The Byzantine forewarning might have also enabled the capture of Jerusalem in 1097–98 CE by the Fatimid vizier al-Afḍal Ibn Badr al-Jamālī. Ibn al-Athīr's chronicle maintains the perspective that the success of the Fatimid capture of Jerusalem was also based on the disunity of the Seljuq Turks, their lack of

In Kommission bei Harrassowitz, 1961); Ibn Taghrībirdī, *Nujūm al-ẓāhira*, vol. 5 (Cairo: Maṭba'at dār al-kutub, 1939); trans. and ed. William Popper as *Annals, Entitled 'an-Nujūm az-ẓāhira fi muluk Miṣr wal-Qāhira'*, vol. 5 (Berkeley: University of California Press, 1954). See also Carole Hillenbrand, *Islamic Perspectives*, 31–88; Gerhard Endress, *Islam: An Historical Introduction*, 2nd ed. (New York: Columbia University Press, 2002), 110–21; Hugh Kennedy, *The Prophet and the Age of the Caliphates* (London: Longman, 2004), 307–45; S. Lane-Poole, *A History of Egypt in the Middle Ages*, 2nd. ed. (London: Frank Cass, 1914), 160–70; Hans L. Gottschalk, *Al-Malik al-Kāmil von Egypten und seine Zeit* (Wiesbaden: Harrassowitz, 1958). A good source for general history is Ira M. Lapidus, *A History of Islamic Societies* (Cambridge: Cambridge University Press, 2002).

37. See al-Maqrīzī, *Itti'āẓ al-ḥunafā'*, 164–65; al-Jawzī, *Al-Muntaẓam*, 9:100–108; Al-'Azimi, "La chronique abrégée d'al-'Azimi," ed. Claude Cahen, *Journal Asiatique* 230 (1938): 353–448; and Ibn al-Athīr, *al-Kamil*, 10:187–90.

38. Hillenbrand, *Islamic Perspectives*, 44–45.

cohesion, and the weakening of their power as a result of the battle of Antioch (lines 282–83).

The brief section of the Frankish capture of Jerusalem in Ibn al-Athīr's chronicle in fact alludes to the transfer of power of the city of Jerusalem from the Seljuqs to the Fatimids of Egypt. This reference transitions the narrative to the description of yet another shift in power over the city. Within the section devoted to the invasion of Jerusalem, the image of the Franks and their destruction of significant physical monuments within the city calls to mind the city under the rule of the Umayyads but also reveals two other competing images of the city. As Ibn al-Athīr explains,

> The Franks did indeed take the city from the north in the forenoon of Friday, seven days remaining of Shaʿban [July 1099]. The inhabitants became a prey for the sword. For a week the Franks continued to slaughter the Muslims. A group of Muslims took refuge in the Tower of David and defended themselves there. . . . In the Aqsa Mosque the Franks killed more than 70,000, a large number of them being imams, ulema, righteous men and ascetics. . . . The Franks took forty or more silver candlesticks from the Dome of the Rock, each of which weighed 3,600 dirhams, and also a silver candelabrum weighing forty Syrian rotls.[39]

Ibn al-Athīr's description of the invasion of the Franks on the city of Jerusalem not only focuses on the sites in the city built under the Umayyads, which hold significance for the Islamic faith, but through these physical edifices exposes Islam's internal conflicts and its confrontation with the Franks. By drawing attention to the *ḥaram*, or holy sites, within Jerusalem—such as the Miḥrāb, or Tower of David; the al-Masjid Aqṣā mosque; and the Qubbat al-Ṣakhra, or the Dome of the Rock—the glory of the Islamic past is set in contrast to the internal strife of the contemporary present that leads to the eventual loss of the city of Jerusalem.

In addition to outlining four different moments of domination over the city, Ibn al-Athīr's testimony exposes two sets of conflicts within its narrative. The first tension appears within the earlier part of the account, where the text summarizes the dispute between the Seljuqs and the Fatimids and

39. Ibn al-Athīr, *al-Kāmil*, 10:283–84; [ʿIzz al-Dīn Ibn al-Athīr,] *The Chronicle of Ibn al-Athīr for the Crusading Period, from al-Kamil fiʾl-Taʾrikh*, vol. 1, trans. D. S. Richards (Aldershot, England: Ashgate, 2006), 21–22.

their quarrels over the city of Jerusalem (among other territories). In this earlier portion, the anxiety over the loss of Jerusalem is internally Muslim. The swaying of power between the two powers is due to a lack of cohesion, a religious schism, and disunity. Despite these factors, the city is still in Muslim hands. Badr al-Jamālī's acquisition and dismissal of Suqmān and Īlghāzī are in fact presented in an agreeable light when the text claims, "Al-Afḍal treated Suqmān, Īlghāzī, and their followers well, gave them generous gifts and sent them on their way to Damascus. Subsequently they crossed the Euphrates. Suqmān took up residence in Edessa and Īlghāzī moved to Iraq."[40]

This internal tension, which is eventually resolved by the narrative through the amicable departure of Badr al-Jamālī's two sons, is disrupted with the shift to the description of the arrival of the Franks, which produces a higher magnitude of conflict. In this section, the strife is not internal but external, since the invader of the city is a foreigner who not only disrespects the terrestrial Jerusalem through acts of destruction and looting but also slaughters the Muslims in their holy places. The physical edifices built under the Umayyads—symbols for the centuries of Muslim rule over the city—are disrupted by the penetration of the Frankish powers from the west. This invasion and acquisition of the Franks not only drives a wedge into the narrative of past centuries of Muslim domination over the city but also exploits and benefits from Islam's contemporaneous disarray. The narrative clearly sees this invasion of the Franks as not only threatening but also, in its contemporary moment, a means of dislocating the power of Islam and disrespecting its past majesty.

Considering the positioning of Ibn al-Abīwardī's panegyric verses within the account of Ibn al-Athīr's chronicle reveals a secondary function of the poem. The section preceding the poem is one that describes a series of Muslim dominators over the city of Jerusalem, ending with the city completely lost from their hands and acquired by the crusaders from the west. The positioning of the poem after the capture of the city to the Franks within Ibn al-Athīr's account becomes a transition point within the narrative that reflects on the disunity of the Muslim people, their movement away from the faith, and the consequences of such actions. The account of the fall of the city and the descriptions of Muslim disunity and the eventual conquest by the cru-

40. Ibn al-Athīr, *al-Kamil*, 10:283; [Ibn al-Athīr,] *The Chronicle*, 21.

saders becomes both considered and synthesized within Ibn al-Abīwardī's call for Islamic unity and jihad. The lamentation of Jerusalem becomes the channel through which Ibn al-Athīr's chronicle represents a somewhat failed leadership of the past and thus sets up a discussion of the great Muslim leaders who will come in the future, such as Ṣalāḥ al-Dīn, who will eventually reconquer the city and place it once again in the hands of the Muslim people. Ibn al-Athīr is actually believed to have seen the conquest of Jerusalem, and possibly may have met Ṣalāḥ al-Dīn at the siege of Krak des Chevaliers, though he does not explicitly state this in his narrative.[41]

The examination of the image of the city of Jerusalem within both the narrative of Ibn al-Athīr and the lament of Ibn al-Abīwardī reveal Jerusalem's role as a metaphorical interlude between past and present. Jerusalem becomes the channel through which both authors further their call for Islamic unity and promote the campaigns of the Muslim powers in the Levant. The testimony of the capture of Jerusalem by the Franks serves to provide a forum through which Islamic transgressions can be exposed, and also functions as an intermediary that links Jerusalem to temporal, geographical, and cultural events in the Arabo-Islamic world. Jerusalem becomes an emblem for the disjointed and fragmented state of the Islamic powers before the Frankish movement into the Levant. At the same time, the fall of the city becomes the catalyst for a call for the unification of the Muslim people, for a return to the faith and those geographic spaces sacred to it.

What both Ibn al-Abīwardī's lamentation and Ibn al-Athīr's chronicle also demonstrate is that to speak of Jerusalem in the medieval Mediterranean, one must first lament Jerusalem.

41. See D. S. Richards, "Introduction," in [Ibn al-Athīr,] *The Chronicle*, 1–9; and Khallikān, "ʿIzz al-Dīn Abūʾl-Ḥasanʿ Alī b. Muḥammad al-Jazarī," in *Wafayāt al-Aʾyān wa-anbāʾ abnāʾ al-zamān*, 288–90.

Chapter 3

Papal Lamentations

The First Crusade and the Victorious Mourning for Jerusalem

Fresh blows the wind
To the homeland
My Irish child
Where do you wait?

Frisch weht der Wind
Der Heimat zu
Mein Irisch Kind,
Wo weilest du?

—Richard Wagner, *Tristan and Isolde*

In order to speak of Jerusalem, one must first lament Jerusalem.

The inception of movement of a large group of western Europeans to the Levant in the late eleventh century, more commonly referred to as the First Crusade, is argued by scholars to be the result of a series of speeches delivered by Pope Urban II at the Council of Clermont, November 18–27, 1095 CE. According to these same accounts, moved by the efforts of the Greek emperor Alexius I Comnenus and the attacks of the Seljuqs on Byzantine lands, the pope is believed to have preached for the liberation of the city of Jerusalem from the hands of the Muslim powers. Why would the pope be concerned with obtaining the physical city of Jerusalem, when the heavenly Jerusalem was for so many years privileged and internalized in Latin Church doctrines? Why did the control of Jerusalem suddenly become a point of contestation for the Latin Church, when the city had been under the rule of

Muslim powers since the middle of the seventh century? And why do the handful of chronicles that attribute the beginning of the crusading movement to the pope present the city as a Christian space that needs to be reconquered from the enemy?

Our answer is where we began: with city lamentation.

Although the accounts of Pope Urban II's speeches at Clermont are embedded within larger narratives of the victories of the crusaders at Jerusalem (and other regions of the Mediterranean), they initially present the city as a lost Christian space that should be recaptured from Muslim powers. The critical argument I make in this chapter is that these accounts begin their narratives by lamenting the city of Jerusalem in order to assert Christian claims to the city and justify both the crusader movement to Jerusalem and its eventual capture by the Latin West. This mode of lamenting reflects a Christian supersessionism in that these accounts first transfer the image of the earthly Jewish city into the creation of a Latin Christian Jerusalem. By establishing their own earthly Jerusalem, these accounts then rely on the exemplum of lamenting Jerusalem in the Hebrew Bible, which becomes appropriated to the history of the Latin Church and its relationship to Jerusalem. Whereas the attitudes toward the city of Jerusalem by the Latin Church prior to Pope Urban II's call to crusade reflect an understanding that the earthly city was the city of the Jews, that a pilgrimage to Jerusalem was not necessary, and that the goal of the Christian believer was to enter the heavenly, these accounts produced after the victory of the First Crusade reveal a brief shift in Christian thought where the earthly Jerusalem receives a higher status than it had in the past and thus becomes an object of lamentation.[1] It is precisely this shift in theology that allows for Pope Urban II's voice to become the channel through which the "reconquest" of Jerusalem is preached. It is also this movement toward the physical Jerusalem that exposes the ways in which these chronicles draw from the tradition of ancient city lamentations, allowing for a recursive lament of Jerusalem to resurface and for its conquest to be textually actualized. By attributing the onset of the crusading movement to Pope Urban II, these chronicles also expose efforts to create an official version of the victory at Jerusalem in 1099 CE, and to demonstrate through lamentation the an-

1. For more on lamenting Jerusalem in the Old Testament, and Christian attitudes toward the city of Jerusalem prior to the First Crusade, see the introduction to this book.

Figure 2. Illumination of Pope Urban II at the Council of Clermont in *Livre des Passages d'Outre-mer*, c. 1490. Bibliothèque nationale de France, MS. Fr. 5594, fol. 9.

cient connection of Jerusalem to the Latin Church. Crusader historians have debated whether or not Jerusalem was initially the goal of the Crusades or if the conquest of the city came as part of the larger advancements toward the eastern Mediterranean.[2] The attribution of the victory of the capture of Jerusalem by the Franks to the pope Urban II, reframes earlier accounts by establishing the city of Jerusalem as the motivation for the First Crusade. Through the mode of lamentation, these testimonies seek to

2. The question of whether Jerusalem was the central focus of the movement of western Europeans into the Levant and Jerusalem has been debated for decades among crusading historians, who have considered theological, political, and social changes in the period leading up to the First Crusade as reasons behind a European interest in the Levant and the Holy Land in the early eleventh century. Carl Erdmann, *Die Entstehung des Kreuzzugsgedankens* (Stuttgart: Kohlhammer, 1955), argues that the Crusades emerged from a growing "papal militarism" prior to the First Crusade, and that Jerusalem was a secondary goal, a lure to appeal to all aspects of medieval society (the layperson and the religious person alike). The works of E. O. Blake, H. E. J. Cowdrey, and Jonathan Riley-Smith, among others challenge Erdmann's thesis regarding the significance of the city of Jerusalem in the crusading movement. See E. O. Blake, "The Formation of the 'Crusade Idea,'" *Journal of Ecclesiastical History* 21 (1970): 11–31; H. E. J. Cowdrey, "Pope Urban II's Preaching of the First Crusade," *History* 55 (1970): 177–88; Jonathan Riley-Smith, *The First Crusade and the Idea of Crusading* (Philadelphia: University of Pennsylvania Press, 1986); and John Gilchrest, "The First Crusade and the Idea of Crusading by Jonathan Riley-Smith" (review), *Speculum* 63, no. 3 (1988): 14–17.

further establish the relationship between Pope Urban II, his recorded speeches in contemporary historiographic accounts, and the place of Jerusalem in the Latin West.

Jerusalem Foregrounded: The Inclusion of Pope Urban II's Speeches at Clermont

Christian attitudes toward the city of Jerusalem prior to the First Crusade reflect a position that not only considered the earthly city as inferior to the heavenly but also discouraged movement toward the physical Jerusalem. Similarly, the Christian Church associated laments for the city with non-Christian behavior, and more specifically a Jewish and pagan genre, though we know that in the secular realm lamentation was a continued practice. What, then, can we make of the accounts that try to celebrate and authenticate their claim of the Frankish victory at Jerusalem? How can we understand the call of the pope Urban II and his supported for a large movement of pilgrims from western Europe toward the Levant and Jerusalem? Let us begin by first looking more closely at our sources.

In the plethora of material that was produced after the Frankish conquest of Jerusalem in 1099 CE, only the following five accounts provide a version of the speeches at Clermont, attributing the inception of the crusading movement to the pope Urban II: *Gesta Francorum Iherusalem Peregrinantium* (The deeds of the Franks on their journey to Jerusalem) of Fulcher of Chartres, the *Historia Iherosolymitana* (History of Jerusalem) of Robert the Monk, the *Historia Jherosolimitana* (History of Jerusalem) of Baldric of Dol, the *Gesta Dei per Francos* (The deeds of God through the Franks) of Guibert of Nogent, and the *Gesta Regum Anglorum* (The deeds of English kings) of William of Malmesbury.[3] A closer examination of four of these sources reveals

3. Fulcher of Chartres, *Gesta Francorum Iherusalem Peregrinantium*, in RHC Occ. 3:322–24; Fulcher of Chartres, *A History of the Expedition to Jerusalem 1095–1127*, trans. Frances Rita Ryan, ed. Harold S. Fink (Knoxville: University of Tennessee Press, 1969); Robertus Monachus [Robert the Monk], *Historia Jherosolimitana*, in RHC Occ. 3:727–30; Robert the Monk, *Robert the Monk's History of the First Crusade: Historia Iherosolimitana*, trans. Carol Sweetenham (Aldershot, England: Ashgate, 2005); Baldric of Dol, *Gesta Dei per Francos*, in RHC Occ. 4:12–15; Guibert of Nogent, *Gesta Dei per Francos*, in RHC Occ. 4:137–40; Guibert of Nogent, *The Deeds of God through the Franks: A Translation of Guibert de Nogent's Gesta Dei per Francos*, trans. and ed. Robert Levine (Woodbridge, England: Boydell and Brewer, 1997); William of Malmesbury, *Gesta Regum*

three qualities: first, that there was a deliberate attempt to create an "official" version of the victory at Jerusalem, which attributed the onset of the crusading movement to Pope Urban II;[4] second, that collectively these accounts also reveal a shift in Christian attitudes toward Jerusalem by placing the earthly Jerusalem in a higher position than they had in the past; and third, with the preference now being given to the physical obtainment of the city, these historiographic sources rely on an already established model of lamenting Jerusalem in the Hebrew Bible. Jerusalem is first presented as a lost Christian city, and subsequently celebrated as reconquered space for Latin Christendom.

Pope Urban II was born under the name Odo in the diocese of Soissons in northern France. He was educated at Rheims, after which he entered the great monastery at Cluny in Burgundy.[5] In many ways, the histories of Robert, Baldric, and Guibert share a similar policy. As Carol Sweetenham notes, they form "part of a deliberate attempt to create an official version, historical and theological, of the events of the crusade, driven perhaps by Cluny."[6] All three of these figures were Benedictines who came from areas of Northern France that had a Capetian sphere of influence.[7] Robert of Reims, or Robert the Monk, claims to have composed his *Historia* in "a cloister of a certain monastery of St-Rémi" [*claustrum cujusdam cellae Sancti*

Anglorum, vol. 2, ed. and trans. R. A. B. Mynors, R. M. Thomson, and M. Winterbottom (Oxford: Oxford University Press, 1998), 592–609. A translation of Urban's speech can be found in A. C. Krey, *The First Crusade: The Accounts of Eyewitnesses and Participants* (Princeton, NJ: Princeton University Press, 1921), 33–36. All subsequent references to these texts are taken from these editions and translations, with the exception of Baldric of Dol, the translations of which are my own. The original Latin texts will also be referenced throughout this chapter by indicating the corresponding volume and page numbers in RHC Occ. Apart from these five accounts, there are a number of letters and references to Pope Urban II's presence at Clermont, as well as fragmentary reports of other sermons he preached in France; they are not included here.

4. The exception here is the version of William of Malmesbury, who provides the only English account of the First Crusade. The discussion of William's version will be returned to later in this section.

5. Frank J. Coppa, "Pope Urban II," in *The Great Popes through History: An Encyclopedia*, vol. 1 (Westport, CT: Greenwood, 2002), 107.

6. Sweetenham, in Robert the Monk, *Robert the Monk's History*, 14.

7. A fourth Benedictine figure and contemporary of these authors, Gilo of Paris, who later would become cardinal-bishop of Tusculum, composed a verse history of the First Crusade in the first decade of the twelfth century that began with the events at Nicaea. Gilo of Paris, *The Historia Vie Hierosolimitanae of Gilo of Paris*, ed. and trans. C. W. Grocock and J. E. Siberry (Oxford: Oxford University Press, 1997). Robert's text shows extensive parallels with Gilo's account; see Sweetenham, in Robert the Monk, *Robert the Monk's History*, 29–35.

Remigii] (3:721–22). Guibert of Nogent was the abbot of Nogent-sous-Coucy in the Ile de France, and Baldric of Dol was the archbishop of Dol-en-Bretagne.[8]

Believed to be a participant in the First Crusade, Fulcher of Chartres provides the most detailed account of Pope Urban II's speeches and the crusader expedition to Jerusalem. Born around 1059 CE in Chartres, Fulcher was later appointed as chaplain of Baldwin of Boulogne in 1097 CE. He was part of a group of nobleman including Stephen of Blois and Robert of Normandy who made their way through southern France and Italy; he joined their army in Constantinople in 1097 CE. After the success of the First Crusade, Fulcher traveled with Baldwin to Jerusalem and became the canon of the Church of the Holy Sepulcher in 1115 CE until his death. In Jerusalem he had an intimate connection to Baldwin of Boulogne, who was named the first king of crusader Jerusalem in 1100 CE.[9] In the prologue to his *Deeds of the Franks*, Fulcher reveals the foundation for the composition of his work:

> For this reason, moved by the repeated requests of some of my comrades, I have related in careful and orderly fashion the illustrious deeds of the Franks when by God's most express mandate they made a pilgrimage in arms to Jerusalem in honor of the Savior.
>
> Unde comparium meorum quorumdam pulsatibus aliquotiens motus, Francorum gesta in Domino clarissima qui Dei ordinatione cum armis Iherusalem peregrinati sunt. (3:319)

The parallel between the date of the composition of these sources and Bohemond I of Antioch's tour of France may also have had a direct impact on the composition of these histories. According to Sweetenham, Robert the Monk composed his work in 1106–7 CE.[10] Robert Levine dates the composition of the history of Guibert of Nogent around the same year as Robert's, 1107 CE.[11] Baldric of Dol is also believed to have composed his

---

8. Jay Rubenstein, *Guibert of Nogent: Portrait of a Medieval Mind* (New York: Routledge, 2002); Krey, *The First Crusade*, 33–36.

9. Fulcher of Chartres, *A History of the Expedition to Jerusalem*, 1–56.

10. Sweetenham, in Robert the Monk, *Robert the Monk's History*, 4–7.

11. For historical background on the text, see Robert Levine, "Introduction," in Guibert of Nogent, *The Deeds of God*, 1–19.

account in the later part of his life, around 1107 CE, when he was appointed the archbishop of Dol-en-Bretagne.[12] Fulcher completed the first part of his history at an earlier date than the others, in 1105 CE; and his account serves a source text for others.[13] Thus, all four accounts of the First Crusade, which include information pertaining to Pope Urban II's sermons at Clermont, are written after the capture of the city by the Franks in 1099 CE and are contemporaneous with Bohemond I's return to France and his arrangements for a new crusade.[14]

In the aftermath of the First Crusade the anonymous eyewitness account known as the *Gesta Francorum et aliorum Hierosolimitanorum* (The deeds of the Franks and other [pilgrims] to Jerusalem; hereafter *GF*) appeared around 1100.[15] The historian, who seemed to be a compatriot of Bohemond I, provides a narrative of the First Crusade, ending with the Battle of Ascalon in 1099 CE. The *GF* became the exemplary textual source on which a number of subsequent Western chronicles of the First Crusade relied, including those of the aforementioned authors.[16] Although they recognized the *GF* as a textual source, Fulcher, Baldric, Robert, and Guibert saw this account as an initial version with a number of problematic features, the most significant of which was that the chronicle focused heavily on the city of Antioch.

The various hindrances of the *GF* catalyzed a textual movement by these authors to produce their own version of the capture of Jerusalem by the Franks. The historiographic accounts, which also included now testimonies of Pope Urban II's speeches at Clermont, saw a number of hindrances in the version provided in the *GF*. The first criticism of the *GF* was its unrefined and rustic language. In the preface to his work, Guibert states,

12. Krey, *The First Crusade*, 33–36.

13. Due to the detailed nature of his account, some historians argue that Fulcher might have been present at Clermont.

14. Orderic Vitalis, *The Ecclesiastical History of Orderic Vitalis*, vol. 1, *General Introduction*, ed. Marjorie Chibnall (Oxford: Oxford University Press, 1969), 5; Radulfo Cadomensi [Ralph of Caen], *Gesta Tancredi in Expeditione Hierosolymitana*, in RHC Occ. 5:713–14; William of Malmesbury, *Gesta Regum Anglorum*, 2:454.

15. *Gesta Francorum: The Deeds of the Franks and other Pilgrims to Jerusalem*, ed. and trans. Rosalind Hill (Oxford: Oxford University Press, 2002).

16. John France, "The Use of the Anonymous *Gesta Francorum* in the Early Twelfth-Century Sources of the First Crusade," in *From Clermont to Jerusalem: The Crusades and Crusader Societies 1095–1500*, ed. Alan V. Murray (Turnhout, Belgium: Brepols, 1998), 29–42.

> A version of this same history, but woven out of excessively simple words, often violating grammatical rules, exists, and it may often bore the reader with the stale, flat quality of its language.
>
> Erat siquidem eadem historia, sed verbis contexta plus aequo simplicibus et quae multotiens gramaticae naturas excederet, lectoremque vapidi insipiditate sermonis saepius exanimare valeret. (4:119)

Robert also names the text as inarticulate in that "the composition was uncertain and unsophisticated in its style of expression" [*litteralium compositio dictionum inculta*] (3:721).

A secondary and more significant problem of the *GF* was the belief that the text was both unsophisticated and lacking in content, as indicated by Baldric:

> In fact, by no means am I amazed by the astonishing spirit of the aforementioned book, which I am mindful to check and polish—a book by a sciolist, which is a little rugged, contains no real knowledge and especially does not dare to mention its composer.
>
> Non minimum vero obstupescendo miror quo animo libellum praefatum ad compescendum et poliendum direxerit insciolo et pene nullius scientiae gutta rigato, quum praesertim nullus poetarum id praesumere audeat. (4:8)

One of the main goals of these authors was to "correct" the *GF*, a desire that is also expressed by Guibert in his preface: "Therefore, I believe the assaulting model of this very history must be corrected or even corrupted." (Corrigendum igitur nescio an corrumpendum, historiae ipsius aggressurus exemplar; 4:120.)[17] The *GF*'s content, which focused its narrative primarily on the Frankish conquest of Antioch, did not offer the same for the city of Jerusalem. In chapter 10, the text provides an account of the "sanctorum locorum Hierusalem" but does not give any details about the Frankish invasion into Jerusalem, their battle with the Muslim powers controlling the city, and their eventual victory. What in fact is provided is a catalog of places to visit for those on pilgrimage: "If anyone, coming from the western lands, wishes

17. This is my translation, since the manner in which Levine translates the verbs in this sentence gives the impression that Guibert's account is corrupted, whereas I see the line claiming that the author wants to change the account corrupted by the *GF*.

to go to Jerusalem, let him direct his course due eastwards, and in this way he will find stations for prayer in the lands in and around Jerusalem, as they are noted here." (Si quis ab occidentalibus partibus Hierusalem adire voluerit, solis ortum semper teneat, et Hierosolimitani loci oratoria ita inveniet, sicut hic notatur.)[18] The *GF*'s version of the onset of the crusading movement is brief, and it mentions neither Pope Urban II nor Clermont by name. It merely claims that when the words of the pope were spread to all the duchies and counties of Frankish lands, many people decided to set out from their homes:

> For even the pope set out across the Alps as soon as he could, with his archbishops, bishops, abbots and priest, and he began to deliver eloquent sermons and to preach, saying, "If any man wants to save his soul, let him have no hesitation in taking the way of the Lord in humility, and if he lacks money, the divine mercy will give him enough."
>
> Apostolicus namque Romanae sedis ultra montanas partes quantocius profectus est cum suis archiepiscopis, episcopis, abbatibus, et presbiteris, coepitque subtiliter sermocinari et predicare dicens, ut si quis animam suam salvam facere vellet, non dubitaret humiliter viam incipere Domini, ac si denariorum ei deesset copia, divina ei satis daret misericordia.[19]

The subsequent chronicles of Fulcher, Baldric, Robert, and Guibert set out to create a more grammatically sound account of the crusaders but, more important, they develop the basis of the narrative of the capture of Jerusalem by beginning with Clermont. The *GF* was most probably already circulating in connection with Bohemond's drive to raise men for a new crusade in the early eleventh century. Bohemond had arrived in France in early 1106 CE, at which point he visited the Shrine of St. Leonard and undertook a triumphant tour, offering relics from the East to various churches and monasteries.[20]

The four chroniclers' motivation to begin their historiographic works with the speeches of Pope Urban II not only materializes from their disapproval of the *GF*'s style and focus but also functions as the means to which their

18. Hill, ed. and trans., *Gesta Francorum*, 98.
19. Hill, *Gesta Francorum,* 1.
20. Riley-Smith, *The First Crusade*, 137.

narratives can achieve two main goals: first, to uphold the figure of Pope Urban II as the initiator of the western crusading movement and promote the victorious undertakings of the Franks as agents of God; and second, to forefront the image of the city of Jerusalem by shifting the focus from Antioch (in the *GF*) toward Jerusalem. It is their inclusion of the events at Clermont, rather than the absence of this information, that makes the works of these four chronicles distinctive, since almost all the Western accounts of the First Crusade in some form mention Pope Urban II's role in the crusading effort but do not make a point of providing an account of his speeches at Clermont.[21]

Both Robert and Guibert also claim to have composed their accounts for an ecclesiastical patron: Robert for the mysterious Abbot B., and Guibert for Lisiardus, bishop of Soissons. In his *Sermo Apologeticus*, Robert claims he was commissioned to write his history by a presiding abbot because Robert was present at Clermont, "so he instructed me, since I had been present at the council of Clermont, to add the beginning which was missing and to improve its style for future readers" [*praecepit igitur mihi ut, qui Clari Montis concilio interfui, acephalae materiei caput praeponerem et lecturis eam accuratiori stilo componerem*] (3:721–22). Robert's prologue draws attention directly to the *GF* and its "missing beginning," the Council of Clermont, and the pope from Rheims, Urban II. Robert's position at Rheims and the composition of his work were most likely a joint attempt to further the agenda at the Council at Clermont, where according to Steven Runciman, "the primacy of the see of Lyons over those of Sens and Reims was established."[22]

The desire to foreground the city of Jerusalem in the testimonies of these writers further reflects a shift in Christian attitudes toward Jerusalem in the early crusader period. These efforts point to directing attention to the earthly Jerusalem as a means of establishing a past history between the city and the Latin Church, and to promote armed pilgrimage, or crusade, to the eastern Mediterranean. The Crusade is also presented as a war of reconquest and the return of Latin Christians back to Jerusalem. The efforts of these texts

21. An exception is the account of Albert of Aix, or Aachen, produced between 1125 and 1130 CE. This account is not dependent on the *Gesta* tradition and attributes the preaching of the crusade to Peter the Hermit. Albert of Aachen, *Historia Ierosolimitana: History of the Journey to Jerusalem*, ed. and trans. Susan B. Edgington (Oxford: Oxford University Press, 2007).

22. Steven Runciman, *A History of the Crusades*, vol. 1, *The First Crusade and the Foundation of the Kingdom of Jerusalem* (Cambridge: Cambridge University Press, 1987), 42.

to focus the centrality of the crusading effort on Jerusalem is also significant in that these chronicles envision their own Jerusalem through a Latin Christian topography, the sanctity of the earthly city for the Christian faith, and the contested nature of the city. It is this Jerusalem that then becomes the object of lamentation for our chronicles, and thus the main focus of the initiative of Pope Urban II and his call for crusade.

A Latin Christian City: The Earthly Jerusalem Reclaimed

The ways in which the city of Jerusalem becomes represented in the accounts of Pope Urban II's speeches at Clermont reveals a shift in attitude toward the earthly city of Jerusalem. In their accounts, the four chroniclers interpret the history of the city through a supersessionist hermeneutic that attempts to transfer Jewish traditions of the earthly Jerusalem into a Latin Christian one. The assertion of a Latin Christian Jerusalem also allows for the object of lamentation to be the city and for the call to crusade to be justified in these narratives through a Christian theological rhetoric, which is used to assert claims over the physical Jerusalem.

Jerusalem as the locus for Christ's Passion, place of burial, and resurrection become the ways in which these accounts attempt to solidify a Latin Christian Jerusalem. As Robert the Monk claims, "Our redeemer dignified it with his arrival, adorned it with his words, consecrated it through his Passion, redeemed it by his death and glorified it with his burial." (Hanc redemptor humani generis suo illustravit adventu, decoravit conversatione, sacravit passione, morte redemit, sepultura insignivit; 3:729.) Similarly, Baldric states, "it is this city, in which, as you all know, Christ himself suffered for us" [*ipsa civitas, in qua, prout omnes nostis, Christus ipse pro nobis passus est*] (4:13). Guibert also writes that "Christ is our seed, in whom lies salvation and blessing for all people, then the earth and city in which he lived and suffered is called holy by the testimony of the scripture" [*et semen nostrum Christus est, in quo salus et omnium gentium benedictio est: ipsa terra et civitas in qua habitavit et passus est, scripturarum testimonio sancta vocatur*] (4:137).[23] These

23. The passage continues, "Si enim haec terra Dei haereditas et templum sanctum, antequam ibi obambularent ac pateretur Dominus, in sacris et propheticis paginis legitur quid sanctitatis, quid reverentiae obtinuisse tunc creditur, quum Deus majestatis ibidem incorporator, nutritur

narratives further reference a past that stands as a reminder of the centuries of Christian presence in a city that once accommodated the holy men of Israel, the apostles and the first Christians, and—above all—Christ himself, the incarnate God. Jerusalem, a relic that housed the memories of Christ's life on earth—his baptism in the waters of the Jordon, his crucifixion at Golgotha, and his resurrection from the Holy Sepulcher—is described in its contemporary moment as being threatened by the advancing Muslim powers. Yet these chroniclers all claim that the rightful ownership of the city belongs to the Christians, since Jerusalem was once part of the Christian Roman Empire.[24]

Along with the evocation of the figure of Christ in connection with the city of Jerusalem, the chroniclers also draw on the divine authorized wars of the Israelites described in the Old Testament to suggest that the Crusade is the supreme manifestation of divine approval than that of any other historical battle, an opinion that is explicitly stated by Guibert:

> If we look carefully at the wars of the pagans and the kingdoms they traveled through by great military effort, we shall conclude that none of their strength, none of their armies, by the Grace of God, is comparable in any way to ours. Although we have heard that God was worshipped among the Jews, we know that Jesus Christ, as he once was among the ancients, today exists and prevails by clear proofs among the moderns.
>
> Si enim praelia gentilium et regna multo armorum labore pervasa perpendimus, nullas eorum vires, nulla prorsus exercitia nostris, per Dei gratiam, aequiparanda censebimus. Si Deum in Judaico populo magnificatum audivimus, Jesum Christum, sicut heri apud antiquos, ita et hodie apud modernos, esse et valere certis experimentis agnovimus. (4:123)

For Guibert, God had magnified the crusaders as he had once done for the Jews, but the difference resided in the goal of the crusaders. Guibert claims that the Israelites had fought their wars for carnal pleasures (4:221) and that

adolescit, corporali vegetatione hac illacque perambulat aut gestatur; et, ut cuncta quae longo verborum gyro narrari possunt, digna brevitate constringam ubi Filii Dei sanguis, coelo terraque sanctior, effusus est, ubi corpus, paventibus elementis mortuum in sepulchro quievit? quid putamus venerationis emeruit?" Guibert of Nogent, *Gesta Dei per Francos*, 4:137–38.

24. Robert the Monk, *Historia Jherosolimitan*, 3:750, 792; Guibert of Nogent, *Gesta Dei per Francos*, 4:204; Baldric of Dol, *Gesta Dei per Francos*, 4:74.

the story of the capture of Jerusalem by the Franks is much more deserving of dignitary writing than the history of Jewish warfare, since he claims the Jews fought for old laws and rituals, and for temples, while the crusaders fight for the propagation of the faith and a spiritual desire that is rewarded with a divine power never seen before in history.[25] Guibert supports his claim with a reference to the Maccabees and declares that the crusaders deserve just as much praise for their protection of Jerusalem:

> If the Maccabees once deserved the highest praise for piety because they fought for their rituals and their temple, then you too, O soldiers of Christ, deserve much praise for taking up arms to defend the freedom of your country.
>
> Si Machabaeis olim ad maximam profuit pietatis laudem, quia pro cerimoniis et Templo pugnarunt: et vobis' o milites Christiani, legitime conceditur, ut armorum studio libertatem patriae defendatis. (4:138)

Guibert's outlook is also shared by Baldric of Dol, who in two instances compares the struggle of the crusaders to that of the children of Israel against the Jebusites:

> The Children of Israel, who were led out of Egypt, and who prefigured you in the crossing of the Red Sea, have taken that land, by their arms, with Jesus as leader; they have driven out the Jebusites and other inhabitants and have themselves inhabited the earthly Jerusalem, the image of the celestial Jerusalem.
>
> Filii Israel ab Aegyptiis educti, qui Rubro Mari transito, vos praefiguraverunt, terram illam armis suis, Jesu duce, sibi vindicaverunt; Jebuseos et alios convenas inde expulerunt; et instar Jerusalem coelestis, Jerusalem terrenam incoluerunt. (4:14)

Later on he also compares the Jebusites to the Turks:

> And under Jesus Christ, our Leader, may you struggle for your Jerusalem, in Christian battleline, most invincible line, even more successfully than did the sons of Jacob of old; and assail and drive out the Turks who are in these lands,

25. Guibert of Nogent, *Gesta Dei per Francos*, 4:120, 138, 162, 192–94, 207, 221–22, 225, 232, 241.

more impious than the Jebusites. You may deem it beautiful to die for Christ in a city in which Christ died for us.

et sub Jesu Christo, duce nostro, acies Christiana, acies invictissima, melius quam ipsi veteres Jacobitae, pro vestra Jerusalem decertetis; et Turcos qui in ea sunt, nefandiores quam Jebuseos, impugnetis et expugnetis. Pulchrum sit vobis mori in illa civitate pro Christo, in qua Christus pro vobis mortuus est. (4:15)

Baldric's evocation of the Jebusites, the Canaanite tribe that inhabited the region around Jerusalem before its capture by King David, is noteworthy for a number of reasons. In these statements, Baldric compares the image of the Turks to the Jebusites as the former inhabitants of the region before its conquest by the crusaders and the Israelites, respectively. The Jebusites, who had contested David's entrance into Jerusalem (Sam. 2:6–8), find similarities to the Turks who stand in the way of Christian pilgrims desiring to enter the city of Jerusalem. The claim that the Turks are "more impious than the Jebusites" supports the reading provided by Guibert that the victory of the crusaders is an even greater one that that of the Israelites. Just as the Israelites once drove out the Jebusites, the crusaders are presented as being even more successful in their acquisition of the city by driving out the Turks. Most important, the parallelism created with the Israelites is one that suggests that, like the Jews, Christians also have a claim to the earthly Jerusalem.

These numerous references to the Israelites also supports the reading that Pope Urban II's speeches see the capture of the city of Jerusalem as a fulfillment of prophecies foretold in the Christian Bible and draw on a number of Old Testament sources to illustrate the biblical presaging of the Frankish capture of Jerusalem. Although Jonathan Riley-Smith claims that these authors had "no common ground in any tradition of exegesis that could be applied to these events," they all utilized different prophetic passages from the scriptures to focus on the earthly Jerusalem, and to connect the earthly city with Christianity, reflecting a shift in the belief of the Church Fathers (discussed in the introduction to this book), who promoted the understanding present in the Pauline doctrines.[26] Guibert writes a long exposition of Zacharias 12:1–10 within which he identifies Judah with the

26. Riley-Smith, *The First Crusade and the Idea of Crusading*, 142.

crusaders (4:237–40). Robert mostly makes reference to the great prophecy of the future Jerusalem in Isaiah 9:9–11 and 15–16 (3:764, 880, 882). Baldric refers to Psalm 44:4 (4:15) and Canticle 1:4 (4:28), where God is asked to command victories for Jacob. Fulcher recalls Leviticus 26:8 in his description of the capture of the city (3:376). All these passages are used by the authors to suggest that the capture of the city was believed to have come from a decision of God, just as that of the occupation of the Promised Land by the Israelites. Moreover, the belief was that Latin Christians were also strongly connected to the physical city of Jerusalem, since it was prophesied for them to capture and inhabit the city.

Along with the belief that the capture of Jerusalem was a prophetic fulfillment comes an expression of necessity: Christians should have a hold of Jerusalem for the fulfillment of the prophecies of the Last Days. Guibert claims that Pope Urban II recalled how the scripture foretold the coming of the Antichrist to Jerusalem (4:137), and includes an interpretation of the prophecy present in Daniel 7:24:

> According to Daniel and Jerome his interpreter, his tent will be fixed on the mountain of olives, and he will certainly take his seat as the Apostle teaches, In Jerusalem, in the *temple of God, as though he were God* [2 Thess. 2:4.], and according to the prophet, he will undoubtedly kill three kings pre-eminent for their faith in Christ, that is, the kings of Egypt, of Africa, and of Ethiopia. This cannot happen at all, unless Christianity is established where paganism now rules.
>
> Juxta enim Danihelem et Iheronimum, Danihelis interpretem, fixurus est in Oliveti monte tentoria; et Iherosolimis, in *Dei templo, tanquam sit Deus*, certum est, apostolo docente, quod sedeat, et juxta eumdem prophetam tres reges, Aegypti videlicet, Affricae ac Aethiopiae, haud dubium quin pro Christiana fide primos interficiat. (4:138–139)

Jerusalem's connection to the prophetic tradition combines corporeal, spiritual, and ecclesiological qualities of the city. The earthly Jerusalem emulates the heavenly city as a significant locus for the fulfillment of the eschaton and Apocalypse and the connection between the earthly and the heavenly is presented as more than sequential: the entrance into the terrestrial Jerusalem is not only a means by which one can enter into the heavenly Jerusalem but also a place that the Christian believer is now able to inhabit.[27] This belief presents a shift from those of the early Church Fathers such as Augustine, Eusebius, Jerome, and Origen, who interpreted the books of Lamentations and Revelation—the basis for Christian eschatology—as spiritual allegories. According to Augustine, the church has existed since the beginning of humankind, and the people of Israel can call themselves God's people by virtue of a heavenly fellowship that manifests itself into an earthly form.[28] Augustine views the history of salvation as an ongoing process and the appearance of Christ as not an absolute moment but a contemplative pause in the history of the city of God.[29] For Jerome, the prophecies of the Old Testament were already fulfilled with the coming of Christ, and for Eusebius the earthly city was regarded as insignificant, since the most important edifices were those of the soul.[30] The notion of apocalypticism, along with those of martyrdom, provided a motive for the movement of the crusaders to the city of Jerusalem: to die in a city where Christ himself died for the sins of humankind. It is a metaphor that furthers the notion of the *milites Christi* that begins in the accounts of Pope Urban II's call to crusade, and one that develops its full potential at the time of the Third Crusade.[31] In opposition to the attitudes toward the earthly city displayed by the early Church Fathers, these narratives consider the earthly city as part of the larger trajectory of the significance of Jerusalem for the universal Christian church. Rather than attempting to fully reject the Jewish city (as was done by the Church Fathers), these authors both envision and remap Judaic concepts of the temple, transferring the image of the Jewish Jerusalem into a Christian one. As Baldric notes, "and others have themselves inhabited earthly Jerusalem, the image of celestial Jerusalem" [*et alios*

27. Baldric of Dol, *Gesta Dei per Francos*, 4:14, 100–101; Robert the Monk, *Historia Jherosolimitan*, 3:881–82.

28. See Augustine, *De Civitate Dei*, in PL 16.2, 17.16, and 18.47, esp. 16.2, 17.16, and 18.47

29. Augustine, *De Civitate Dei*, 18.45–47. See also Adriaan H. Bredero, "Jérusalem dans l'Occident medieval," in *Mélanges offerts à René Crozet à l'occasion de son 70e anniversaire par ses amis, ses collégues, ses élèves et les membres cu C.E.S.C.M.*, vol. 1, ed. Pierre Gallais (Poitiers, France: Societé d'Études Médievales, 1966), 259–71.

30. Hieronymus, *Commentariorum in Isaiam libri XII–XVIII*, in *Esaiam paruula adbreviatio*, CCSL 73A; Eusebius, *Eusebius: the Ecclesiastical History*, vol. 10, ed. H. J. Lawlor (Cambridge, MA: Harvard University Press, 1980), 44–60.

31. Fulcher of Chartres, *Gesta Francorum*, 3:322; William of Malmesbury, *Gesta Regum Anglorum*, 2:602; Baldric of Dol, *Gesta Dei per Francos*, 4:14–15. For a discussion of the development of the *milites Christi* during the period of the Third Crusade, see chapter 5 of this book.

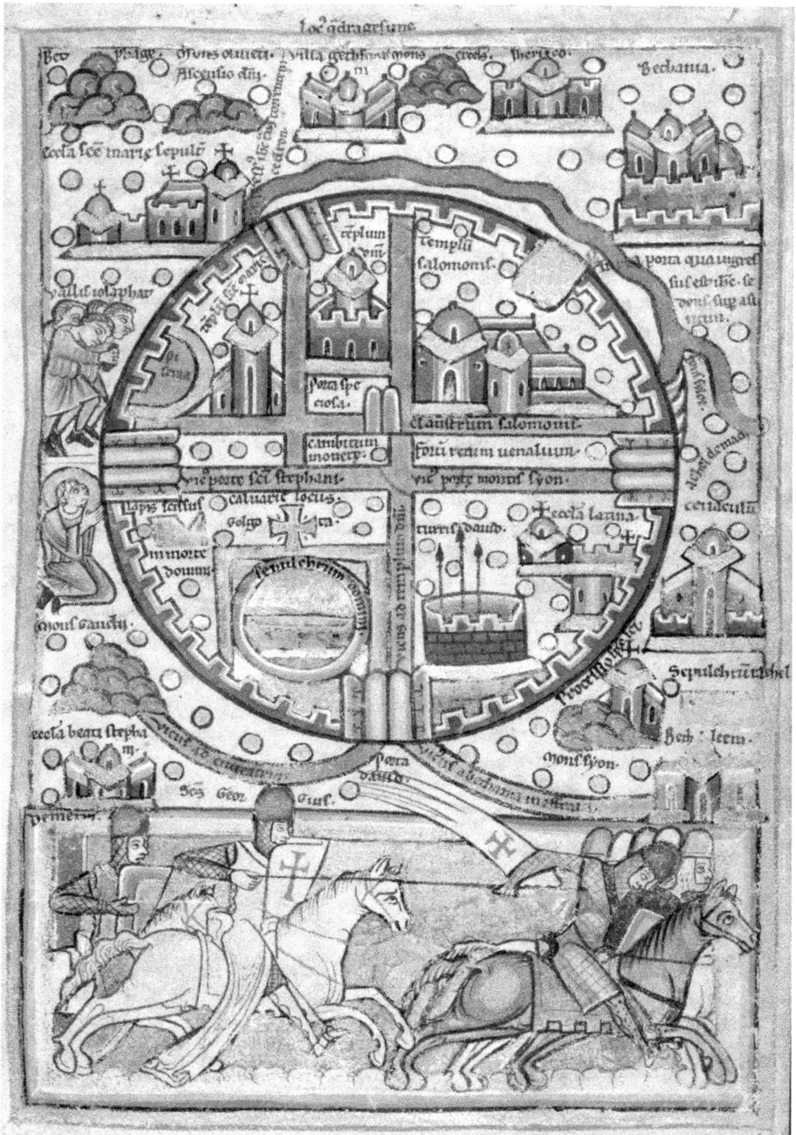

Figure 3. T-O map of crusader Jerusalem. Koninklijke Bibliotheek, 76 F. 5, fol. 1r.

convenas inde expulerunt; et instar Jerusalem coelestis, Jerusalem terrenam incoluerunt] (4:14).

Fulcher's account further outlines this transfer through a topographical description of a Latin Christian Jerusalem:

> It is generally conceded that the city is laid out in such proper proportion that it seems neither too small nor too large. Its width from wall to wall is that of four bowshots. To the west is the Tower of David with the city wall on each flank; to the south is Mount Zion a little closer than a bowshot; and to the east, the Mount of Olives a thousand paces outside the city. . . . In the same city is the Temple of the Lord, round in shape, built when Solomon in ancient times erected the earlier magnificent Temple. Although it can in no way be compared in appearance to the former building, still this one is of marvelous workmanship and most splendid appearance. The Church of the Lord's Sepulcher is likewise circular in form. It was never closed in at the top but always admits the light through a permanent aperture ingeniously fashioned under the direction of a skillful architect. . . . Another Temple, called the Temple of Solomon, is large and wonderful, but it is not the one that Solomon built. This one, because of our poverty, could not be maintained in the condition in which we found it. Wherefore it is already in large part destroyed.
>
> Constat civitas haec condecenti magnitudine facta per circuitum, ita ut nec parvitate nec magnitudine cuiquam videatur fastidiosa, quae interius a muro usque ad murum, quantum jacit arcus sagittam, est lata. Habet siquidem ab occasu turrim Daviticam, utroque latere supplentem civitatis murum; montem Syon a meridie, paulo minus quam jaciat arcus sagittam; ad orientem Oliveti montem mille passibus ab urbe distantem . . . et est in eadem urbe Templum dominicum, opera rotundo compositum, ubi Salomon alterum prius instituit mirificum quod quamvis illi priori scemati nullatenus sit comparandum, istud tamen opere mirabili, forma speciosissima, factum est. Sepulcri dominici ecclesia forma rotunda similiter, quae nunquam fuit tecta, sed semper foramine patulo architecti sapientis magisterio artificiose machinato, hiatu perpetuo aperta claret in summo. . . . Alterum templum, quod dicitur Salomonis, magnum est et mirabile. Non est autem illud idem qoud Salomon fabricari fecit, quod quidem non potuit, propter inopiam nostram, in statu quo illud invenimus sustentari; quapropter magna jam ex parte destruitur. (3:355–57)

The narrative's attention to the four sacred sanctuaries—the Tower of David, the Temple of the Lord, the Church of the Holy Sepulcher, and the

Temple of Solomon—coalesce into an image of Jerusalem as a Christian city in the text's present moment.[32] Fulcher's topographical map of Jerusalem, which concentrates mostly on the southern portion of the city, also focuses on the very area that was significant for the crusader conquest of the city. Fulcher explains that the attack of Raymond and his men on the first day came from the side of Mount Zion, although he does not specify the position of Godfrey, Robert of Normandy, and Robert of Flanders.[33] The monuments of the earthly or Jewish Jerusalem become reassigned to reflect sacred Christian edifices, the most important being the Church of the Holy Sepulcher. Fulcher's map of Jerusalem also asserts the new position of the earthly Jerusalem as a means to reaching the ethereal Jerusalem.[34] Robert the Monk in fact praises the earthly city at the heading of chapter 2: "Regarding the praise of the city of Jerusalem. Jerusalem rejoice! Praise is everlasting for you without deceit." (De laude urbis Iherosolimitanae. Jerusalem gaude: tibi constat laus sine fraude; 3:729.) Jerusalem's geographic position as the center of the earth is also noted: "Jerusalem is the navel of the earth, a fruitful land more than others, almost another earthly Paradise." (Iherusalem umbilicus est terrarum, terra prae ceteris fructifera, quasi alter Paradisus deliciarum; 3:729.) Later, the work reiterates this concept, referring to "this royal city at the center of the world" [*Haec igitur civitas regalis, in orbis medio posita*] (3:729).[35] By the twelfth century, the theological concept of Jerusalem as the center of the earth, deriving from the Old Testament and a Midrashian

---

32. The Templum Domini of the crusaders is the octagonal mosque Qubbat aṣ-Ṣakhrah, or the "Dome of the Rock," built by the caliph ʿAbd al-Malik in 691 CE over the rock from which it is believed Muḥammad ascended to heaven.

33. Other sources indicated their position to be as far south as the Tower of David. See Benjamin Z. Kedar, "The Jerusalem Massacre of July 1099 in the Western Historiography of the Crusades," in *Crusades*: vol. 3, ed. Benjamin Z. Kedar, Jonathan Riley-Smith, Helen Nicholson, and Michael Evans (New York: Routledge, 2004), 15–75.

34. For a study of the physical setting, topography, events, administration and institutions of Jerusalem see Adrian J. Boas, *Jerusalem in the Time of the Crusades: Society, Landscape, and Art in the Holy City under Frankish Rule* (London: Routledge, 2001); and Joshua Prawer, "The Jerusalem the Crusaders Captured: A Contribution to the Medieval Topography of the City," in *Crusade and Settlement: Papers Read at the First Conference of the Society for the Study of the Crusades and the Latin East and Presented to R. C. Smail*, ed. Peter W. Edbury (Cardiff, Wales: University College Cardiff Press, 1985), 1–16. For a map of twelfth-century Jerusalem, see Michel Join-Lambert, *Jerusalem* (London: Elek, 1958), 193.

35. The penultimate section of Robert's account discusses the naming of the city, which the rubric claims indicates its founder. Robert concludes his account with a commentary on the opulence of the city. In book 9, chapter 24 the text also bestows on the reader the manner in which the

interpretation of Ezekiel, became an accepted belief that also became translated in our texts into geographic and cartographical terms, as seen in Fulcher's description of the city.[36] Jerusalem's centrality is even a significant part in William of Malmesbury's account, where he re-creates a T-O (*terra-oceanus*) version of the map of the world (*mappa mundi*) by outlining the three parts of the world (Asia, Africa, and Europe) and describing how each of these areas is being threatened by the advancement of Muslim powers.[37] William, a Benedictine monk, librarian and the precentor of Wiltshire Abbey, provides the only surviving English account of the First Crusade in book 4 of his *Gesta Regum Anglorum*, composed about thirty years after the Council of Clermont.[38] These easterners, whom he calls "ad inimicos Dei," now dwell in Asia. They threaten the Christians who inhabit the land, and also have a hold on the city of Jerusalem, where they suppress Christians and require them to pay taxes. The text then moves to describe how the past conquests of these enemies of God have led them to also occupy Africa. The concern is that these same people who have overrun the Balearic Islands and Spain are also threatening the rest of Europe. These descriptions of the peril of this tripartite world at the hands of the Turks are interwoven with historical claims to Christian presence in each of these parts: Asia, regarded for its connection of the land to the Apostles and the beginnings of Christianity; Africa, a land that produced famous

prophecy in Isaiah 60:11 is actualized through the Frankish conquest of Jerusalem. Robert the Monk, *Historia Jherosolimitan*, 3:880.

36. Sylvia Schein, *Gateway to the Heavenly City: Crusader Jerusalem and the Catholic West, 1099–1187* (Aldershot, England: Ashgate, 2005), 141.

37. For more on medieval maps, see Brigitte Englisch, *Ordo orbis terrae. Die Weltsicht in den Mappae mundi des frühen und hohen Mittelalters* (Berlin: Akademie Verlag, 2002); and Schein, *Gateway*, 143–45. For a detailed discussion of the T-O cartographic tradition, see chapter 4 of this book.

38. William's account of Pope Urban II's speeches at Clermont relies heavily on Fulcher's *Gesta Francorum*, at times citing Fulcher verbatim. His testimony also draws from the account of Guibert of Nogent, and from people whom he claims had heard the speech. While the chronicle acknowledges the Council at Clermont as a significant event in Latin Church history, William's inclusion of Pope Urban II's name reflects a criticism of the ecclesiastical schisms and controversies of his day. For William, Urban was a representative of the venalities of the Rome, and his motives for preaching the First Crusade stem from his desire to hire auxiliary troops and overrun the Rome he had been driven from by Wibert of Ravenna's violence. Wibert was made antipope in 1080 CE during the Investiture Controversy between Gregory VII and Henry IV. See Rodney M. Thomson, *William of Malmesbury* (Woodbridge, England: Boydell, 1987), 1–98.

men of genius; and Europe, the continent that houses the majority of Christians (600).

Lamenting Jerusalem: The Call for Crusade

The establishment of a Latin Christian Jerusalem solidifies the theological position of the earthly Jerusalem and enables these chroniclers to then lament their city—a Jerusalem they can claim as their own sacred space. In their testimonies about Pope Urban II's speeches at Clermont, these accounts present the call to crusade as a reaction to this lost Christian Jerusalem, which they describe as being destroyed and disrespected by the Muslim enemy. In order to call for crusade, to announce a movement toward the conquest (or reconquest) of the city, the narratives begin by lamenting the loss of Jerusalem. Just as a Christian Jerusalem was asserted in these accounts through the supersessionism of a Jewish earthly Jerusalem, the texts also rely on common devices of the lamenting of Jerusalem in the Hebrew Bible to mourn the fall of the city to the enemy. As outlined in the introduction to this book, these tropes include the attribution of the fall of the city due to the sins of its inhabitants; intense and graphic descriptions of its destruction and desolation; a plea for forgiveness for the people's sins; the desire for God's mercy; and the movement through God's will toward the recapture of the city. For our narratives, this redemption is believed to happen only through the new pilgrim, or crusader, who is advised to make the journey to liberate Jerusalem.

In his account of Clermont, Fulcher writes how, "in the sorrowing voice of a suffering church, [Pope Urban II] told of its great tribulation" [*sub Ecclesiae lugentis voce querula planctum non minimum expressit*] (3:321). Here it is the pope who, like Jerusalem itself, is lamenting the city's destruction and loss. The pope suffers because Jerusalem and the Latin Christians are suffering. His lamentation through the voice of the city also reflects the newly imagined earthly Jerusalem in Christian thought: a place to inhabit and to defend, and a place that, it is believed, will lead the faithful Christian to the heavenly Jerusalem of the afterlife. The pope and the Holy Sepulcher stand as symbols of Christianity in both the physical and the spiritual, representing the earthly and the heavenly city, respectively. The pope's delivery of his speech through the perspective of the desecrated church further suggests that the events in the Holy Land and are not that distant from France. In lamentation, he calls for Latin Christians to faithfully defend the rights of the holy church and move toward the liberation of Jerusalem:

> Since, oh sons of God, you have promised Him to keep peace among yourselves and to faithfully sustain the rights of the Holy Church more sincerely than before, there still remains for you, newly aroused by Godly correction, an urgent task which belongs to both you and God, in which you can show the strength of your good will. For you must hasten to carry aid to your brethren dwelling in the East, who need your help for which they have often entreated.
>
> Quoniam, o filii Dei, si pacem apud vos tenendam et Ecclesiae jura conservanda fideliter sustentare virilius solito polliciti Deo estis, exstat operae pretium ut insuper ad quoddam aliud Dei negotium et vestrum, emendatione deifica nuper vegetati, probitatis vestrae valitudinem versetis. Necesse est enim, quatinus confratribus vestris in Orientali plaga conversantibus, auxilio vestro jam saepe acclamato indigis, accelerato itinere succurratis. (3:323)

Pope Urban II's call to crusade is further presented as an effort for Christian peace and a reaction to internal Christian strife.[39] The sins of the Christian population and their movement away from the faith have resulted in the fall of the city as a punishment from God. Fulcher testifies to the pope's evocation of this disregard of conviction:

> Moreover seeing the faith of Christendom excessively trampled upon by all, both by the clergy and by the laity, for the princes of the land were incessantly at war, quarrelling between themselves with someone or another. He saw that people stole worldly goods from one another, that many captives were taken unjustly and were most barbarously cast into foul prisons and ransomed for excessive prices, or tormented there by three evils, namely hunger, thirst, and cold, and secretly put to death, that holy places were violated, monasteries and villa consumed by fire, nothing mortal spared, and things human and divine held in derision.

39. Philip I of France was excommunicated at the Council of Clermont by Pope Urban II because of his bigamous relationship with Bertranda de Montfort, an incident that both William and Fulcher allude to and condemn; see William of Malmesbury, *Gesta Regum Anglorum*, 2:594; Fulcher of Chartres, *Gesta Francorum*, 3:321.

> Videns autem Christianitatis fidem enormiter ab omnibus, tam clero quam populo, pessundari, et terrarum principibus incessanter certamine bellico, nunc istis nunc illis inter se dissidentibus, pacem omnino postponi; bona terrae alternatim diripi; multos injuriose vinctos captivari, et in carceres teterrimos truculentissime subrui, supra modum redimi, vel intus trifariam angariatos, scilicet inedia, siti, algore, obitu clandestino exstingui; loca sancta violari, monasteria villasque igne cremari, nulli mortalium parci, divina et humana ludibriis haberi. (3:321)

Baldric describes the sinful believer of the past as the Christian who kills other Christians:

> You girt about with the badge of knighthood, are arrogant with great pride; you rage against your brothers and cut each other in pieces. This is not the soldiery of Christ which rends asunder the sheepfold of the Redeemer.
>
> Vos accincti cingulo militae magno superbitis supercilio; fratres vestros laniatis, atque inter vos dissecamini. Non est haec militia Christi, quae discerpit ovile Redemptoris. (4:14)[40]

These actions are shameful for Baldric, and for this reason God has withdrawn from the city, leaving it polluted by foreign invasion:

> Of holy Jerusalem, brethren, we dare not speak, for we are exceedingly afraid and ashamed of it. This very city, in which, as you all know, Christ himself suffered for us, because our sins demanded it, has been reduced to the pollution of paganism and, I say it to our disgrace, withdrawn from the service of God. Such is the heap of reproach upon us who have so much deserved it!
>
> De sancta Jerusalem, fratres, hucusque quasi loqui dissimulavimus, quia valde loqui de ea pertimescimus et erubescimus: quoniam ipse civitas, in qua, prout omnes nostis, Christus ipse pro nobis passus est, peccatis nostris exigentibus, sub spurcitiam paganorum redacta est, Deique servituti (ad ignominiam nostram dico) subducta est: quod enim ita est improperii nostri cumulus est, qui ita promeruimus. (4:13)

---

40. See Robert the Monk, *Historia Jherosolimitan*, 3:728, 748; and Guibert of Nogent, *Gesta Dei per Francos,* 4:138.

For William of Malmesbury, the Christian of the past has indulged in criminal behavior, resulting in this calamity:

> For besides the criminal behavior in which individuals used freely to indulge, all men this side of the Alps had reached such depths of calamity that for the very slightest reason or none at all anyone would take another man prisoner and not let him go free except on payment of heavy ransom.
>
> Nam preter flagitia quibus singuli licenter incubabant, ad hoc calamitatis omnes Cisalpini deuenerant, ut nullis uel minimis causis extantibus quisque alium caperet, nec nisi magno redemptum abire sineret. (594)

In contrast, Guibert's account attributes the lamentable status of the city to the eastern pilgrim:

> However, the faith of easterners, which has never been stable, but has always been variable and unsteady, searching for novelty, always exceeding the bounds of true belief, finally deserted the authority of the church fathers.
>
> Orientalium autem fides, quum semper nutabunda constiterit, et rerum molitione novarum mutabilis et vagabunda fuerit, semper a regula verae credulitatis exorbitans, ab antiquorum patrum auctoritate descivit. (4:125)

Guibert blames the Greeks for their movement away from church history, claiming that they have committed heresies and focused their commentaries on useless questions—clearly an attack on the faith of Eastern Christians. Since Constantine was responsible for the erection of the Holy Sepulcher, Guibert claims that a genealogical accountability remains with the Greek powers. He criticizes the Greeks, suggesting that institutions that endured under the Romans, such as Jerusalem, were not able to sustain themselves under the Byzantine Empire (4:125). Guibert advises that the heretic nature present in Eastern books (but not in the Roman world), their improvident attitudes toward the Eucharist, and their location of the apostolic see have contributed to a failed test of faith and the loss of Jerusalem (4:126).

Though Guibert attacks the Greeks for their inability to sustain the faith, Pope Urban II presents his call for crusade as a motivation by the Greek emperor Alexius I Comnenus, who has been complaining of Seljuq advancements on Christians in the eastern Mediterranean. These accounts therefore lament the attacks on the city, the destruction of Jerusalem by the

Muslim people, and the disrespect of Christian holy sites in Jerusalem. Baldric describes this lamentable sentiment be evoking Psalm 79 when he writes,

> We weep and wail, brethren, alas, like the Psalmist, in our inmost heart! We are wretched and unhappy, and in us is that prophecy fulfilled: "God, the nations are come into thine inheritance; thy holy temple they have defiled; they have laid Jerusalem in heaps; the dead bodies of thy servants have been given to be food for the birds of heaven, and flesh of thy saints unto the beasts of the earth. Their blood they have shed like water round about Jerusalem, and there was none to bury them." Woe unto us brethren! We who have already become a reproach to our neighbors, a scoffing, and derision to them round about us, let us at least with tears condone and have compassion upon our brothers! We who are become the scorn of all peoples, and worse than all, let us bewail the most monstrous devastation of the Holy Land!
>
> Ploremus, fratres, eia ploremus et cum Psalmista medullitus plorantes ingemiscamus. Nos miseri, nos infelices quorum prophetia ista complete est: *Deus, venerunt gentes in haereditatem tuam: polluerunt templum sanctum tuum; posnerunt Jerusalem in pomorum custodiam: posuerunt morticina servorum tuorum escas volatilibus caeli, carnes sanctorum tuorum bestiis terrae*: *Effuderunt sanguinem eorum, tanquam aquam in circuitu Jerusalem, et non erat qui sepeliret.* Vae nobis, fratres! Nos, qui jam *facti sumus opprobrium vicinis nostris, subsannatio et illusio his qui in circuitu nostro sunt*, condoleamus et compatiamur fratribus nostris, saltem in lacrimis! Nos *abjectio plebis* facti, et omnium deteriores, immanissimam sanctissimae Terrae plangamus devastationem. (4:14)

This passage from the opening lines of Psalm 79 makes reference to the destruction of the Jewish temple and Jerusalem under Nebuchadnezzar II. Here Baldric parallels the bewailing Christian believer to the psalmist, who also laments the destruction of Jerusalem when others have come into the inheritance of the holy temple. The rest of the Psalm references the deplorable position of the people at the time in their sin, a petition to God for their relief, and the desire to praise God and ask for pardon. For Baldric, however, the current destruction of the Jerusalem is the most monstrous because, due to their sins, the Christians have become the scorn of all people. Baldric's use of Psalm 79 to parallel the current condition of Jerusalem and the Christian people further reflects how these authors have reframed notions of lamenting the loss of Jerusalem in the Hebrew Bible into a contemporary Latin

Christian Jerusalem. The destruction of the Jewish temple then transfers to lamenting the current status of the Temple of the Lord—or, more specifically, the Church of the Holy Sepulcher, as Fulcher attests:

> All the Saracens held the Temple of the Lord in great veneration. Here rather than elsewhere they preferred to say the prayers of their faith although such prayers were wasted because [they were] offered to an idol set up to Mohammed. They allowed no Christian to enter the Temple.
>
> Hoc Templum dominicum in veneratione magna cuncti Sarraceni habuerant, ubi precationes suas lege sua libentius quam alibi faciebant, quamvis idolo in nomine Mahumet facto eas vastarent, in quod etiam nullum ingredi Christianum permittebant. (4:357)

The destruction of the Church of the Holy Sepulcher becomes the central focus for lamentation in these accounts. As Robert asserts, "We all have but one goal: the liberation of the Holy Sepulcher [*nostra omnium una sit intentio, sancti scilicet Sepulcri deliberatio*] (3:731).[41] Guibert recalls the chief figure responsible for the construction of this church in his account:

> In the time of the faithful Helen, the mother of the ruler Constantine, throughout the regions known for the traces of the Lord's sufferings, churches and priests worthy of these churches were established by this same Augusta.
>
> A temporibus fidelis Helenae, Constantini principis matris, per loca dominicorum suppliciorum vestigiis insignita, basilicae sunt per eamdem Augustam et ministeria digna basilicis instituta. (4:125)

The construction of the Church of the Holy Sepulcher in Jerusalem under Constantine's proclamation of a New Jerusalem, or *omphalos*, was a conscious effort to separate the Jerusalem of the pagan and Jewish past from the Christian present. Constantine's plan included construction on an area where all the soil from the past two centuries was to be removed and a new founda-

41. Robert's section on the crusaders' arrival and capture of Jerusalem is brief. The account does not provide any topographical evidence pertaining to the city, and focuses on the Holy Sepulcher and the image of the crusaders praying and bowing their heads to the church (bk. 9, chap. 1). Robert's testimony of the capture of the city is also highly based on Fulcher's account, whom he mentions by name (bk. 5, chaps. 12–13).

tion placed on the location declared to be the site of Christ's crucifixion, Golgatha, as attested to by the emperor's mother Helena.[42] Guibert's evocation of Constantine's erection of the church reflects this very transfer of meaning of Jewish sites to Christian ones. The Church of the Holy Sepulcher seems to stand as a metonym for the city of Jerusalem in these accounts. Thus, to speak of the destruction of a Christian Jerusalem means to reference the status of the Church of the Holy Sepulcher, the location that was also accepted to be the closest to "the navel of the earth" in the twelfth century.[43] It is also interesting to note that within Fulcher's testimony, the name Jerusalem never makes an appearance.[44] What we have, however, is the pope lamenting (through the voice of the church) the very destruction of the Church of the Holy Sepulcher.

Pope Urban II's call to crusade, therefore, is a declaration for the movement toward Jerusalem because of the threatened status of this holy space for Christendom. Embroidered descriptions of devastation, death, and disrespect for not only the Christians in the city but also, and most specifically, the Church of the Holy Sepulcher paint a susceptible picture of Jerusalem and further create a tone of immediacy for the obtainment of the city. Speaking of the vulnerable status of the city is yet another trope for lamenting the loss of Jerusalem in the Hebrew Bible, as attested by Baldric when he writes,

> But why do we pass over the Temple of Solomon, nay of the Lord, in which the barbarous nations placed their idols contrary to law, human and divine? Of the Lord's Sepulcher we have refrained from speaking, since some of you with your own eyes have seen to what abominations it has been given over.

42. See Paul Ciholas, *Omphalos and the Cross: Pagans and Christians in Search of a Divine Center* (Macon, GA: Mercer University Press, 2003), 13–26.

43. Schein, *Gateway*, 144.

44. Janus Møller Jensen, in fact, questions whether Urban even mentioned Jerusalem in his speeches at Clermont because, Fulcher, the most significant source does not mention its name—a point Jensen uses to support his argument that Urban did not intend to start a crusading movement, nor produced one, and that the "notion of crusade changed during the twelfth century because of the practical and ideological experiences of crusading, which contributed to forming and developing the more institutionalized features recognizable in the writings of the theologians and the canon lawyers toward the end of the twelfth century and in the thirteenth." Janus Møller Jensen, "War, Penance and the First Crusade: Dealing with a Tyrannical Construct," in *Medieval History Writing and Crusading Ideology*, ed. Tuomas M. S. Lehtonen and Kurt Villads Jensen (Helsinki: Finnish Literature Society, 2005), 51–63.

> Sed quid Templum Salomonis, immo Domini praetermisimus, in quo simulacra sua barbarae nationes contra jus et fas modo collocata venerantur? De Sepulcro Dominico ideo reminisci supersedimus, quoniam quidam vestrum oculis vestris vidistis quantae abominationi traditum sit. (4:13)

William of Malmesbury attacks the inability of Christian pilgrims to freely enter the city when he exclaims,

> Nay more, they claim as theirs the Lord's sepulchre, that supreme monument of our faith, and take money from our pilgrims for entrance to a city that ought to be open exclusively to Christians, if they yet had in them some vestige of their wonted valour.
>
> Quid quod Dominicum monimentum, unicum fidei pignus, ditioni suae uendicant, et eius urbis introitum peregrinis nostris uenditant quae solis Christianis patere deberet, si aliquod solitae uirtutis uestigium eis inesset? (600)

Guibert even provides ornamented description of the evil nature of the Muslims who torture Christians desiring to visit the Sepulcher:

> The brutality of these evil-doers was so great that, suspecting that the wretches had swallowed gold and silver, they gave them purgatives to drink, so that they would either vomit or burst their insides. Even more unspeakable, they cut their bellies open with swords, opening their inner organs, revealing with a hideous slashing whatever nature holds secret. Remember, I beg you, the thousands who died deplorably, and, for the sake of the Holy Places, whence the beginnings of piety came to you, take action.
>
> Crudelitas nefandorum ad hoc usque perducitur, ut aurum vel argentum miseros absorbuisse putantes, aut, data in potum scamonia, usque ad vomitum vel etiam eruptionem eos vitalium urgent; vel ferro, quod dici nefas est, discissis ventribus, intestinorum quoromque . . . distendentes, quicquid habet natura secreti, horribili concisione aperiunt. Recolite, precor, eorum millia qui detestabiliter perierunt, et pro sanctis locis agite, unde vobis pietatis rudimenta venerunt. (4:140)

The imagery of turmoil and despair utilized in the description of the contemporaneous state of the Holy Sepulcher becomes a distorted pictogram of the physical church, which serves as a symbol for Jerusalem, suggesting a greater importance of the earthly city in Christian thought than in the past. In addition to the threatened status of the Holy Sepulcher is the anxiety over the pilgrim who desires to enter the church and is unable to do so because of brutal and monetary hindrances. In turn, what seems lamentable in these accounts is not what is described to be the abominable situation of the Holy Sepulcher (or Jerusalem), but the inability of the church to tailor itself to the needs of both the believer in the Levant and future pilgrims (or crusaders) who come to it to seek salvation. The expression of a lack of reassurance for the spiritual traveler in the Levant becomes a channel through which Pope Urban II's speeches place Jerusalem into a position of conflict and also becomes a temporary means of offering a solution to the problem of the sinful Christian believer of the past.

The pilgrim in these accounts appears in a twofold context: the pilgrim who is now suffering as a result of the infidels, and the pilgrim of Europe who has been called to liberate Jerusalem and subsequently the suffering Christian pilgrims of the East. The current pilgrim represents the city under the hands of Muslim powers, a city in which a true Christian virtue cannot be expressed. In the case of the latter, the pilgrim of Europe is the savior figure, the *milites Christi* named in Pope Urban II's oratories, the soldier who, just like Christ, will bring about salvation for the city and its Christian inhabitants.[45] Fulcher's account of the conclusion of the speech ends with this very declaration:

> Then as a suppliant he exhorted all to resume the powers of their faith and arouse in themselves a fierce determination to overcome the machinations of the devil, and to try to fully restore the Holy Church, cruelly weakened by the wicked, to its honorable status as of old.
>
> Deinceps, rogitatu supplici cunctos exhortatus est, ut resumptis fidei viribus, cum ingenti sollicitatione ad expungnandas Diaboli machinationes viriliter se animarent, et Ecclesiae sanctae statum, crudelissime a nefandis debilitatum, in honorem pristinum competenter erigere conarentur. (3:321)

The image of the pilgrim also parallels that of Jerusalem through a dual connotation. As a secular individual on a spiritual journey, the pilgrim

45. Fulcher of Chartres, *Gesta Francorum*, 3:324; Baldric of Dol, *Gesta Dei per Francos*, 4:14.

becomes a textual reflection of what Jerusalem or the Holy Sepulcher represents in a now developed Christian thought that takes into account the earthly city. The pilgrim, as a representative of the Christian faith, temporarily takes on the role of Jerusalem in the areas that refer to the current status of the city. In these instances, which proclaim the journey to the city and a Christian procession difficult, the European pilgrim replaces the role of the Sepulcher, just as the pope is paralleled to the lamenting church.[46] The anticipated journey of the Western pilgrim to the Holy Land and the subsequent liberation of the city are described as being the most adequate means through which the crusader may reach the heavenly. The role of this armed pilgrim is also meant to present the texts' call for mercy, their desire for redemption from God, and repentance for the past sins that led to the fall of the Christian Jerusalem. As William of Malmesbury asserts, "this same road will lead you to the fatherland that you have lost, for indeed 'We must through much tribulation enter into the kingdom of God" [*sed haec eadem uos amissam ducet ad patriam; per multas nimirum tribulationes oportet nos introire in regnum Dei*] (602). Jerusalem is therefore Latin Christianity's *patria*, a homeland that these pilgrims have a right to enter, inhabit, and claim as their own. Baldric expresses this very sentiment when he writes,

> The Holy Church keeps for herself an army which comes to the aid of her own people, but you have perverted it with knavery. To speak the truth, the preachers of which it is our duty to be, you are not following the path that leads you to life. You oppressors of orphans, you robbers of widows, you homicides, you blasphemers, you plunderers of others' rights; you hope for the reward of brigands for the shedding of Christian blood, and just as vultures nose corpses you watch and follow wars from afar. Certainly this is the worst course to follow because it is utterly removed from God. And if you want to take counsel for your souls, you must either cast off as quickly as possible the belt of this sort of knighthood and go forward boldly as knights of Christ, hurrying swiftly to defend the Eastern Church.
>
> Sancta Ecclesia ad suorum opitulationem sibi reservavit militiam, sed vos eam, male depravatis in malitiam. Ut veritatem fateamur, cujus praecones esse debemus, vere non tenetis viam per quam eatis ad vitam: vos pupillorum

46. According to Guibert, the pilgrims were being taxed at all the Christian stations: Guibert of Nogent, *Gesta Dei per Francos*, 4:140.

> oppressores; vos viduarum praedones, vos homicidae, vos sacrilegi, vos alieni juris direptores: vos pro effundendo sanguine Christiano expectatis latrocinantium stipendia; et sicut vultures odorantur cadavera, sic longinquarum partium auspicamini et sectamini bella. Certe via ista pessima est, quoniam omnino a Deo remota est. Porro si vultis animabus vestris consuli, aut istiusmodi militae cingulum quantocius deponite, aut Christi milites audacter procedite, et ad defendendam Orientalem Ecclesiam velocius concurrite. (4:14)[47]

It is the pilgrim of the future who now travels to Jerusalem and dies for the faith in the name of the Lord, who can only replenish the seed of the holy church. These narratives then claim that Jerusalem's lamentable state can only be redeemed through the journey of the crusader. For Guibert, the visualization of the freeing of the Holy Land is presented as a task that can only be achieved by the West and, more specifically, a task willed by God that the French are only capable to perform. He wants to know

> upon whom did Pope Urban call for aid against the Turks? Wasn't it the French? . . . I say, truly, everyone should believe it, that God reserved this nation for such a great task.
>
> ad quos papa Urbanus contra Turcos praesidia contracturus divertit? nonne ad Francos? . . . .Fateor vero, et omnibus credibile est, huic tanto gentem istam Deum reservasse negotio. (4:136)[48]

For our narratives, to speak of Jerusalem, to call on the notion of armed pilgrimage to liberate the city, can only be achieved in two ways: first, by temporally and topographically envisioning a Latin Christian Jerusalem, and second, by lamenting this Jerusalem as a lost Christian space. With their inclusion of Pope Urban II's sermons at Clermont and their discussion of the deficient qualities of the *Gesta Francorum*, these accounts display an interest in reframing their own narratives toward the city of Jerusalem and celebrating the acquisition of the city by attributing the crusade to Pope Urban II. These constructions, which attempt to reject the Jewish Jerusalem, paradoxically

47. See Robert the Monk, *Historia Jherosolimitan*, 3:728; Guibert of Nogent, *Gesta Dei per Francos*, 4:128; and the translation of the latter in Riley-Smith, *The First Crusade and the Idea of Crusading*, 149.

48. See William of Malmesbury, *Gesta Regum Anglorum*, 2:602; Fulcher of Chartres, *Gesta Francorum*, 3:140; and Baldric of Dol, *Gesta Dei per Francos*, 4:16.

incorporate Jewish models of representing the loss of cities in the Hebrew Bible and reveal a temporary shift in Christian attitudes toward the earthly city that consider Jerusalem as space that Christians have an inherit right to claim and inhabit. The earthly Jerusalem in the accounts is also presented as a locus to the heavenly city of the afterlife, a shift from the Christian position toward Jerusalem prior to the First Crusade. Considering also that these chronicles were written after the crusader victory at Jerusalem in 1099 CE, the lamentable anxiety within them is solved through the image of the liberating crusader, a new topography that reflects the presence of the European Christian believer and God's reward and acceptance of repentance with the actuality of creating a Latin Christian Jerusalem. It is this capture of the earthly Jerusalem that retrospectively allows for these narratives to engage in a victorious lamenting of Jerusalem—a city they claim as their own until its loss again in 1187 CE.

Chapter 4

Jerusalem's Prince Levon

Lamentation and the Rise of the Armenian Kingdom of Cilicia

Behold! I exclaim the lamentable sound,
I lament all in tears,
I leave my strength to the heaven above,
I turn to speak to the earth below,
I call the two instead of one,
To become the mourner of my being,
I narrate my melancholic anger
I tell of my weeping pain.

Ահա ձայնեմ ձայն ողբագին,
Կական բառնամ արտասուագին,
Զձեռս ձգեմ յերկին վերին,
Դառնամ խօսիմ յերկիր ներքին,
Կոչեմ զերկուսս ընդ միակին,
Լինել սգակից իմոյս անձին,
Պատմեմ զվիշտս իմ տրտմագին,
Ասեմ զցաւս իմ լալագին.[1]

In order to lament Jerusalem, you must first claim Jerusalem.

1. Grigor Tłay, *Asac'eal ban ołbergaḳan vasn aṙmann Erusałēmi*, in *Grigor Tłay: Banastełcutiwnner ev Poemner*, ed. A. Š. Mnac'akanyan (Erevan: Armenian SAH GA, 1972), 244–333, and notes, 431–34. All translations from the poem are my own, and line numbers will hereafter be cited parenthetically in the text. An abbreviated form of the poem (lines 1–2395), accompanied by a French translation, can be found in: E. Dulaurier, "Élégie sur la prise de Jérusalem," in RHC Doc. Arm. 1:269–307. According to the colophon (lines 2793–96), the poem was composed in the year 668 of the Armenian calendar, which is the year 1189 in the Gregorian calendar.

So begins Jerusalem's lamentation in Middle Armenian, reacting to the fall of the city in 1187 CE to the great Islamic leader, Ṣalāḥ al-Dīn Yūsuf Ibn Ayyūb, better known as Saladin in western Europe. In 1189 CE, two years after the capture of the city, the Catholicos or high patriarch of all Armenians, Grigor IV Tłay, composed his creation of over four thousand lines, *Asacʿeal ban ołbergakan vasn aṙmann Erusałēmi* (Poem of lamentation over the capture of Jerusalem). Grigor's poem, told from the point of view of the fallen city of Jerusalem, begins with a declaration of mourning, later calling for others to join in bewailing the city's loss to Ṣalāḥ al-Dīn. Relying on ancient tropes of lamenting Jerusalem in the Hebrew Bible, the poem describes the advancement of Ṣalāḥ al-Dīn and the eventual capture of the city, provides details of the loss and desolate state of Jerusalem, reflects on the sins and disunity of the Christian population and the subsequent fall of the city, expresses pleas for redemption, and appeals to God to aid in the city's eventual reconquest.[2] Grigor's lament concludes by presenting the Cilician Armenian prince Levon II as the savior of Jerusalem, the figure who can reclaim the city for Christianity. This chapter argues that Grigor's lament posits the contemporary sociopolitical position of the Cilician Armenians within this ancient model of city lamentation as a way of furthering its political motive of establishing an independent kingdom of Armenian Cilicia, with Prince Levon II as its monarch.

Grigor Tłay, or Grigor the Boy, was the son of Prince Vasil Pahlawuni, a descendant of a prominent Armenian family often called the Second Pahlawunis who traced their lineage to Grigor Lusaworičʿ, the figure believed to have converted the Armenian King Trdat to Christianity at the turn of the fourth century.[3] Grigor Tłay grew up in his father's castle of Karkaṙ, near Kʿesun in east Cilicia. In 1148 or 1149 CE, when the Ortoqid prince of Diyārbekir, Kara Aslan, took his father prisoner, Grigor's mother Maremik surrendered the fortress to spare her husband's life. He then moved to Hṙomklay, the see of the Armenian Catholicosate at the time, where he lived

2. For a more detailed discussion of lamenting Jerusalem in the Hebrew Bible, see the introduction in this book.

3. For more on Grigor Tłay and his family, see Theo Maarten van Lint, "The Poem of Lamentation over the Capture of Jerusalem Written in 1189 by Grigor Tlay Catholicos of All Armenians," in *The Armenians in Jerusalem and the Holy Land*, ed. Michael E. Stone, Roberta R. Ervine, and Nira Stone, Hebrew University Armenian Studies 4 (Leuven, Belgium: Peeters, 2002), 121–42.

with his two uncles, the current Catholicos Grigor III and later Catholicos Nersēs Šnorhali, the latter considered also one of the greatest poets in Armenian literary history. In 1173 CE, Grigor succeeded his uncle Nersēs as Catholicos and contributed widely to the literary, political, and theological developments of Armenian Cilicia—all of which become reflected in his poem of lamentation over Jerusalem.

Grigor's poetic work not only contextualizes Jerusalem within the greater political climate of Armenian Cilicia but also furthers the trajectory of the established tradition of city lamentations. The opening lines of the poem reference the earthly and the heavenly Jerusalem, calling "the two instead of one" [Կոչեմ զերկուս ընդ միականին] (5). Here the poem is already linking the events on the earthly Jerusalem to the heavenly city but, more important, asserting the position of the lamentation as one that will expose an ancient Armenian presence and connection to Jerusalem. After the initial lines of the poem that call on others to bewail the city's current status, Jerusalem further declares, "Let me be the ancient Jerusalem" [Երուսաղեմն իցեմ ես հին] (13).[4] This line of verse exposes the symbolic role of the city in the poem's anticipation for the future kingdom of Armenian Cilicia. For Grigor's lament this ancient Jerusalem is fashioned in two major ways, both of which link the city to the Armenians. The first manner is through a textual re-creation of the map of the world through the point of view of Jerusalem, where the city acknowledges the presence of Cilician Armenians and their far-reaching history. The second is the multiple allusions in the poem to Mount Zion, the area in the old city linked to the Armenian Quarter. For Grigor's lament, this remapping and direction toward a specific topographical area in the city provides the channel through which the text can both draw attention to the presence of the Armenians in the medieval Mediterranean world and establish a connection between them and the city of Jerusalem. This past and contemporary position of the Armenians becomes posited into the model of lamenting Jerusalem in the Hebrew Bible.

If one were to read the verb "be" (իցեմ) in the line "Let me be the ancient Jerusalem" [Երուսաղեմն իցեմ ես հին] (13) in the future tense, as

4. Dulaurier's translation of this line in "Élégie sur la prise de Jérusalem," 272, reads as follows: "Je suis la Jérusalem antique." Dulaurier's choice to translate the verb *ic'em* (first-person singular subjunctive of the verb "to be") as "suis" does not create the same sense of the hypothetical in the Armenian as perhaps translating the line as "Suis je la Jérusalem antique."

opposed to the subjunctive (as rendered in both classical and middle Armenian), it exhibits the poem's anticipation for the creation of a new Jerusalem: "I will be the ancient (or former) Jerusalem."[5] This Jerusalem is the anticipated Christian city of the future, possibly liberated through the coming of a new crusade from western Europe. It is this ancient city that housed the beginning of Christianity—a city that could once again be regained by the Christians in this upcoming crusade but also through the efforts of the Cilician Armenians, and especially Prince Levon II, who is presented in the poem as the savior king of Jerusalem. By drawing parallels between this Cilician prince and ancient heroes of Europe, the lament further establishes a connection between the Armenians, the Holy Land, and Rome. The poem's anxiety over the loss of the city and its longing for the liberation of Jerusalem become the channel through which the text foregrounds the image of Prince Levon II, establishes an Armenian alliance to the Roman papacy (which has just called for the Third Crusade, or Kings' Crusade), and anticipates a Christian Jerusalem of the future through the establishment of an Armenian kingdom of Cilicia.

Acquiring a Crown for Cilicia: Grigor Tłay, Prince Levon II, and the Roman Papacy

In order to understand the ways in which the lament of Catholicos Grigor Tłay anticipates the possibility of a future kingdom of Armenian Cilicia, a number of significant moments in Cilician Armenian political and ecclesiastical history should be briefly noted. Key developments in the decade leading up to the capture of the city of Jerusalem by Ṣalāḥ al-Dīn's forces were crucial in shaping Cilicia's position at the onset of the Third Crusade, also referred to as the Kings' Crusade because of the leadership of three European kings: Frederick Barbarossa, the Holy Roman emperor, Phillip II of France, and Richard I (or Richard Lionheart) of England. These developments not only resulted in a shift of Armenian Church policy from the Greeks to the Latin Church but also paved the opportunity to receive a crown from the pope and the Holy Roman emperor.

5. In Middle Armenian, as in the classical language, the subjunctive can also render the future. These two verb moods also share the same form.

In 1179 CE, Catholicos Grigor Tłay convoked a synod at Hṙomklay, where Archbishop Nersēs of Lambron became the primary spokesperson for the union of the Armenian and Greek Churches. A decade earlier Emperor Manuel Comnenus I had laid down before the Armenian Church nine demands concerning dogma and liturgy. Although the Armenian high patriarch Nersēs Šnorhali rejected the terms of the union, the Byzantine ambush by the Seljuqs at the Battle of Myriokephalon resulted in the withdrawal of eight of the nine points, leaving only the question of the nature of Christ. The Armenian Church had already separated from the (as yet undivided) Greek and Latin Churches as a result of the Council of Chalcedon in 451 CE. The Armenians held firm to Cyril of Alexandria's wording at Ephesus regarding the single nature of Christ, officially rejecting Chalcedon's definitive statement concerning the two natures at the Council of Dvin in 506 CE.[6] The church officials at Hṙomklay and their spokesman Nersēs of Lambron realized the need for a firm guarantee of aid against the Muslim threats and agreed to join with the Greek Church and affirm its belief in the dual nature of Christ.[7] Before the letters from Hṙomklay reached Constantinople, Emperor Manuel had died and the Armenians politely ignored the results of the council. In the aftermath of the council, Grigor Tłay realized that the possibility of a Greek union could no longer be an actuality under the policy of the new emperor, Alexius II Comnenus, who started persecutions against the Armenian people. It is then that Grigor turned his attention to Rome.[8]

In 1184 CE, Grigor Tłay addressed a letter to Pope Lucius III and entrusted it to a Latin-speaking bishop, Gregory of Philippopolis, who met the pope that year at Verona. According to Vardan Arewelecʿi, Grigor wished to recount in his letter "the tribulations that the Armenians were suffering

6. See Nina Garsoïan, *L'église arménienne et le grand schisme d'orient* (Leuven, Belgium: Peeters, 1999), which places the date later, in 522 or 607 CE; Karekin I. Sarkissian, *The Council of Chalcedon and the Armenian Church* (Antelius, Lebanon: Armenian Church Prelacy, 1964), esp. 171–200; V. Inglisian, "Chalkedon und die armenische Kirche," in *Das Konzil von Chalkedon*, vol. 2, ed. A. Grillmeier and H. Bacht (Würzburg, West Germany: Echter Verlag, 1953), 361–417.

7. Alexander Balgy, *Historia Doctrinae Catholicae inter Armenos* (Vienna: Typis Congregationis Mechitaristicae, 1878), 49.

8. In the aftermath of Hṙomklay, Nersēs of Lambron continued to advocate his policy of cooperation with other Christian churches. He was the son of the Hetumid prince of Lambron, and his family tradition emphasized a loyalty to Constantinople, although he also had a genuinely theologically motivated ecumenical attitude.

because of the Greeks, and to solicit his prayers and blessing as his predecessors had done."[9] In response to this letter, the pope gave the messenger Gregory a miter, a pallium, a ring, and liturgical books of the Latin Church. A letter also accompanied the gifts requesting that Armenians celebrate Christmas on December 25, put water in the Eucharistic wine, and consecrate holy oil during the week prior to Easter. Nersēs of Lambron translated this letter into Armenian upon Gregory's return to Cilicia.[10] The interaction between the Catholicos Grigor Tłay and Pope Lucius III became one of the first significant exchanges in this period between the Armenians and the Latin Church. At this time Latin liturgical vestments and uses also made their way into Armenian Church ceremonies. These relations also paved the way for future interactions with Rome, such as the correspondence between Catholicos Grigor Tłay and Pope Clement III prior to the Third Crusade.

In 1189 CE the Armenian Prince Levon and Catholicos Grigor received a letter from Pope Clement III informing them that the Third Crusade had been organized and formally requesting from the Catholicos and the rising Cilician prince financial and military assistance for the crusading army. After the capture of Jerusalem by Ṣalāḥ al-Dīn, Prince Ruben II, ruler of the principality of Cilicia, handed over his rule to Levon and retired to a monastery. The crusaders and Levon had found Ṣalāḥ al-Dīn, the emperor Isaac Angelus, the Seljuqs, and the Turkomen tribes who invaded Anatolia as common opponents. Levon offered a loan to Bohemond I of Antioch, and married Sybil, an Antiochene princess. He also drafted a letter to Emperor Frederick Barbarossa and the pope, asking to be crowned king when Barbarossa arrived for the crusade, in return for the aid of the Cilician Armenians to the crusaders. Both the pope and Barbarossa agreed to combine the Armenians lands in Cilicia into an independent kingdom.[11] According to its col-

9. Vardan Arewelec'i, *Havakumn Patmutiwn*, in RHC Doc. Arm. 1:438; Vardan Arewelec'i, "The Historical Compilation of Vardan Arewelec'i," trans. Robert W. Thomson, *Dumbarton Oaks Papers* 43 (1989): 209.

10. The Armenian version of the letter appears in Ł. Alishan, *Léon le Magnifique*, ed. G. Baian (Venice: St. Łazar, 1888), 161.

11. Yerevan, Madenataran MS 1206, ff.167v-174v; Venice, Mxitarist Monastery at St. Lazarus: MS 297, f.173r; Vienna, Mxitarist Monastery: MS 610, f.11. For the Armenian translation by Nersēs of Lambron of the series of letters between Grigor Tłay, Levon, and Pope Clement III, see Ł. Alishan, *Sisuan Hamagrut'iwn Haykakan Kilikioy ew Levon Mecagorc* (Venice: St. Lazarus Armenian Monastery, 1885), 463–76. My extensive search for the original letters of Pope Clement III

ophon, Grigor Tłay's poem of lamentation is composed in the same year these exchanges and negotiations were being made, 1189 CE.

These series of exchanges between Frederick Barbarossa, Grigor Tłay, Pope Clement III, and Prince Levon II leading up to the Third Crusade (and Grigor's composition of his poem of lamentation) suggest the following: Levon II was promised a crown from both Barbarossa and the pope upon the arrival of the crusaders in exchange for their aid of the crusading armies; the composition of Grigor's lament occurred after his exchange of letters with Pope Clement III; and the lament's contemporaneous moment exists in the realm of hopefulness for the possibility of the establishment of an autonomous Armenian kingdom of Cilicia. Taking into consideration the political circumstances surrounding the composition of Grigor's *Asacʻeal ban ołbergakan vasn aṙmann Erusałēmi*, the remainder of this chapter examines the ways in which the genre of the city lament becomes the framework that not only reflects on the loss of the city of Jerusalem and the call for a new crusade but also, by establishing connections between the city and the Armenians, becomes the channel through which the lament can further its political desires for an autonomous Armenian kingdom of Cilicia through the figure of Prince Levon II.

Jerusalem's View: Armenia in the T-O Map of the World

In its stratagem to present Prince Levon II as the savior of Jerusalem (a symbol for the future Armenian kingdom of Cilicia) and gain a crown from Rome and the Holy Roman emperor, Grigor's *Asacʻeal ban ołbergakan vasn aṙmann Erusałēmi* posits the physical city of Jerusalem into the context of Greater Armenia and a medieval worldview. At the start of the poem appears a textual representation of the map of the world with Jerusalem as its center. As the rest of the section demonstrates, this map combines Eastern

has thus far been unsuccessful, which brings me to believe that perhaps the Armenian translations might be the only surviving copies. Arab historians from the period also record a letter from Grigor Tłay Ṣalāḥ al-Dīn to *Saladin*, though there have been several arguments against Grigor's authorship and its authenticity; sources for the letter include Abū Shāma, *Kitāb al-rawḍatayn fī akhbār al-dawlatayn al-Nūriyya wa-l-Ṣalāḥiyya*, RHC Or. 4:435–36; Bahāʾ al-Dīn, *al-Nawādir al-Sultāniyya wa al-Mahāsin al-Yūsufiyya*, in RHC Doc. Or. 3:164–66. See also the translations and discussion in Assadour Antreassian, *Jerusalem and the Armenians* (Jerusalem: St. James, 1968), 46–48.

and Western topographical traditions, and through these models advances the social and political motives of this lament.

Around twenty lines into Grigor's poem appears a geographic description of the world through the point of view of the city of Jerusalem:

> I am not unfamiliar to the four corners of the earth,
> Which they call the tripartite world.
> I am neither a foreigner to Europe,
> Nor am I distant from Africa,
> Asia is near the border
> And close to my region.
>
> Չեմ անծանօթ քառակուսին,
> Որ եռամասն երկիր ասին:
> Եւ ոչ օտար եմ Եւրոպին,
> Ոչ հեռաւոր եմ Լիբէին.
> ԶԱսիայ մերձ է սահմանին
> Եւ առընթեր իմ նահանգին:.
>
> (24–29)

The description then continues with the naming of major bodies of water:

> What shall I say of the Pontus?
> Or about the Black, which is somewhat resembling. . . .
>
> Or what of the ocean they name
> The great Caspian.
> And what of the sea of Egypt
> Which is close to Mount Sinai, . . .
>
> That, which they call the Red,
>
> The same and the sea Mediterranean.
>
> Զի՞նչ ասացից զՊոնտոսին
> Եւ կամ զՍեւն, որ կից նմին:
>
> Կամ զի՞նչ զծովս զանուանին՝
> ԶԿասբիականն զպանծալին:
> Զի՞նչ եւ զծովս Եգիպտոսին,
> Որ հուպ լերինն է Սինային,

Այն, ում Կարմիրն կոչէին,

Նոյն եւ ծովակք միջերկրային.

(35–36, 42–45, 49, 51)

These references to both the landmasses and bodies of water at the start of the poem textually re-create a view of the world through the concept of the medieval *rota terrarum* or *orbis terrae*. This construction is better known today as the Psalter map or T-O *(terra-oceanus)* map of the world. Cosmas Indicopleustes first introduced the schematic for the cartographic representation of the world through the T-O structure at the beginning of the Christian era in his *Topographia Kristianikē*. Moving away from the science of cartography to the teachings of the scriptures, Cosmas replaced the spherical structure of the earth with a disk-shaped one that was divided into continents and oceans.[12]

The seventh-century scholar Isidore of Seville, who became the influential figure of the T-O map structure through the Middle Ages, further developed Cosmas's model.[13] In chapter 14 of his *Eytmologiae Sive Originum*, Isidore describes the world as such:

> The mass of solid land is called round after the roundness of a circle, because it is like a wheel. . . . Because of this, the Ocean flowing around it is contained in a circular border, and is divided in three parts, one part being called Asia, the second Europe, and the third Africa.
>
> Orbis a rotunditate circuli dictus, quia sicut rota est. . . . Undique enim Oceanus circumfluens eius in circulo ambit fines. Divisus est autem trifarie: e quibus una pars Asia, altera Europa, tertia Africa nuncupatur.[14]

Isidore's description of the world produces a map that represents the world through a *T*, the edges of which are surrounded by an encircling *O*. The three

12. Wanda Wolska, *La Topographie chrétienne de Cosmas Indicopleustès: Théologie et science au VIe siècle*, Bibliothèque Byzantine, Études 3 (Paris: Éditions du Cerf, 1962).

13. David Woodward, "Medieval *Mappaemundi*," in *The History of Cartography*, vol. 1, *Cartography in Prehistoric, Ancient, and Medieval Europe and the Mediterranean*, ed. J. B. Harley and David Woodward (Chicago: University of Chicago Press, 1987), 294–304.

14. [Isidore of Seville,] *Isidori Hispalensis episcopi: Etymologiarum sive originum*, ed. W. M. Lindsay, vol. 14 (Oxford: Clarendon, 1911) chap. 14; John Henderson, *The Medieval World of Isidore of Seville: Truth from Words* (Cambridge: Cambridge University Press, 2007) 166–69.

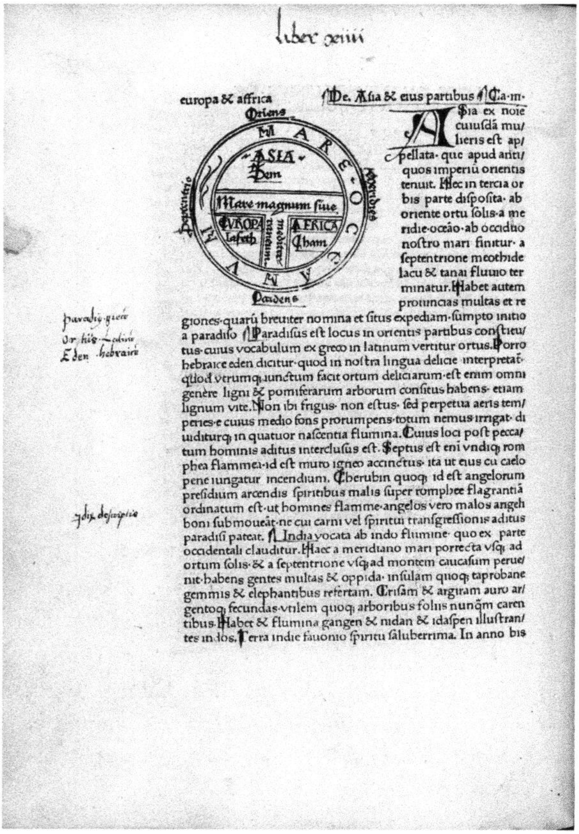
Liber xiiii

europa & affrica

De. Asia & eius partibus Ca. iii.

Asia ex noie cuiusdã mu/lieris est ap/pellata. que apud anti/quos imperiũ orientis tenuit. Hec in tercia or/bis parte disposita. ab oriente ortu solis. a me/ridie. oceão. ab occiduo nostro mari finitur. a septentrione meothide lacu & tanai fluuio ter/minatur. Habet autem prouincias multas et re/giones. quarũ breuiter nomina et situs expediam. sumpto initio a paradiso. Paradisus est locus in orientis partibus constitu/tus. cuius vocabulum ex greco in latinum vertitur ortus. Porro hebraice eden dicitur. quod in nostra lingua delicie interpretatũ. quod vtrumq; iunctum facit ortum deliciarum. est enim omni genere ligni & pomiferarum arborum consitus habens. etiam lignum vite. Non ibi frigus. non estus. sed perpetua aeris tem/peries. e cuius medio fons prorumpens. totum nemus irrigat. di/uiditurq; in quatuor nascentia flumina. Cuius loci post pecca/tum hominis aditus interclusus est. Septus est eni vndiq; rom/phea flammea. id est muro igneo accinctus. ita ut eius cũ caelo pene iungatur incendium. Cherubin quoq; id est angelorum presidium arcendis spiritibus malis super romphee flagrantiã ordinatum est. ut homines flamme. angelos vero malos angeli boni submoueãt. ne cui carni vel spiritui transgressionis aditus paradisi pateat. India vocata ab indo flumine. quo ex parte occidentali clauditur. Haec a meridiano mari porrecta vsq; ad ortum solis. & a septentrione vsq; ad montem caucasum perue/nit. habens gentes multas & oppida. insulam quoq; taprobane gemmis & elephantibus refertam. Crisam & argiram auro ar/gentoq; fecundas. vtilem quoq; arboribus foliis nunq̃m caren/tibus. Habet & flumina gangen & nidan & idaspen illustran/tes indos. Terra indie fauonio spiritu saluberrima. In anno bis

Figure 4. T-O map of the world from the first printed version of the *Etymologiae* of Isidore of Seville, with the three known continents labeled with the names of the three sons of Noah: Sem (Shem), Iafeth (Japeth), and Cham (Ham). Vollbehr Collection, Library of Congress, Washington, DC.

landmasses of the world—Asia, Europe, and Africa—are divided by the *T*, which represents the Mediterranean, the Nile, and the Don River (*Tanais*, in its Greek form). Asia occupies the top of the map and is twice as large as Europe and Africa, which appear to the bottom left and right, respectively. The upper part of the *T* represents the Mediterranean Sea, which separates the landmass of Africa from that of Europe. The Red Sea, which occupies the right side of the crossbar, separates Africa from Asia, whereas the left side of the crossbar, representing the Black Sea, the Don River, and the Sea of Azov, separates Europe from Asia.[15]

A significant feature of the T-O map is that it also possesses an eastern orientation. The reasoning behind this placement comes from the direction of the rising sun. This eastern point of reference was further influenced by the belief that the long-lost Garden of Eden or the terrestrial paradise lay at the farthest eastern point of the earth.[16] In Christian attempts to organize and theologize space, Jerusalem occupies the center of the map.[17] The *T* may be a symbol both representing the cross and reflecting the city where Christ was crucified.[18]

The appearance of the textual T-O map of the world at the start of Grigor's poem both allows for further analysis of the representation of Jerusalem within this particular lament and reveals an interchange between the Armenian, Byzantine, and Roman cartographic traditions. A closer examination of the specifics of the T-O model in this Armenian poem not only uncovers the map's form as a symbolic product of interpretations of the world but also exposes the uniqueness of this textual map through its addition of two geographic areas, the Caspian Sea and the Pontus region. The identification of specific topographical loci, along with the utilization of various traditions within the textual T-O map in Grigor's poem, reveal the political and social motives of the work: to bring recognition to Cilicia and its Prince Levon through an anticipation of the liberation of Jerusalem with a new crusade.

Although an extensive study of the Armenian cartographic tradition has not yet been performed, the works of the seventh-century Armenian geographer and mathematician Ananias of Širak reveal that the Armenian tradition, influenced by the Greek tradition, also envisioned a tripartite view of the world. In his *Geography*, Ananias describes the world as such:

---

15. For early examples, see Woodward, "Medieval *Mappaemundi*," 297, 302–3.

16. James W. Flanagan, "Mapping the Biblical World: Perceptions of Space in Ancient Southwestern Asia," in *Mappa Mundi: Mapping Culture/Mapping the World*, ed. Jacqueline Murray (Windsor, ON: Humanities Research Group at the University of Windsor, 2001), 11–12.

17. Cf. Ezekiel 5:5: "This is Jerusalem. I have set her in the center of nations with countries round her."

18. Jaroslav Folda, *Art of the Crusaders in the Holy Land, 1187–1291* (Cambridge: Cambridge University Press, 1995), 44; Adrian J. Boas, *Jerusalem in the Time of the Crusades: Society, Landscape, and Art in the Holy City under Frankish Rule* (London: Routledge, 2001), 199–200.

> The earth is further divided into three parts: Europe, Libya, and Asia. Europe and Libya occupy the western part. Europe is to the northwest as far as the river Tanais. To the southwest is Libya, which extends as far as the Red Sea [MS L1881]. . . . Asia, however occupies the north, south, and middle of the east side as far as an unknown land. It is larger than the other parts of the world and it is the foremost among them having countries and limits vaster than those of Europe. Libya comes second; Europe is third. It seems to me the three parts are Shem, Ham and Japheth [MS S1819].

> Նոյնպէս եւ զերկիր բաժանեալ յերիս, յԵւրոպիայ, ի Լիբիա, յԱսիա եւ ունի զարեւմտական հիւսիսային կողմանէ Եւրոպիա մինչեւ ի Տոնաւիս գետ. եւ զարեւմտական հարաւայնով կողմամբ Լիբիա մինչեւ զԿարմիր ծովս. . . . Իսկ յարաւելս կոյս՝ զհարաւ եւ զհիւսիսի եւ զմէջն՝ Ասիա ունի մինջեւ զԱնծանօթ երկիր վասն որոյ մեծագոյն է քան զայլ հատածսն. եւ սա է առաջին բաժին աշխարհի. եւ զի Լիբիա մեծագոյն է սահմանօք քան զԵւրոպիա, սա երկրորդ է Ասիա, եւ երրորդ Եւրոպիա: Ինձ թուի Սեմայ, Քամայ, եւ Յաբեթի.[19]

According to Rouben Galichian, Armenian medieval maps dating from the eleventh to the fourteenth centuries did in fact produce T-O maps of the world.[20] An interesting example of T-O cartography in the medieval Armenian tradition can be found in manuscript 1242 (MS 1242) of the Yerevan Matenadaran.[21] As Galichian notes, "This anonymous T-O map is from an Armenian manuscript, which based on the analysis of its inscriptions is dated no later than 1206."[22] Although the author does not offer any information regarding the location of the map, the presence of the map suggests that Armenians not only knew of the tradition of the T-O map but also adhered to its system in their cartography. The presence of this map also suggests that

19. According to the Armenian historian Movsēs Xorenacʻi, Armenians descended from Japheth through Torgom, the father of the heroic ancestor of the Armenians, Hayk. Attempts to interpret T-O maps through the positioning of Noah's three sons and their descendants were commonplace in medieval cartography. See Philip S. Alexander, "Notes on the *Imago Mundi* in the Book of Jubilees," *Journal of Jewish Studies* 33 (1982): 197–213; and Philip S. Alexander, "Geography and the Bible (Early Jewish Geography)," in *Anchor Bible Dictionary*, vol. 2, *D–G*, ed. David Noel Freedman (Garden City, NY: Anchor, 1992), 982.

20. Rouben Galichian, *Historical Maps of Armenia: The Cartographic Heritage* (London: Taurus, 2004), 15.

21. MS 1242, Matenadaran, Yerevan, Armenia, in Galichian, *Historical Maps of Armenia*, 57.

22. Galichian, *Historical Maps of Armenia*, 56.

Armenians were working within multiple and even competing topographical traditions.

Galichian's catalog entry for MS 1242 also provides further information about characteristics of Armenian T-O maps:

> The centre of the map [MS 1242] is occupied by the city of Jerusalem, drawn out of proportion, showing its gates and quarters. Mount Sinai can be seen to its south-east with the Red Sea to its south. The left of the stem of the T bears the inscription *This side is Europa*, then the cartographer carries on with the names of the countries of *Bulgars*, *Alemans*, *Franks*, and *Spania*. . . . Here the Black and Azov seas are represented as lines, which are the extensions of the River Don. . . . It is curious to note that while the majority of similar maps produced in the Christian west show Armenia, Mount Ararat and Noah's Ark, the Armenian author has chosen not to mention Armenia on his circular map.[23]

Galichian's query regarding the absence of symbols denoting Armenia on the MS 1242 T-O map elicits a similar question as regards the textual map of the world at the start of Grigor's lament, which includes two areas uncharacteristic to T-O maps: the Caspian and the Pontus.

To recall, the description of the T-O map at the start of Grigor's lamentation names four seas: the Black, the Caspian, the Mediterranean, and the Red. The Black, Mediterranean, and Red are the three bodies of water characteristically featured in medieval T-O maps. Variants would also include the River Don and the Sea of Azov, as noted in Galichian's description of the medieval Armenian T-O map. Yet Grigor's lament also names the Caspian as one of the featured bodies of water. The three continents, Europe, Africa, and Asia, are also accompanied by what seems to be an uncharacteristic reference to the geographic region of the Pontus. Although the reference to these regions may seem atypical, the inclusion of the Caspian Sea and the Pontus within the poem's reconstruction of the T-O map becomes the channel through which the text can posit the city of Jerusalem within the geographic context of the Armenians. The geographic region between the Caspian and the Pontus (the area south of the Black Sea) is the

23. Ibid.

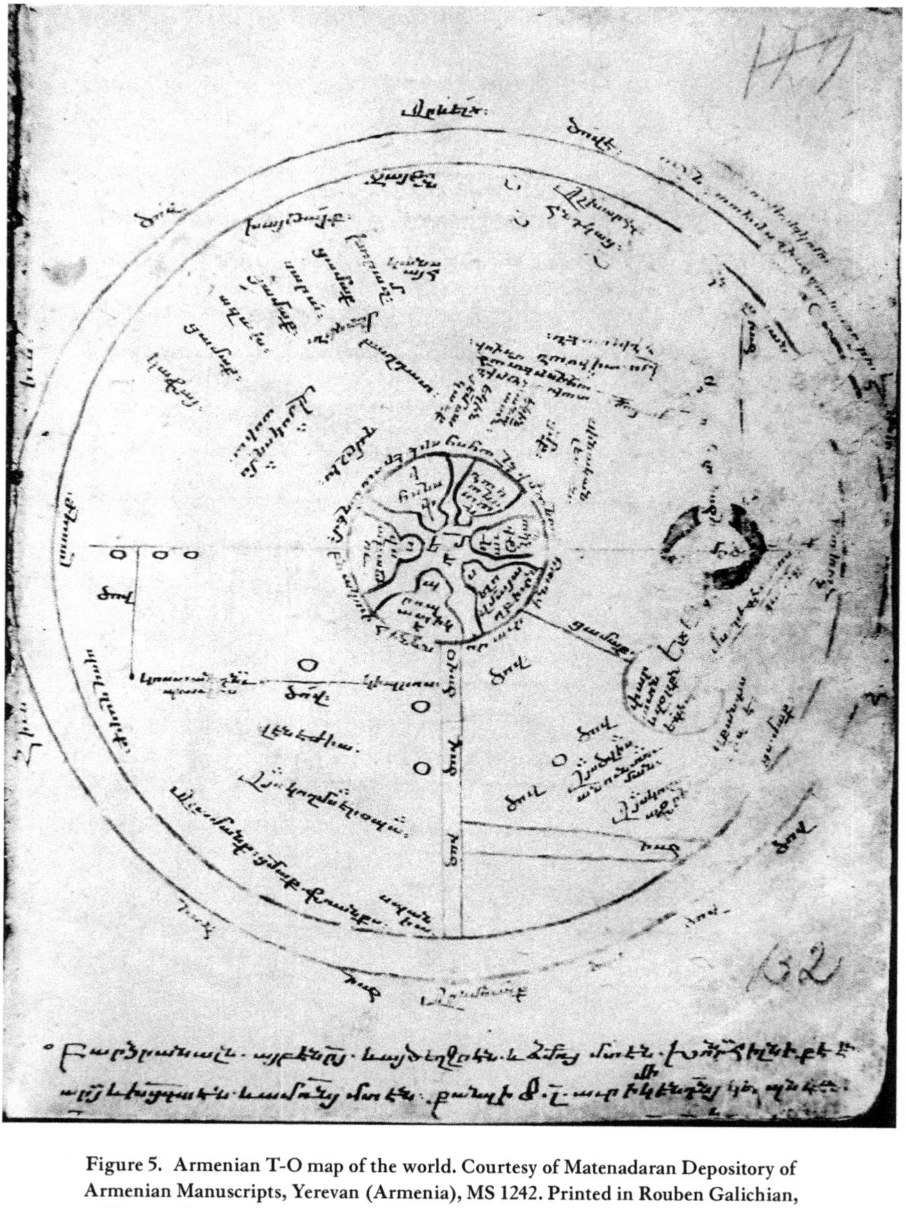

Figure 5. Armenian T-O map of the world. Courtesy of Matenadaran Depository of Armenian Manuscripts, Yerevan (Armenia), MS 1242. Printed in Rouben Galichian, *History of Armenian Cartography: Up to the Year 1918* (Yerevan: Zangak, 2017).

area of Greater Armenia in its historical geographic setting.[24] The seventh-century *Geography* of Ananias of Širak, which provides detailed information on the provinces attributed to Armenia, also situates the Armenians in relation to the Caspian and the Pontus, respectively:

> The third sea is that of Hyrcania which is called the Sea of the Caspians. It is surrounded by Europe. It extends from the mouth of the Araxes and Cyrus rivers as far as the River Politimetus. . . . The Armenians occupy the west shore, while the northwestern is inhabited by the Albanians and the Massagetae, and the northeast by the Scythians.
>
> Asia is the first among the general divisions of the world. It has several countries of which the first is Asia Minor, which lies between the Grecian Sea and the Pontus. . . . Cappadocian Pontus is east of the Polemoniac Pontus [extending] from the sea to the mountains which separate it from Greater Armenia. It has three mountains and four rivers. Such is the description of Asia Minor.
>
> Երրորդ ծով՝ Վրկանին է, որ կոչի Կասբից. եւ ձգի եկայնութիւն նորայ ի բարանոյ Երասխայ եւ ի Կուր գետոյ մինչեւ զՊաւլիտ իմիտոս գետոյ. . . . եւ սահմանէ յարեւմտից՝ Հայօք. իսկ յարեւմտից հիւսիսոյ՝ Աղուանիք եւ Մասքթօք. իսկ յարեւելից հիւսիսոյ Սկիւթացւովք.
>
> Առաջին բաժին երկրի ընդհանուր Ասիա է, եւ ունի կողմունս եւ նախ զկողմն Միջերկրեայս, որք մտանեն ընդ մէջ Յունաց ծովս եւ Պոնտոսի. . . . Պոնտոս Կապատովկիոյ յելից կալով Պողմոնական Պոնտոսին առ երի ծովուն ի ցամաքական լերինան որք բաժանեն ընդ նա եւ ընդ Հայս: Ունի լերինս երիս եւ գետս չորս: Ահա կատարեցան Միջերկրեայքս կոչեցեալք:.[25]

Therefore, what does the T-O map structure, with the inclusion of the Caspian and the Pontus, reveal about the textual map of the world at the start of Grigor's lament? According to Robert Hewsen's study of Širak's *Geography*, the allusion to the land of Armenia through a reference to the geographic

24. Robert H. Hewsen, *Armenia: A Historical Atlas* (Chicago: University of Chicago Press, 2001). 127; Robert H. Hewsen, "The Geography of Armenia," in *The Armenians from Ancient to Modern Times*, vol. 1, *The Dynastic Periods: From Antiquity to the Fourteenth Century*, ed. Richard G. Hovannisian (New York: St. Martin's, 1997), 1–17.

25. [Ananias of Širak,] *The Geography of Ananias of Širak: Ašxarhac'oyc', the Long and the Short Recensions*, trans. Robert H. Hewsen (Wiesbaden: Reichert, 1992), 45a.

area of the Caspian and the Pontus is the result of the influence of the Byzantine cartographic tradition. Hewsen notes,

> The chief sources for the *Ašxarac'oyc'* [Geography] are known to us, for our author cites several of them by name in his introduction: Ptolemy, Pappus of Alexandria, Marinus of Tyre, "Constantine of Antioch," Hipparchus, "Diodorus of Samos," "Dionysius," and "Apollo." . . . The text is based, as the author himself tells us, on the lost *Khorographia Oikoumenikē* of Pappus of Alexandria, which was itself most likely an abridgement of Ptolemy's *Gēographikes Hyphēgēsis* while the other classical authors cited, not already quoted by Ptolemy, were probably found cited in Pappus' work to begin with.[26]

Productions of Ptolemaic maps are known to have continued through the late fifteenth century, and the influences of the works of Ptolemy on western Europe were particularly strong in the twelfth.[27] Therefore, in concordance with the Ptolemaic maps of the world, the *Geography* of Ananias of Širak also locates Armenia Major and Minor between the Pontus Euxinus and the Caspian (Hyracanean) Sea.[28]

Yet the description of the world at the beginning of Grigor's lament does not adhere to the Ptolemaic tradition (the one most influential on Armenian cartography) but to the tradition of Isidore through the T-O structure. In T-O maps of western Europe where Armenia is noted, either Noah's ark or Mount Ararat (representative symbols of Armenia) appear in the northwest corner.[29] The textual map of the world at the start of Grigor's lamentation first utilizes a Latin model to describe the world through the viewpoint of the city of Jerusalem and then posits the geographic region of the Armenians based on the Ptolemaic model. The synthesis between this Latin model through the representation of the T-O worldview and the Ptolemaic model—through the inclusion of the Caspian and the Pontus—symbolically reflects the possible positioning of the Armenians of Cilicia within the context of an expanding western Europe at the onset of a new crusade.

26. Hewsen, *Geography*, 28, 32; see also 15–16; 29–35, 42–46, image a.
27. Woodward, "Medieval *Mappaemundi*," 299.
28. Galichian, *Historical Maps of Armenia*, 85, and maps 32, 32a, 36.
29. Ibid., maps 14, 18, 20.

The geographic area of the Caspian and the Pontus also calls to mind the significance of the area in the time of early Christianity. Under Diocletian, the Pontus was divided into four provinces, one of which was Armenia Minor, with Sebastia as its capital.[30] Inhabitants of the Pontus were believed to be the very first converts to Christianity and are mentioned as one of the groups present during the Day of Pentecost (Acts 2:9). Acts 18:2 mentions a Jewish couple from Pontus that convert to Christianity, and the apostle Peter addresses the Pontians (in 1 Pet. 1:1) as the εκλεκτοις, or "chosen ones." The Pontus also connects the Armenians to the early days of Christianity and calls to mind their conversion under King Trdat (Tiridates)—the genealogical line from which the family of Catholicos Grigor Tłay is believed to have descended.[31]

The allusion to the Armenians through the Caspian and the Pontus in the representation of the world through the T-O/Ptolemaic structure at the start of the Grigor's lament reflects both the contemporary geopolitics of the Cilician Armenians during the time of the early Crusades and their desire to position themselves within this sociopolitical sphere through their own autonomous kingdom. The insertion of the geographic areas inhabited by the Armenians within a competing and simultaneous image of the world, as it appears at the start of Grigor's lament, reflects further the intermediary position of the Armenians and their political motives of gaining a crown for the Armenian prince Levon II. Moving away from the established Greek tradition of cartography into the T-O structure, the lamentation's map also reflects the shift of Levon II and Grigor Tłay toward Rome and the crusaders as a means of furthering their own political positions. It is through the point of view of Jerusalem that this map of the world is established at the beginning of the lament. Jerusalem therefore constructs a world that is mindful of the long-standing relationship between the city and the Armenians and continues to assert and solidify this relationship throughout the entirety of the poem.

30. Hewsen, *Armenia: A Historical Atlas*, 64–74, and maps 57, 59.

31. Agatʻangełos, *History of the Armenians*, ed. and trans. Robert W. Thomson (Albany: State University of New York Press, 1976).

Jerusalem's Topography: Mount Zion and the Armenians

The allusion to the geographic area of historic Armenia in the textual T-O map of the world at the start of Grigor's lament is accompanied by recurring allusions to a physical landmark at the southern border of the city, Mount Zion. Through its references to Mount Zion, the lamentation draws further attention to the presence of Armenians in the Holy Land by foregrounding their position in Jerusalem during the period of the Crusades. It is through the image of Mount Zion that the lament also promotes its political narrative by both reinforcing the past and contemporary presence of the Armenians and also connecting the area of Mount Zion to a linked Armenian and Roman past. For Grigor's lament, the image of Mount Zion functions as a metonym for the physical city of Jerusalem, as suggested in a three-hundred-line refrain in the middle of the poem, where Jerusalem occupies the second part of the verse: "Mount Zion, Jerusalem" [Լեառն Սիոն, Երուսաղեմ] (1348).

Armenian presence in Jerusalem dates back to early Christianity, with a documented presence in the fifth century.[32] According to Adrian Boas, Armenians were predominantly concentrated around the area of Mount Zion during the crusader period: "The Armenian community in Jerusalem had earlier been located in different parts of the city. These probably included the area to the north-west, outside the city walls, which is now occupied by the Musrara neighbourhood, the part of Mount Zion within the present city walls where the Armenian Quarter is now located, and an area on the summit of the Mount of Olives. By the Crusader period it seems that the areas outside the city walls were no longer occupied by them [the Armenians], but they retained their quarter in the southwest of the city."[33] Armenian pres-

32. Kevork Hintlian, *History of Armenians in the Holy Land* (Jerusalem: St. James, 1976); Victor Azarya, *The Armenian Quarter of Jerusalem: Urban Life behind Monastery Walls* (Berkeley: University of California Press, 1984), 57–73; Avedis K. Sanjian, *The Armenian Communities in Syria under Ottoman Dominion* (Cambridge, MA: Harvard University Press, 1965), 4–8; Amnon Linder, "Christian Communities in Jerusalem," in *The History of Jerusalem: the Early Muslim Period 638–1099*, ed. Joshua Prawer and Haggai Ben-Shammai (New York: New York University Press,1996), 157–59.

33. Boas, *Jerusalem in the Time of the Crusades*, 39. According to the Arab historian Mujīr al-Dīn, in 1191 CE Ṣalāḥ al-Dīn carried out plans to repair the city. This included the rebuilding of a new wall in the south to include Mount Zion within the fortifications of the city and the Armenian Quarter, a measure which was carried out by Ṣalāḥ al-Dīn's brother al-Malik al ʿAdīl. If we

ence in the southwest portion of Jerusalem during the period of the Crusades was also linked to the history of the Cathedral of Sts. James. In the middle of the eleventh century the Georgians secured the ancient martyrium of St. Menas on Mount Zion in Jerusalem, and in 1070 CE they built a church on the same site dedicated to St. James the Major. In the following century, for an unknown reason, they ceded this church and monastery to the local Armenian community. Subsequent to the visit of Catholicos Grigor, the Armenians erected the large Cathedral of Sts. James, consisting of a complex of sanctuaries including the chapels containing the tombs of St. Makar and St. Menas. The accommodations of the monastery were also enlarged for the benefit not only of the local monastics but also the large number of Armenian pilgrims who annually arrived in the Holy City.

According to the Armenian tradition, Mount Zion was the location of the house of Caiaphas, the high priest of the Jews, and the locus of Christ's arrest and delivery to crucifixion (John 18:24). The Armenians' claim to their quarter near Mount Zion comes from the belief that that the small room on the upper level of the house of Caiaphas on the mountain was being used as a church in the early years of Christianity. Following the Ascension, it is also an accepted tradition among Armenians that the apostles elected as the first bishop James the Younger, who establishes his seat on Mount Zion, the location of the site of the Armenian Cathedral of Sts. James. The cathedral is also believed to be the site of the beheading and burial of James the Great, brother of John the Evangelist, by Herod Agrippa in 44 CE.[34]

According to Joshua Prawer, the development of the Cathedral of Sts. James as a locus for the Armenians was connected to the visit of the Catholicos Gregory or Grigor III Pahlawuni, who attended the Latin Church Council at Antioch in 1141 CE, and then accompanied the papal legate and cardinal bishop of Ostia, Alberic, on a pilgrimage to Jerusalem, where he was given a place of honor at the Second Latin Council. As Prawer notes, "It appears as a result of Bahlavouni's pilgrimage the Cathedral of St. James was enlarged and a hospice was added. Many architectural parts of St. James are

---

were to trust the colophon in the dating of the lament, this reconstruction would have occurred after the composition of Grigor's lament.

34. Ewsebios Kesarecʻi, *Patmutyun Ekełecʻwoy*, ed. H. Abraham (Venice: St. Łazar, 1877); Tigran Sawalaniancʻ, *Patmutyun Erusałēmi*, vol. 1 (Jerusalem, 1931), 34; Sanjian, *Armenian Communities*, 95–101; Azarya, *Armenian Quarter*, 59, 109; Antreassian, *Jerusalem and the Armenians*, 36.

undoubtedly from the Crusader Period, though they show Georgian and Armenian influences. . . . The original cupola on pendentives followed a Crusader pattern before it was replaced by the Armenian one."[35] The Council of Jerusalem in 1140 CE, summoned by Alberic, solidified the relationship between the Armenians and Rome. According to William of Tyre, Gregory promised to confirm the Armenian credo in a way that was acceptable to the Roman Catholic Church in the areas inhabited by Armenians who were not pro-Roman.[36] With the fall of Edessa to Zengi in 1144 CE and the continuing Byzantine persecution of the Armenians, Gregory VII once again turned to Rome, sending delegates on his behalf to Eugenius III. According to Otto of Freising, the Armenian delegates agreed to accept liturgical traditions of the Latin Church upon their return to the East.[37] Although Armenian sources do not mention this conformity, Pahlawuni's visit to Jerusalem and attendance at the Councils of Antioch and Jerusalem became a significant moment in Armenian ecumenical relations with the Roman Catholic Church. Although Pahlawuni's successor, Nersēs Šnorhali (Nersēs the Gracious), centered his attention on relations with Byzantium, the inception of the Third Crusade renewed the interactions between the two current high patriarchs.[38] As is the case with the T-O map at its start, the lament of Grigor Tłay, through its references to Mount Zion, presents two important elements for the political narrative of the poem. First, the lament draws a connection between the Armenians and Jerusalem and establishes their presence in the city from the times of early Christianity to the Crusades. Second, Mount Zion becomes the symbol for an established relationship between the Armenians and the Latin Church as the locus for the Second Council of Jerusalem, where interactions between the two churches took place. Through an understanding of Jerusalem as a space linked to the Armenians and Rome, and through

35. Joshua Prawer, "The Armenians in Jerusalem under the Crusaders," in *Armenian and Biblical Studies*, ed. Michael E. Stone (Jerusalem: St. James, 1976), 228–29.

36. William of Tyre, *Historia rerum in partibus transmarinis gestarum*, in PL 201, bk. 9, col. 630; *Sacrorum Conciliorum nova et amplissima collection*, vol. 21, ed. J. D. Mansi (Paris: Welter, 1903) 505–8. See also Prawer, "The Armenians in Jerusalem," 227–31; Hugues Vincent and F.-M. Abel. *Jérusalem Nouvelle* (Paris: Gabalda, 1914), 522; Joshua Prawer, *Latin Kingdom of Jerusalem: European Colonialism in the Middle Ages* (London: Weidenfeld and Nicolson, 1973), 252.

37. Otto of Freising, *"Chronica de duabus civitatibus,"* in *Ausgewählte Quellen zur Deutschen Geschichte des Mittelalters*, vol. 16, ed. A. Schmidt (Berlin: Rütten & Loening Verlag, 1957), 554.

38. Charles A. Frazee, "The Christian Church in Cilician Armenia: Its Relations with Rome and Constantinople to 1198," *Church History* 45, no. 2 (1976): 166–84.

a reconception of the city within a medieval worldview that also includes the Armenians, the Grigor Tłay's poem positions its lament, and the narration of the events surrounding the fall of Jerusalem to Ṣalāḥ al-Dīn, within a contemporary politics that links the Armenians and the Latin Church. The approaching advancement of the new crusade toward Jerusalem is presented as one with a strong Armenian alliance through the figure of the Cilician prince Levon II, who is presented in the lamentation as the redeemer of Jerusalem and an ally of Rome and the crusaders.

The Fallen City: Armenian Cilicia and the Jerusalem Lament

The link between the Armenians, the Roman papacy, and the city of Jerusalem becomes the focal point through which Grigor's lament sets up its support for a new crusade and its desire for an autonomous Armenian kingdom of Cilicia in the figure of Prince Levon II. At its start the lament establishes a connection to the physical city of Jerusalem through a textual T-O map and in its references to Mount Zion. Whereas the constructed city was presented as a space in connection with the Armenians through the image of Mount Zion, the name Zion (and in some instances Mount Zion) stands as a metonym for the Promised Land or the heavenly city.[39] By relying on the model of lamenting cities in the Hebrew Bible, the text brings together all these elements to then speak of both the loss and the possible future of the city of Jerusalem.

Mount Zion was the physical token of God's munificence, the axis between the sacred and the terrestrial realms, and the locus above which lay Zion, the kingdom of God. The transfer of the symbol of God's dwelling place from Sinai to Mount Zion in the Hebrew Bible appears through David's transfer of the Ark of the Covenant (2 Sam. 6) and the eventual building of Solomon's Temple. Thereafter, from the temple period onward, Zion symbolized the idea of the heavenly Jerusalem. This transcendent image of Zion later shifted into eschatological thought in the postexilic period.[40] The

39. Psalm 48:6, 9, 13–14; Psalm 132:8, 13–14. See also the description in Revelation 19:1–8.

40. J. D. Levenson, *Sinai and Zion: An Entry into the Jewish Bible* (San Francisco: Harper and Row, 1985), 148–51; John S. Kselman, "Sinai and Zion in Psalm 93," in *David and Zion: Biblical Studies in Honor of J. J. M. Roberts*, ed. Bernard F. Batto and Kathryn L. Roberts

idea of the heavenly Jerusalem as a model of the earthly city was originally a Jewish concept developed in Christian thought in the book of Revelation, where the New Jerusalem achieved autonomous status. Zion's symbolic function as an expression of Israel's political and religious idealism further transfers to the person and the works of Christ in the New Testament.[41] As outlined by Kiwoong Son, the connection to the image of Zion and the ministry of Christ is threefold: "First, Zion as a symbol of God's presence is transferred to Jesus describing him as a mother Jerusalem who weeps over the fate of her children Jerusalem. Secondly, the theological significance of the new covenant is described in relation to the transcendent symbol of Zion. Thirdly, the death and resurrection of Jesus symbolizes the destruction of the earthly Jerusalem temple and the election of the eschatological new temple of Zion that is the Christian community."[42] Throughout the lament, Jerusalem continuously stresses the significance of Zion, "But they should not forget about Zion / Since the laws of God arise [from there]" [Բայց Սիոն լեառն չմոռանին, / Ուստի օրէնքն Տեառն ելին] (943–44). The befallen city requests, "Gather round the injured / And in Zion let them rest again" [Վիրաւորեալքն պատանին / Եւ ի Սիոն դարձեալ հանգչին] (948–49). Jerusalem reiterates how through Zion one can "rise to the house of Christ" [Եւ բարձրանայ տուն Քրիստոսին] (955).

Acceding to the Christian theological interpretations of the concept of Zion, the lament of Grigor Tłay posits the destruction of Jerusalem into both the biblical and historical Armenian narrative. Grigor's poetic work finds itself part of the Armenian literary tradition of the *ołb*, or lament (the roots of which date back to the biblical lamentations over Jerusalem sung by the prophet Jeremiah) and also as continuing the trajectory of the standards set by two of his predecessors: Grigor Narekac'i in his *Matean Ołbergut'ean* (Book of lamentations) and Nersēs Šnorhali (Grigor's uncle and predecessor) in his

(Winona Lake, IN: Eisenbrauns, 2004), 74–76; Kiwoong Son, *Zion Symbolism in Hebrews* (Waynesboro, GA: Paternoster, 2005), 29–63; Herbert G. May, "Cosmological Reference in the Qumran Doctrine of the Two Spirits and the Old Testament Imagery," *Journal of Biblical Literature* 82 (1963): 1–14.

41. Kim Huat Tan, *The Zion Traditions and the Aims of Jesus* (Cambridge: Cambridge University Press, 1997).

42. Son, *Zion Symbolism in Hebrews*, 64–74.

Ołb Edesioy (Lament on Edessa), which was written in 1144 CE after the fall of the principality to Nur al-Din.[43]

This tradition of the lament dates back to early Armenian literary history, where laments were included as part of long historiographical prose narratives, the first of which appears in the historical work of the figure considered the father of Armenian history, Movsēs Xorenac'i. Other examples of prose laments include Davt'ak K'ert'oł's *Ołb i mahn Ĵewanširi meci išxanin* (Lament for the death of the great prince Zevanshen) in the seventh century and the laments in the *Patmut'iwn* (History) of Aristakes Lastivertc'i. It is significant to note that the first Armenian work written entirely in verse form appeared in the eleventh century, composed by Grigor (Magistros) Pahlawuni. During his visit to Constantinople in 1045 CE, Grigor Magistros met an Arab poet named Manuč'e who argued that the Muslim Qur'an was superior to the Bible because it was written in monorhyme verse. Magistros's response was that he could compose the Bible in verse in forty days. Manuč'e, considering the task impossible, promised to convert to Christianity if Magistros succeeded. Magistros's creation set important groundwork for Armenian poetry, particularly for those authors who composed city lamentations. His work includes influences that remained within the medieval (and sometimes later) Armenian poetic tradition, such as the Arabic epic genre of the *qaṣīda*, which also had its influence in Persian courts. Magistros had chosen the end rhyme of *-i*, which would maximize the possibilities of variation throughout his work. His use of isosyllabic lines may also have been influenced by Syrian prototypes. Finally, the Persian lyric form of the *ghazal* contributed to the creation of the couplet and quatrain structure. Magistros's work of "a thousand lines" became a common term used by later poets to describe lengthier pieces of writing.

Grigor Tłay's lamentation over Jerusalem assumes a system of commonplaces already associated with the representation of fallen cities as they appear in the Hebrew Bible (an influence also on Grigor's literary predecessors) and situates the loss of Jerusalem to Ṣalāḥ al-Dīn within this model of

43. Numerous studies have assessed the lament of Grigor Tłay as one inferior to Šnorhali's *Ołb Edesioy*, comparing the structure, theme, and rhetorical techniques of the two laments. The goal of this section is not to perform such a task, but to comment on Grigor's poetic reaction to Ṣalāḥ al-Dīn's conquest of Jerusalem as a reflection of the repercussions of the capture of the city on the Cilician Armenian people.

lamentation. As in the Hebrew Bible, personified cities are almost always condemned and destroyed, and their destruction is subsequently lamented. The tropes and rhetorical techniques utilized in Grigor's lament follow this model in representing the events surrounding the befallen city through descriptions of Ṣalāḥ al-Dīn's victory over the city (419–40, 1692–1700), the destruction and desecration of Jerusalem (670–82) and its inhabitants (2801–2), and the contamination of the city at the hands of the enemy (204–5; 224–34). Numerous references to the wrath of God (2373, 2695–2700) and the fall of the city as a result of the sins of the Christian population are also recalled (455–60, 2215–18). Mourning for the city is combined with a plea to God (2709–20) and hope for liberty and restoration. The desire for independence from the hands of the enemy is further entwined with statements calling for political organization and military advancements (1968–2022).[44]

The lament's consideration of Jerusalem also reflects Christianity's ongoing confrontation with Judaism.[45] Numerous references to Old Testament figures and events anticipate and foreshadow the ministry of Christ: Moses's parting of the Red Sea (48–49) and his leading of the Israelites from Egypt to Palestine (2505–11); Abraham's offering and God's last-minute replacement of Isaac by the ram (2473–82); the story of Noah and the flood (2460–72), and Jacob's ladder (960–74). The fall of the city of Jerusalem as a result of the sins of the inhabitants appears in the references to both the past, through the Jews, and the present, through the Christians (308–9). Jerusalem recalls sinners such as Adam (2426) and Cain (2430, 2447, 2451) and describes the movement away from faith and the abandonment of God, "For it became the will of the Creator / As a result of our evil deeds, they say" [Քանզի դարձաւ կամք արարչին, / Ըստ չարութեան մեր, ասէին] (457–58).

In addition to these characteristics associated with the lamentation of cities is the practice of personifying the city as female—a rhetorical technique that developed from the ancient Near Eastern understanding of capital cities as goddesses who were married or were counterparts to the patron gods

44. For an extensive study of city laments in the Armenian tradition, see P. M. Xačʻatryan, *Hay mijnadaryan patmakan olber* (Yerevan: Armenian SAH GA, 1969).

45. Joshua Prawer, "Christian Attitudes towards Jerusalem in the Early Middle Ages," in *The History of Jerusalem: The Early Muslim Period, 638–1099*, ed. Joshua Prawer and Haggai Ben-Shammai (New York: New York University Press, 1996), 311–47. See also the discussion of the Christianity's confrontation with Judaism vis-à-vis Jerusalem in chapter 1 of this book.

of the city.[46] From its beginning, the lament casts the city of Jerusalem into the voice of a mourning woman, narrating the cause of her grief and calling on others to mourn as well. This female city describes herself as contaminated (203), indecent (260), and bestial (292–94). The images of the virgin (443) and bridegroom (1238) are paired with descriptions of fallen crowns (774), the cutting of nuptial veils and embellished coverings (773), and a woman clothed in dresses of mourning (772). The female city also claims herself to be barren and infertile (1215–16); she is a mother whose milk and wine have been drunk by the invaders (259–60).

Jerusalem recalls many things that happened "within her." Drawing from both biblical and contemporary history, the city speaks of her neglect, abandonment, and desecration. She is described as feeble, and "demoted" from her status, in the same manner that God's honor has been devalued by his believers. Her shame and humiliation, presented through images of nakedness and the ripping of nuptial clothing, further suggest a loss of purity; her barrenness points to a city that becomes void of Christian rule, and her sexual pollution is a reflection of the contamination of the holy places within the city. The sinful nature of the female city becomes a reflection of the sins of the inhabitants or of Christians, their movement away from God, and their avariciousness—all of which the text attributes to God's wrath and the subsequent fall of the city to the enemy powers (1215–38).

The positing of contemporary events in the city of Jerusalem into established literary tropes surrounding the destruction of cities produces not only an allegorical interpretation of the Bible but also an interpretation with a definite purpose. As Theo van Maarten van Lint argues:

> *Babelac'i*, Babylonian, becomes the name not only of the people who carried the Jews into captivity six centuries before Christ was born, but also of the enemies of the young Christian state. The enemy is always Babylonian, whether his name is Nebuchadnezzar, Zengi, or Saladin. This presentation not only opens up the personal dimension of fighting evil within oneself, the internal Babylon, but a political struggle for a free Christian state. The principle of loss of political freedom as a consequence of personal transgression combines the public and the personal domains and fuses them. Humanity's

46. For a more detailed discussion of the history of city laments in the ancient Mesopotamian world, see the introduction to this book.

> sins bring disaster upon it, but the instrument by which this disaster is brought about is held in God's hand. In this way a medieval Christian could be reconciled to the loss of sacred places to Muslim conquest, or at least to be presented with an explanation.[47]

Thus the regular alteration between the Old Testament, the New Testament, and contemporaneous events in the lament links the history of the Israelites not only to the image of Christ but also to that of the crusaders. The lament portrays Jerusalem within a continuum of the past, but also as means to invite a possible future; the link is an example between Armenian and crusader. The text assumes a system of commonplaces already associated with representing the destruction of cities and then shapes and extends these rhetorical techniques to suit its political motive of presenting Prince Levon as the liberator of Jerusalem—an analogy for his position as the first monarch of the Armenian kingdom of Cilicia.

The Cilician City: Prince Levon II and the Conquest of Jerusalem

The rhetorical technique of equating the city of Jerusalem with a female persona plays a significant role in the political narrative of the poem and its declarations for the reconquest of Jerusalem. A noteworthy section begins with the Jerusalem's pronouncement, "I was a barren virgin to the bridegroom" [Էի ամուլ կոյս փեսային] (1215), after which Jerusalem explains the reasons behind her current state—the presence of "foreigners," Arab princes, who entered into her, trampled and crushed her, and then adorned her as their own bride (1215–38). The continuous allusions to the city's invasion and destruction anticipate both a concern for future aid and also set these enemies in opposition to a liberator. The redemption of the city, in its female form, is represented as a shift in domination from male figures who are presented as evil and faithless (Nebuchadnezzar, Ṣalāḥ al-Dīn, and Zengi) to a desired and more redeemable male warrior, Levon. A catalog of people and places that neglected to come to Jerusalem's aid anticipates the arrival of not only the crusaders but also the aid of the Armenians through Levon, setting

47. Van Lint, "The Poem of Lamentation," 139.

forth the lament's political motive through its dual solution for the liberation of Jerusalem: to turn to the Latin West and the Armenian prince.

Although the female Jerusalem acknowledges the attack of Ṣalāḥ al-Dīn, she also reprimands other places and groups of people who neglected these events and refused to come to her aid. Positioning its narrative in the tradition of the Hebrew Bible, the lament recalls the destruction of other important centers such as Ascalon (578), the First Temple of Solomon (623; 2691), and Sodom (621), but it also draws on contemporary situations and circumstances, naming specifically the city of Antioch. Jerusalem seeks from its "sister" Antioch a sense of understanding for its current status. The lament acknowledges the similarity between the two sisters—they have both, at one point in time, been captured by a Muslim power. The female city describes how the Muslims took over Antioch; how they destroyed and overthrew the city; and how they ransacked the churches and enslaved her (1915–26). Acknowledging the city's past tribulations, Jerusalem calls on the "sister city" to now come to her aid:

> Let me call upon Antioch,
> The mother-city of Syria,
> Which was my strength and valor,
> Brother and sister of the same family.
>
> Ձայնեմ յառաջ Անտիոքին,
> Մօր քաղաքացն Սիւրացին,
> Որ էր իմ ուժ եւ զօրութիւն,
> Եղբայր եւ քոյր համատոհմին:
> (367–70)

The unanswered cries of Jerusalem result in her reprimanding Antioch for not being a "good sister" (865–68). Jerusalem is angered by Antioch's disregard and mistreatment (383–88) and reminds her sister of the events of her destruction. The appeal to Antioch concludes with a statement about how Antioch's story must be "boring for the listener" [Զի այս ձանձրոյթ է լսողին] (392), directing the attention once again to Jerusalem's lament (399–400).[48]

48. With the help from the fleets of the Italian city-states, Antioch survived Ṣalāḥ al-Dīn's assault on the kingdom of Jerusalem in 1187 CE and was not a participant in the Third Crusade. See

In addition to mentioning the city of Antioch, several sections in the poem allude to various groups that did not support Jerusalem during the invasion of Ṣalāḥ al-Dīn. In the middle of the lament, Jerusalem provides a catalog of the people who neglected her in time of need and those who were not able to save her from destruction, such as the king of the Greeks (787) and the army of the Franks (788). She continues then to name geographic regions and people of Europe, such as Bologna (810), the Limousin (804), Normandy (808), Provence and Vienna (802), Sicily (794), Spain (839), and the people of Tanais or the Don River (805), among others. The dismissal of these groups is followed by Jerusalem's description of her solemn state:

> I sat alone in the house—silent,
> Putting my hands on my breast,
> Those, who were my brothers and sisters,
> Abandoned me—they hated me,
> and they loved more
> Those who wounded me, through and through.
>
> Նստայ միայն ի տան լռին՝
> Եղեալ ըզձեռս իմ ի ծնօտին.
> Զի որք եղբարք եւ քոյրք էին՝
> Ի բաց թողեալ զիս ատեցին,
> Եւ առաւել զայն սիրեցին,
> Որք խոցոտեալ զիս խեթկեցին:.
>
> (822–26)

Yet among the record of people and places that chose to abandon her, Jerusalem also names the city of Rome:

> In the middle of the great war,
> I turned to the glorious Rome
> And I called on Saint Jacob.

Itinerarium Peregrinorum at Gesta Regis Ricardi: Untersuchungen uber einige englische chronisten des zwölften und des beginnenden dreizehnten jahrhunderts, vol. 1, ed. Hans Lamprecht (Torgau, Germany: Nitschke, 1937), 5; Guillaume de Tyr [William of Tyre], *Le Continuation de Guillaume de Tyr*, in RHC Occ. 4, bk. 1, chap. 42; Ambroise, *The History of the Holy War: Ambroise's Estoire de la Guerre Sainte*, ed. and trans. Marianne Ailes and Malcolm Barber (Woodbridge, England: Boydell, 2003), lines 615–830. See also Tamar M. Boyadjian, "Crusader Antioch: The Sister-City in the Armenian Laments of Nersēs Šnorhali and Grigor Tłay," in *East and West in the Medieval Eastern Mediterranean*, vol. 3, *Antioch from the Byzantine Reconquest until the end of the Crusader Principality*, ed. Krijnie Ciggaar and Michael Metcalf (Leuven, Belgium: Peeters, 2018), 37–50.

And the Pope of Rome did not arrive,
Who was prince to a part of my soul
Neither the archbishops nor the bishops came[49]

Ի մէջ մեծի պատերազմին,
Դարձայ ի Հռոմս պանծալին
Եւ ձայնեցի սուրբ Յակոբին:

Եւ ոչ եհաս պապն Հռոմին,
Որ էր իշխան հոգւոյս բաժին.
Ոչ արծուէսք եւ վէսք եկին.
(836–38; 847–49)

Although the naming of the city of Rome seems to be among the catalog of people and places who failed Jerusalem, a closer look, about thirty lines following this passage, reveals the lament's political motive of praising Rome and the coming of the new crusade: "But behold, two years have passed / And I am still overrun with anguish" [Բայց ահա ամք երկուք անցին / Եւ դեռ ի տապս եմ տագնապին] (877–78). This lament's recognition of Jerusalem's contemporary status, two years after the capture of the city on October 2, 1187 CE, alters the temporal moment of the previous lines from the past to the present. This sequential shift therefore also suggests that the reference to the Roman pope (847) is to Pope Urban III, the church leader during the siege of the city, who according to the legend died shortly after hearing news of the crusader defeat at the pivotal Battle of Hattin, which resulted in the subsequent capture of Jerusalem by Ṣalāḥ al-Dīn.[50]

The claim that the pope was only a "prince to a part of my soul" (848) further reinforces the failure of Urban III and the Latin Army to secure the principality and city of Jerusalem. As such, this line could also be alluding

49. I have considered the word *arcvēsk̦* (line 849) from MS 4207, since the spelling and meaning appear to be more conducive to the context of the lines preceding it. Though I have translated it here as "archbishops" and "bishops," *arcvēsk̦* could also possibly translate as "noble eagles," which might refer to "the Latins," since the common symbol of imperial authority in heraldry and vexillology for the Roman Catholic Church was the single-headed eagle. This symbol was also used by the Arsacid Armenian royal family, the Mamikoneans, as well as in medieval Armenia, Byzantium, Persia, and other places. But since the text names the Roman pope two lines before this term, "archbishops" and "bishops" are probably more appropriate.

50. Geoffrey Hindley, *The Crusades: Islam and Christianity in the Struggle for World Supremacy* (New York: Carroll and Graf, 2004), 121.

to the quarrels between Urban III and Frederick Barbarossa, and the rising controversies over the election of the "king of the Romans" and whether the title could be gained only in Germany or if the coronation in Rome consummated one's position as emperor. Rome is "glorious" (837) under the emperor Frederick Barbarossa, who has promised Prince Levon II a crown when he is in the East, and under the papacy of Clement III, who was ordained as pope on December 9, 1187 CE. Despite Jerusalem's criticism of the neglect of other cities, Rome still receives the adjective "glorious" [պանծալի] (837). Jerusalem is still hopeful for the coming aid of the West.

But the great hero of Grigor Tłay's lament is Prince Levon II, "Levon prince of Cilicia" [Լեւոն իշխան Կիլիկեցին] (1968). In the model of linking the biblical story with the defense of the land, Levon II is compared to the warriors of the Old Testament, such as David, Gideon, and Samson (1389). A parallel is also drawn with Alexander the Great, Darius the Great (1989), the Maccabees (which is a common trope in Armenian literature), and the Macedonians (1988) . Levon II is also presented as a successor to the lines of Armenian mythological heroes Artašēs (who was victorious over Croesus), Hayk (who battled Bel), and Tigran (who defeated Crassus).[51] Through these parallels the Armenian prince becomes the symbolic figure through which the text both foreshadows the upcoming military advancements of the West and also exposes Levon II as the champion of Jerusalem and the triumphant leader who will defend the city against the infidels. To strengthen Levon's military position and leadership, the prince is also placed in the forefront following a series of questions relating to the structure of military warfare:

> Where [are] the soldiers, who do not appear
> Or the ones who fight in single combat, who were victorious,
>
> Where [are] the troops in order of battle
> Or the contestants.
> Where [are] the cavalry for the spectators,
> The infantry with their shields
> Where are the archers with their aim,
>
> Where [are] the slingers for its purpose.

51. Van Lint, "The Poem of Lamentation," 140.

Ո՞ւր զինաւորքն, որ չերեւին
Կամ մենամարտքն, որք յաղթէին.

Ո՞ւր կռուարարքն ի ճակատին
Կամ ըմբշամարտքն պատերազմին.
Ո՞ւր ձիավարժքն ի թատերին,
Նիզակակիրքն վահանին.
Ո՞ւր է նետողք նպատակին,

Ո՞ւր պարսաւորք ճահողակին.
(1779–80; 1785–1789; 1791)[52]

The naming of various units of a medieval army (or even perhaps an invocation of the theater of war) then regresses to the model of the Hebrew Bible, once again evoking the metaphor of the female city and its suitor-warrior: "Where is the bridegroom to the flower-garden" [Ո՞ւր է փեսայն ի ծաղկոցին] (1795). The poem's declaration is that Levon is the groom of the city:

Crying out in the name of the Holy Cross
Leaped into battle,
Just like an eagle onto a flock.

Ձայնեց զանուն Սրբոյ Խաչին,
Կայթեաց ի մէջ պատերազմին,
Որպէս զարծիւ իսկ յերամին:
(1971–73)

The section then continues with the description of Levon's numerous victories, his successes in integrating new lands into his leadership, and ends with the proclamation of his faith: "Levon, lover of Christians, / Ally with the right hand of Jesus" [Լեւոնն սիրողն Քրիստոնէին / Խնամեալ աջոփն Յիսուսին] (2022–23). The lament's consideration of Levon II as both the prince of the Armenians and the redeemer of Jerusalem makes apparent the

52. Line 1785 literally translates as "contenders in the front"; line 1788's "Nizakakirk'n" literally translates as "spear bearers" or "lance bearers"; in line 1789, "netołk" is a term that was also used for the Scythians and the Mongols in the later Middle Ages. This passage could also be an invocation of the theater or contests where the narrative might be both commenting on and drawing from the performativity of war.

political narrative of Grigor Tłay's lament and its desire to receive a crown from the West by also linking the image of Levon to the crusaders. The text specifically recognizes Levon as the leader of the Armenians: "Where the ruler of the Armenians [lit., Race of Hayk] was, / the triumphant Levon the brave" [Ո՞ւր իշխեցող էր Հայկազնին/ Մեծայաղթող Լեւոն արին] (1962–63). Similarly, the lament also names the leaders of the West as the Franks: "Who are the princes of the west, / the Arian people of the Franks" [Որք են իշխանքն արեւմտին / Արիական ազգն Ֆռանկին] (2671–72). These two groups are presented as combatants through the image of the *arciv* (eagle). The Armenian prince is metaphorically compared to an eagle attacking a flock (1973), while the army of the West is described as eagle-like (*arcvēsk'*). The lamentation considers the union of the two groups in the liberation of the city of Jerusalem through the coming of a new crusade and the possibility of an autonomous Armenian kingdom of Cilicia.

The lament's declaration is thus made clear. Levon II is the brave warrior who, incomparable to those who neglected Jerusalem in the past, stands as a symbol for the savior of Jerusalem. In Grigor Tłay's *Asac'eal ban ołbergakan vasn aṙmann Erusałēmi,* the city of Jerusalem functions as a metaphorical space that allows for the text to create a link between the long-standing Armenian presence in Jerusalem and its political motives of gaining an autonomous kingdom of Armenian Cilicia. References to Mount Zion and the textual T-O map of the world draw attention to the areas inhabited by Armenians and also pave the way for the praising of the Armenian prince Levon II. The city lamentation, drawing from the exemplum of the Hebrew Bible, not only places the contemporary situation of the Armenians and western Europe in the past but also draws from the historic to foreground the future salvation of Jerusalem. Through the praise and adoration of Prince Levon II, the lament recognizes the prince as the ruler of the Armenians as it also promotes the campaign of his monarchy by inviting Armenian and Crusader to be read alongside one another as allies of the future new Christian Jerusalem.

The arrival of the crusaders did not appear to be that useful early on for the political motives of Cilicia. Frederick of Barbarossa drowned in the Saleph River as his army was approaching Antioch. Although the success of a crown did not come with the armies of the Third Crusade, Prince Levon II was able to secure two crowns: one from the Byzantine emperor, Alexios III Angelos, and the other from the papal legate Conrad of Wittelsbach, the archbishop of Mainz, on behalf of the pope. The prince also received a royal scepter from the chancellor of the German emperor, Conrad of Hildesheim, and was crowned King Levon I on January 6, 1198 or 1199 CE. Catholicos Grigor Tłay had died in 1191 CE and never saw the actuality of an Armenian kingdom of Cilicia, but his lamentation survives today, allowing us to better understand the way in which the medieval Mediterranean world lamented cities while also giving Cilician Armenians a voice with which to compose their own song of lamentation over Jerusalem.

Chapter 5

Forgotten Lamentation

Richard I and the Heavenly Journey to Jerusalem

On the evening of Friday 4 Rabīʿ I 588 (20 March 1192), a letter came from Humfrey, an envoy of Richard the Lionheart [to Ṣalāḥ al-Dīn], which stated that the land should be divided between the two leaders. "Jerusalem will be ours and you can have the Dome of the Rock."

—Bahāʾ al-Dīn Ibn Shaddād,
al-Nawādir al-Sulṭāniyya wa al-Mahāsin al-Yūsufiyya[1]

In order to lament Jerusalem, you must first speak of Jerusalem.

Richard the Lionheart's proposed statement reflects differing notions of how Jerusalem is envisioned within the Latin Church and the Islamic world. Richard sees the Dome of the Rock as the defining marker for a Muslim Jerusalem—and, as chapter 2 explored, the metonym, which stands for both the physical city and one that represents the sacred character of Jerusalem for the Islamic faith. In chapter 3, I argued that the chronicles accounting Pope Urban II's call for the First Crusade also reflected on the Church of the Holy Sepulcher as a symbol for the city of Jerusalem. I further suggested that these accounts relied on the ancient model of lamenting Jerusalem in the Hebrew Bible to construct a newly formed relationship with the earthly

1. Bahāʾ al-Dīn Ibn Shaddād, *al-Nawādir al-Sulṭāniyya wa al-Maḥāsin al-Yūsufiyya*, in RHC Or. 3; Bahāʾ al-Dīn Ibn Shaddād, *The Rare and Excellent History of Saladin, or al-Nawādir al-Sulṭāniyya wa'l-Maḥāsin al-Yūsufiyya*, trans. D. S. Richards (Aldershot, England: Ashgate, 2001), 238.

city, which stood as justification for the call to crusade and the eventual capture of the physical Jerusalem.

This chapter considers the lamentation—or, rather, the rejection of lamentation—over Jerusalem in the anonymous chronicle *Itinerarium Peregrinorum et Gesta Regis Ricardi* (Regarding the itinerary of the pilgrims and the deeds of king Richard; hereafter *IP*) and in some instances also draws supporting examples from one of its source texts, Ambroise's Anglo-Norman verse chronicle *Estoire de la Guerre Sainte* (The history of the Holy War).[2] The *IP* bears testimony to the moment anticipated in Grigor Tłay's lamentation over Jerusalem discussed in chapter 4—the arrival of the Third Crusade from western Europe, later known as the Kings' Crusade, with Richard the Lionheart of England as one of its primary commanders. The textual representation, conceptualization, and attitude toward the city of Jerusalem within the *IP* bear a number of similarities to the lament of Grigor Tłay. Just as Grigor's lament posits the Hebrew Bible model of lamenting Jerusalem into Cilician Armenia's contemporary sociopolitical world with Prince Levon II as savior, the *IP* also models the fall of Jerusalem on this ancient example to shape this moment into a relationship between ruler (in this case Richard I of England) and city. Yet whereas the previous chapter argued that the city of Jerusalem and its link to Prince Levon II furthered the lament's political narrative for an independent kingdom of Armenian Cilicia, Richard's connection to Jerusalem does not bear any anxiety over the physical obtainment of a Latin Christian Jerusalem; instead it signifies a spiritual relationship with the heavenly city. In the *IP*, Richard's position as liberator is formulated in the narrative as one that in multiple occasions dissociates itself from the physical city of Jerusalem. The relationship between Richard's army and its act of pilgrimage reflects developing Christian atti-

2. *Itinerarium peregrinorum et gesta regis Ricardi*, ed. William Stubbs (London: Longman, 1864); trans. Helen J. Nicholson as *The Chronicle of the Third Crusade: The Itinerarium Peregrinorum et Gesta Regis Ricardi* (Aldershot, England: Ashgate, 1997). Ambroise, *The History of the Holy War: Ambroise's Estoire de la Guerre Sainte*, 2 vols., ed. and trans. Marianne Ailes and Malcolm Barber (Woodbridge, England: Boydell, 2003). All subsequent references to and translations of these texts are taken from these editions, unless otherwise noted, and page numbers will hereafter be cited parenthetically in the text. On the influence of Ambroise's chronicle on the *IP*, see Helen J. Nicholson, "Introduction," in *The Chronicle of the Third Crusade*, 1–17. For manuscript traditions and variants, see Hans Eberhard Mayer, *Das Itinerarium peregrinorum: eine zeitgenössische englische Chronik zum dritten Kreuzzug in ursprünglicher Gestalt* (Stuttgart: Hiersemann, 1962).

tudes toward the city of Jerusalem that manifest themselves through a presentation of Richard as the exemplary pilgrim whose symbolic journey to the physical city stands as a model for both crusaders and pilgrims attempting to make their way to the heavenly city of the afterlife.

This desire for the Latin Christian pilgrim to gain access to the Holy City, and specifically the Church of the Holy Sepulcher, was considered in the accounts of Pope Urban II's speeches at the Council of Clermont in chapter 3. These First Crusade chronicles, in their description of the destruction of Christian holy places within Jerusalem, not only utilize the image of the pilgrim as the figure of the *milites Christi* but also provide a reflection for what Jerusalem represents in the Latin Church. The Christian view toward the city of Jerusalem prior to the First Crusade could be characterized as one that sought to sever the connection with the historically Judean city and for the most part considered the position of Jerusalem within a transcendental and apocalyptic sphere. Christianity's anti-Jewish polemic to eliminate the centrality of the Temple Mount, severed the link with the earthly city and transferred Israel's history into symbolic and prophetic implications. Eusebius, in fact, argues in his *De vita Constantini* that the Holy Church is the new Jerusalem, rebuilt after Jesus's crucifixion.[3] Thus, the presence of edifices in a Christian Jerusalem became symbols for a once divine presence in the city. These structures were interpreted as providing proof of the triumphs of Christianity, which also shifted the city from a Jewish past into a Roman Christian existence and, later, the Byzantine Empire. The presence of a Christian Jerusalem eventually repositioned the conceptualization of the city in Christian thought as a city that housed holy relics and the memories of Christ. Though the view of Jerusalem as one with a distinct Christian presence resulted in the city's allure as a destination of pilgrimage, this too was rejected by early church thinkers, such as St. Gregorius Nyssenus (Gregory of Nyssa), who claimed that a pilgrimage should go from within oneself to God and not from Cappadocia to Palestine.[4] In fact, the city of Jerusalem was the last center of Christendom to be given the status of a patriarchate—after Rome, Constantinople, Alexandria,

3. [Eusebius,] *De vita Constantini*, in PG 20, col. 1094, trans. J. H. Bernard in PPTS 1, 6–7.
4. [Gregory of Nyssa,] *Epistola*, in PG 46, cols. 1009–16.

and Antioch—in the year 451 CE, at the Fourth Ecumenical Council of Chalcedon.[5]

The reading of the book of Lamentations by the Christian church in many ways parallels the significance of Jerusalem for Christianity briefly summarized in chapter 1.[6] The accounts of the speeches at Clermont sought to both rewrite and redirect the focus of the preliminary account, the *Gesta Francorum et aliorum Hierosolimitanorum* (The deeds of the Frank and other [pilgrims] to Jerusalem), from the city of Antioch to Jerusalem. Chapter 3 argues that the effort of these authors to focus their narratives on lamenting the city, and then the subsequent capture of Jerusalem (rather than the city of Antioch) reflects an interest in the earthly Jerusalem. This belief contradicted those of the early Church Fathers, who through their exegesis of the Pauline doctrines and the book of Revelation had rejected the earthly city at an early stage.[7]

A further argument presented in chapter 3 is that the dedication of specific sections on the topography of the city within these accounts of Clermont reflects a specific reverence for the earthly Jerusalem (and one that differs from the early patristic period). In Fulcher of Chartres's account, for example, a detailed layout of the physical city is provided, with special attention given to the Christian edifices, primarily the Church of the Holy Sepulcher.[8] Robert the Monk and William of Malmesbury not only posit the city of Jerusalem within a medieval worldview but also draw attention to the significance and benefits of the earthly city.[9] These texts mirror an escalating Christian interest in the physical city of Jerusalem as a result of its capture by the Franks in 1099 CE. The growing position of Jerusalem as a holy site of pilgrimage for both laypersons and crusaders, further resulted in the

5. Jerusalem's elevation to the status of patriarchate at the Council of Chalcedon was purely informal, although in Justinian's *Novellae* Jerusalem appears equal to the others. See [Justinian,] *Novellae*, in *Corpus Iuris Civilis*, vol. 3, *Novellae*, ed. R. Schoell and G. Kroll (Berlin: Apud Weidmannos, 1895) no. cxxiii, col. 3; and Y. Katzir, "The Patriarch of Jerusalem, Primate of the Latin Kingdom," in *Crusade and Settlement: Papers Read at the First Conference of the Society for the Study of the Crusades and the Latin East and Presented to R.C. Smail*, ed. Peter W. Edbury (Cardiff, Wales: University College Cardiff Press, 1985), 169–75.

6. For a lengthier discussion, see the introduction to this book.

7. [Eusebius,] *De vita Constantini*, col. 1094; Hieronymus, *Praefatio Hieronymi in Librum Paralipomenon in* PL 29, col. 401.

8. Fulcher of Chartres, *Gesta Francorum Iherusalem Peregrinantium*, in RHC Occ. 3:355–57.

9. Robert the Monk, *Historia Jherosolimitana*, in RHC Occ. 3:729; William of Malmesbury, *Gesta Regum Anglorum*, vol. 2, ed. and trans. R. A. B. Mynors, R. M. Thomson, and M. Winterbottom (Oxford: Oxford University Press, 1998), 600.

development of the sanctity of the physical city beyond the Church of the Holy Sepulcher. As the physical description of the city in Fulcher's chronicle further suggests, Jerusalem's sacred character slowly grew into a large-scale topographical image.[10]

A third argument made in chapter 3 is that these authors also present an understanding of the Holy Land as Christianity's patria, or homeland: the space that had been both prophesied and promised to the Christian believers.[11] The accounts of the victory of the First Crusade not only narrate the conquest as divinely inspired but also justify this success through what they name to be the chosen people (the Franks), who now undertook the reconstruction of the new Israel. Whereas the heavenly city was believed in early Christian thought to be autonomous from the earthly city, through the mode of lamentations these early crusade chronicles present the earthly city as both a means to and integral part of its heavenly counterpart. One example of this opinion is present in part of a letter from Bohemond I, Godfrey, and Raymond of Normandy to Pope Urban II, calling him to come and take command of the crusade and to "open for us the gates to the two Jerusalems, and liberate the sepulcher of the Lord and make the name of the Christians exalted above all other names" [*portas etiam utrimque Hierusalem nobis aperias et sepulchrum Domini liberum atque Christianorum nomen super omne nomen exaltatum facias*].[12]

In contrast, Richard's relationship to the physical city of Jerusalem in the *IP* reflects developing Christian attitudes that began to revert back to the belief that the earthly city was inferior to that of the heavenly one. Because the Kings' Crusade was unable to actually obtain the physical Jerusalem, the *IP* retrospectively attempts to solve the fragmented relationship between the Latin Church and the earthly city by disassociating itself once again from the earthly Jerusalem and redirecting its focus to the heavenly city. Therefore, the Hebrew Bible model of lamenting the loss of cities—which served as a framework to posit the political narrative of the accounts of Pope Urban II's call for crusade, and also that of Grigor Tłay's lamentation—

10. Fulcher of Chartres, *Gesta Francorum*, 355–57.

11. Cf. Guibert of Nogent, *Gesta Dei per Francos*, in RHC Occ. 4:123; Baldric of Dol, *Gesta Dei per Francos*, in RHC Occ. 4:14; Raimundi de Aguilers [Raymond of Aguilers,] *Historia Francorum qui ceperunt Iherusalem*, in RHC Occ. 3:300.

12. H. Hagenmayer, ed., *Epistulae et chartae ad historiam primi belli sacri spectantes. Die Kreuzzugsbriefe aus den Jahren 1088–1100* (Innsbruck: Verlag der Wagnershen Universitäts-Buchhandlung, 1901), 164; my translation.

becomes rejected in this account. On numerous occasions Richard, along with his group of pilgrims, decides to put off his visit to Jerusalem and to instead embark on other conquests. When Richard's army finally reaches Jerusalem (only after a truce has been made with Ṣalāḥ al-Dīn), the pilgrims perform a procession through the city, visiting those places connected to the life of Jesus. Although it is unclear in the *IP* whether Richard accompanies the people on this pilgrimage, he then leads them on their return home, coming across a number of misfortunes on the way. In contrast to the figure of Prince Levon II in chapter 4, Richard is never presented as the future ruler of the earthly Jerusalem. Rather, the *IP* metaphorically portrays the journey to the physical Jerusalem as an exemplum of the actions believed to be necessary to reach the heavenly city of the afterlife. Moreover, the *IP* does not necessarily channel any anxiety over the loss and eventual retrieval of Jerusalem; instead the narrative both justifies and supports deliberate efforts to abandon the journey to the physical city. Upon eventual arrival to Jerusalem, the text creates a sacred Christian topography, including only those sites connected to Jesus and the Stations of the Cross. The conceptualization of Jerusalem as a political narrative, as seen in the previous chapters in this book, becomes transferred into a purely sacred one. The goal set is thus not the retrieval of the earthly city but the ultimate desire to reach the heavenly one, and for this reason, the lamenting of Jerusalem no longer becomes a rhetoric that serves the political motives of the account. This chapter critically demonstrates how in the text's contemporary moment, the physical Jerusalem becomes connected not only to a Judaic past but also to an Arabo-Islamic one, with a specific tie to Ṣalāḥ al-Dīn. Furthermore, the *IP* reflects an attitude of indifference to the physical city of Jerusalem as a place that is significant to visit but not inhabit. It simply remains as a space that carries the memories of Christ's life and Passion and a means to the heavenly city of the afterlife for the Latin Christian believer.

Lamentation Reconsidered: Earthly Jerusalem as the City of Ṣalāḥ al-Dīn

The ancient model of lamenting the loss of cities, as discussed in the chapters of this book, builds on the exemplum of depicting the destruction of cities based on ancient Mesopotamian traditions that also translate themselves into the Hebrew Bible. Assuming a system of commonplaces already associated with the representation of fallen cities, the narratives position the biblical understanding of loss into their own contemporary moments to understand the past and utilize it to facilitate their interpretation of their own contemporary moments and those of the future. This mode of representation becomes the channel through which these narratives can both further justify their own respective political objectives. Chapter 2 outlines how the *rithāʾ al-mudun* (elegies to fallen cities) model of lamentation in the pre-Islamic poetic tradition became the exemplum used by the poet Ibn al-Abīwardī to call for the liberation of the city through the joint forces of the Muslim powers. By reading this lament within the larger historical compilation of Ibn al-Athīr, the text reveals how Jerusalem is presented as a discursive and competing space, and it is the political goal of both of these narratives, in their lamentation of the loss of the city to the Franks, to channel the contested space as an Islamic Jerusalem of the future, to be liberated through leaders such as Nūr al-Dīn and Ṣalāḥ al-Dīn. In chapter 3's accounts of Pope Urban II's speeches at Clermont, the biblical model of lamentations becomes the model through which these various accounts of the victory of the First Crusade connect the city of Jerusalem to a Latin Christian past, and this in turn serves to strengthen Christian claims to the physical city. The model of the Hebrew Bible then becomes reframed and used as support for the understanding of the capture of Jerusalem as a fulfillment of certain prophecies that favor Christian presence in the city over a Jewish or Muslim one. This exemplum becomes further positioned into the consideration of Jerusalem in a European Christian worldview as the place of the redeemer, setting the foundations for the developing perception of the physical city of Jerusalem as the locus for Christ's Passion and life on earth.

Acceding to the Christian theological interpretations of the concept of Zion, the lament of Grigor Tłay in chapter 4 posits the destruction of Jerusalem within both the biblical and historical Armenian narrative. By geographically reframing Jerusalem into an Armenian worldview, Grigor's lament channels the past model of loss into a contemporary moment by further connecting the figure of the Cilician Armenian prince Levon II to the city of Jerusalem and the crusaders. This link serves the narrative's political goal of both illustrating an Armenian alliance to Rome and also the greater goal of establishing an Armenian kingdom of Cilicia. This model of lamentations becomes the exemplum through which the lament can both represent the events surrounding the conquest by Ṣalāḥ al-Dīn and offer the solution of the reconquest of the physical city of Jerusalem through the figure of the Cilician prince.

In the *IP* the biblical model of lamentations also becomes utilized as the exemplum through which the narrative can comment on Ṣalāḥ al-Dīn's capture of Jerusalem and Richard I's eventual voyage to the Holy Land. Yet as the remainder of this section demonstrates the conceptualization of the loss of Jerusalem through the biblical model becomes associated with a Judaic and Islamic past, which the narrative rejects through the introduction of the figure of Richard. Thus, the image of Ṣalāḥ al-Dīn and his conquest of Jerusalem—which become situated within the Hebrew Bible model of the loss of cities—not only link the Judaic and Islamic traditions but also stand as symbols for a past perception of the earthly city of Jerusalem. In contrast, the introduction of the figure of Richard and his journey to Jerusalem metaphorically represent a temporal shift from the contemporary present to the future. In turn, Richard's movement toward the earthly Jerusalem becomes presented as a journey, the goal of which is not to liberate the city of Jerusalem but to fulfill the vow of pilgrimage as a means to the heavenly city of the afterlife.

The *IP* begins its narrative of Richard's journey to Jerusalem by framing its account of the loss of the city within the Hebrew Bible model of lament. Utilizing the rhetorical practice of personifying the city as female, the *IP* maintains the understanding of the prophetic books of the Hebrew Bible, which transfer the Near Eastern image of the city as a goddess into the image of the city as a weak and mortal female adulteress. Thus the defilement of the city and the temple become metaphorically described through the relationship between God and an unfavorable woman, sometimes referred to as his wife. As the text notes:

> The lady of cities was reduced to servitude; the city who was the inheritance of her sons was subjected to an alien race, because of the evil of those who dwelt within her.
>
> urbemque tam sacram deserit, urbem quae filiorum haereditas alienigenis subditur, a malitia habitantium in ea. Gloriosa civitas Dei Jerusalem, ubi Dominus passus, ubi sepultus, ubi gloriam resurrectionis ostendit, hosti spurio subjicitur polluenda. (22)[13]

---

13. See the discussion in chapter 3 of this book.

The sins of the inhabitants, another common trope in describing the fall of cities in the ancient world, is also alluded to in book 1: "The Lord exterminates the people of Syria because of the people's sins." (Quia pro peccatis populorum Dominus exterminavit populum Syriae; 5.) After making a reference to Pope Urban III, the account then continues by providing a brief catalog of the names of the major rulers of western Europe, such as Frederick Barbarossa, Isaac Angelus, Philip II, Henry II, and William II, who then become juxtaposed with a declaration of God's wrath against his people:

> Then the Lord's hand was aroused against his people—if we can properly call them "His," as their immoral behaviour, disgraceful lifestyle, and foul vices had made them strangers to Him. For shameful practices had broken out in the East, so that everywhere everyone threw off the veil of decency and openly turned aside to filth things.
>
> aggravata est manus Domini super populum Suum, si tamen recte dixerimus Suum, quem conversationis immunditia, vitae turpitudo, vitiorum foeditas fecerat alienum. Jam enim eosque flagitiorum consuetudo proruperat, ut omnes, abjecto erubescentiae velo, palam et passim ed turpia declinarent. (5)

Although the *IP* declares that its goal is to "describe events and not to write a moral tract" [*que res gestas delibare decrevimus, non formare tractatum*] (5), the destruction of Jerusalem is further attributed to the lack of honor and illicit deeds of the people:

> So the region from which other areas had received religion now became an example of all immorality. The Lord saw the land of His Nativity, the place of His Passion, had fallen into the filthy abyss. Therefore He spurned His Inheritance, permitting the rod of His fury, Saladin, to rage and exterminate the obstinate people. Since they had no sense of honour to restrain them from illicit deeds, He preferred the Holy Land to serve the profane rites of Gentiles for a time than for His people to flourish any longer.
>
> et unde regiones caeterae susceperant relligionis exordium, inde totius immunditiae sumebant exemplum. Hinc igitur Dominus terram Nativitatis suae, locum Passionis suae in abyssum turpitudinis, decidisse conspiciens, haereditatem Suam sprevit, et virgam furoris Sui Salahadinum ad obstinatae gentis exterminium debacchari permisit; maluit, enim Terram Sanctam per aliquan-

tum tempus profanis gentilium ritibus ancillari, quam illos florere diutius quos ab illicit nullius honestatis compescebat respectus. (5–6)[14]

The assessment of the role of Ṣalāḥ al-Dīn suggests that the conquest of Jerusalem by this Zengid leader was advanced through the will of God, since Ṣalāḥ al-Dīn's retrieval of Jerusalem is presented as the means through which God punished the unfaithful Christian population for their sins. According to the narrative, God's preference was that the Gentiles inhabit the Holy Land rather than the obstinate people (5). In fact, the *IP* speaks of various disasters that foretell the approaching of these circumstances, offering a possibility to obey God before destruction is brought down as final punishment. Earthly misfortunes such as famine, earthquakes, and frequent eclipses reflect both the wrath of God and the status of sin among the people (5–6), all common of which tropes found in the Hebrew Bible narrative of the destruction of cities. In fact, the *IP* dedicates several sections describing Ṣalāḥ al-Dīn's exploits over a number of geographic areas, which include the Battle of the Springs of Cresson (6–8); his movement into Egypt, Damascus, and Syria (10–11); the capture at Antioch (16–17); the conquest of Beirut and Sidon (20); and the infamous Battle of Hattin (14–16), the victory of which led to Ṣalāḥ al-Dīn's eventual conquest of Jerusalem.[15]

14. This viewpoint is not present in the *Estoire*, which sees the Franks as still a good and chosen people: "His land had been devastated, where His people were so pressed that they did not know what to do. But no-one should be surprised that they were then defeated. They were a good people, a chosen race, but it was the will of God that they should die and that others should come to their aid. They died in body but lived on in heaven. This is what happens to those who die there but who abide in the service of God."

"Da sa terre qui ert guastee, / U sa gent lui fud si haste / Qu'ele ne se sot conseillier; / Mais nuls ne se deit merveiller / S'ele fud lores desconfite, / Ke ço estoit bone gent eslite, / Mais Deus voleit que cil murussent, / E qu'autres genz le sucurrusent. / Cil furent mort corporelment, / Mais il vivent celestielment. /Autresi font cil qui [i] moerent /Qui el servise Deu demuerent." Ambroise, *Estoire*, lines 75–86.

15. See also Ambroise, *Estoire*, lines 2522–72; Ralph [of Coggeshall], *Libellus de Expugnatione Terrae Sanctae per Saladinum* (London: Longmans, Green, Reader, and Dyer, 1875); Roger of Howden, *Gesta Regis Henrici Secundi*, vol. 1, ed. W. Stubbs (London: Longmans, 1867), 10–15, 36–37; Roger of Howden, *Chronica Magistri Rogeri de Houedene*, vol. 3, ed. W. Stubbs (London: Longmans, 1870), 319–20, 340–42; Bahā' al-Dīn, *al-Nawādir al-Sulṭāniyya*, 110–16. It has been argued that the Battle of Hattin was the most pivotal battle for the capture of Jerusalem. See Benjamin Z. Kedar, ed., *The Horns of Ḥaṭṭīn* (Jerusalem: Yad Izhak Ben-Zvi, 1992; London: Variorum, 1992).

Ṣalāḥ al-Dīn's various conquests (including the city of Jerusalem) link the earthly city to this Islamic figure at the beginning of the *IP*. This connection becomes further established within a brief section devoted to the description of the origins and descent of Ṣalāḥ al-Dīn that appears among the accounts of his various conquests. In this succinct segment, the *IP* specifically makes a point of mentioning three specific characteristics about this leader. The first relates to his standing in society: "His parents were not descended from the nobility, but neither were they common people of obscure birth" [*parentum non ingenuorum proles, nec tamen obscuri sanguinis humilitate plebescens*] (8). The second mentions his name: "His father's given name was Job [Ayyūb], and his was Joseph [Yūsuf]" [*Pater ejus Job, ipse vero Joseph*] nuncupatus (8). Finally, the narrative makes a commentary on the tradition of his name as one derived from the Hebrew:

> Giving Hebrew names of circumcision when their sons are circumcised is a rite which thrives among many of the Gentiles and follows Muslim tradition. The princes take their names from the title of the law of Muḥammad, so that their names may remind them to be studious defenders of that law.
>
> Nam juxta Mahumeti traditionem, haec apud plerosque Gentilium viget observantia, ut cum charactere circumcisionis etiam Hebraeorum nomina circumcidendis imponant: principes vero ut nominibus suis admoniti legis Mahumetiae studiosi defensores existant, ab ipso legis vocabulo nomina sortiuntur. (8–9)[16]

Following this brief section, and among the catalog of Ṣalāḥ al-Dīn's conquests, comes another opinion regarding Ṣalāḥ al-Dīn's successes:

> It was the caprice of Fortune that wished for these rapid changes. She raises up a rich man from a pauper, the lofty from the humble, a ruler from a slave. If we measured the value of things by rational judgment and not by general opinion,

16. The *IP*'s source for the information regarding Ṣalāḥ al-Dīn's background here is unclear and erroneous. The account claims that Ṣalāḥ al-Dīn was "de genere Mirmuraeni [Mirmuraenus]." Mayer, *Das Itinerarium peregrinorum*, 250, claims that this is a corruption of the Arabic *Amīr al-Mu'minīn*, "leader of the believers," which was a typical phrase used for the title of caliphs; Nicholson, however, argues in *The Chronicle of the Third Crusade*, 26–27, that the author may have taken it from Ṣalāḥ al-Dīn's letter to Frederick I. This section also incorrectly names the Islamic law as "Hadin" and not *ḥadīth* (*IP*, 9).

we would reckon the power that comes from worldly successes as worthless, since too often it is the most evil and unworthy people who obtain it! That pimp, you had a kingdom of brothels, an army in taverns, who studied dice and rice, is suddenly raised up on high. He sits among princes, no, he is greater than princes! . . . He alone claims the governments of so many kings!

Haec fortunae ludentis potentia, has rerum vicissitudinis voluit; quae de paupere divitem, de humili sublimem, de servo suscitat dominantem. Quod si rerum pretia judicio non opinione, metimur, quantalibet terrenae felicitatis potentia villis aestimanda est, quam pessimi et indignis saepius nanciscuntur. Leno, ille cujus regum in prostibulis, milita in tabernis, studium in aleis et aliis, subito sublimatur; sedet cum principibus immo major principibus . . . et tot regnum solus vendicat principatum. (10–11)

These characteristics about Ṣalāḥ al-Dīn's origins and the opinion expressed about his undeserved accomplishments are significant in that they establish at the start of the narrative a rejection for the earthly Jerusalem. In its opinion about Ṣalāḥ al-Dīn's undeserved gains, the *IP* also claims that Ṣalāḥ al-Dīn's wealth is *terrenae* (10)—or, as Helen J. Nicholson translates, "worldly" (28). Yet it is the very occupation of the *terrenae* (the earthly) and the particular geographic space of Jerusalem that the account is discrediting. Ṣalāḥ al-Dīn's conquests are worldly (in the literal sense) in that his occupation of the physical city of Jerusalem is based on an understanding, also shared in Judaism, of the centrality and significance of the Temple Mount. By claiming that Ṣalāḥ al-Dīn's name was one that was linked to the ceremony of circumcision and a derivative of Hebrew, and by providing the names Job and Joseph instead of Ayyūb and Yūsuf, respectively, the *IP* establishes a link between Ṣalāḥ al-Dīn and the Abrahamic (Judaic) tradition.

The *IP*'s attitude toward the Frankish conquest of Jerusalem also reflects a disregard for the earthly Jerusalem. In its reference to the capture of Jerusalem by the Franks, the *IP* shows no real appreciation for the conquest of the physical city and does not even mention this city by name. Rather, in the section recounting Ṣalāḥ al-Dīn's victory over Jerusalem, it specifically makes a point of mentioning the crusaders' erection of the True Cross, believed in the Christian tradition to be the remnants from the cross upon which Jesus was crucified. The text claims, "There used to be a stone cross which our knights had once erected on the walls in memory of their victorious capture of this city after their capture of Antioch." (Erat crux quaedam lapidea quam olim milites nostri cum hauc urbem post Antiochiam victoriose cepissent, in titulum facti supra murum erexerant; 21.) The narrative's main concern seems to be the loss of the True Cross rather than the loss of the city:

> The terrible enemy also undertook another unspeakable action. There was a cross fixed on top of the spire of the Hospitallers' church. They tied ropes around it and threw it down, spat contemptuously on it, hacked it into pieces, then dragged it through the city dungpits, as an insult to our faith.
>
> Nefas aliud atrocissimi hostes aggressi: crucem quandam quae supra pinnaculum ecclesiae Hospitalariorum posita eminebat, alligatis funibus dejecerunt, et eam turpiter consputam et caesam per urbis sterquilinia in improperium fidei nostrae traxerunt. (22–23)[17]

The *IP*'s discussion of the True Cross—its initial erection with the Frankish conquest of the city and its obtainment during the Islamic conquest—reflects the understanding that the earthly Jerusalem is the city that was home to the life of Jesus, his Passion, and his resurrection. The Church of the Holy Sepulcher, which metonymically functioned as a symbol for Jerusalem in Pope Urban II's sermons at Clermont, becomes reframed into a locus connected specifically to Jesus: "There is no sorrow like this sorrow, when they possess the Holy Sepulchre but persecute the One who was buried there; and they hold the Cross but despise the crucified" [*nec est dolor sicut dolor iste, cum hii sepulchrum possideant, qui sepultum persequuntur; crucem teneat qui Crucifixum contemnunt*] (22). Both the True Cross and Jesus's connection to the city of Jerusalem are also evoked in the *IP*'s description of the pivotal Battle of Hattin:

---

17. H. Frolow, *La relique de la Vraie Croix. Recherches sur le développement d'un culle* (Paris: Institut d'Études Byzantines, 1961), 305–49; Jaroslav Folda, *The Art of the Crusaders in the Holy Land, 1098-1187* (Cambridge: Cambridge University Press, 2005), 125–53; Y. Katzir, "The Vicissitudes of the True Cross of the Crusaders," in *The Crusaders in Their Kingdom: 1095–1291*, ed. B. Z. Kezar (Jerusalem: Yad Izhak Ben-Zvi, 1987), 243–53; Guiseppe Ligato, "The Political Meanings of the Relic of the Holy Cross among the Crusaders and in the Latin Kingdom of Jerusalem: An Example of 1185," in *Autour de la Première Croisade*, ed. Michel Balard (Paris: Publications de la Sorbonne, 1996), 315–30; Alan V. Murray, "Mighty against the Enemies of Christ": The Relic of the True Cross in the Armies of the Kingdom of Jerusalem," in *The Crusades and Their Sources*, ed. John France and William G. Zajac (Aldershot, England: Ashgate, 1998), 217–38.

Even the life-giving wood of the Cross of Salvation, on which our Lord and Redeemer hung, down whose trunk flowed the pious blood of Christ, whose image angels adore, humans venerate, demons dread, through whose help our people had won the victory in war-alas! was now captured by the enemy.

Illud etiam vivificum salutiferae Crucis lignum, in quo Dominus ac Redemptor noster pependit, in cujus stipitem pius Christi sanguis, defluxit, cujus signum adorant angeli, venerantur homines, daemones expavescunt, cujus praesidio nostri semper in bello extitere victores,—heu nun ab hoste capitur. (15)

The opening section of the *IP* establishes its position to the city of Jerusalem, which become extrapolated throughout the remainder of the account, through its descriptions of both the figure of Ṣalāḥ al-Dīn and his conquest of Jerusalem. Criticizing both Ṣalāḥ al-Dīn's character and conquests, the narrative also reveals a dismissive attitude toward the earthly city of Jerusalem, since the city is linked to him. The description of the Frankish conquest of Jerusalem in the *IP* is neither elaborate nor one that possess a yearning nostalgia for the obtainment of the physical city. Rather, the *IP*'s admiration for the Frankish success is one that expresses a glory for the erection of the True Cross within Jerusalem, which then becomes lost with Ṣalāḥ al-Dīn's conquest of the city. By focusing not on the success of the First Crusade but instead on the loss of the True Cross, the *IP* therefore suggests that the obtainment of the physical Jerusalem is not a priority. In contrast to the accounts of Pope Urban II's speeches at Clermont, which both celebrated and venerated the retrieval of the Church of the Holy Sepulcher (a metonym for the city of Jerusalem), at the onset of the *IP* the earthly Jerusalem and the Church of the Holy Sepulcher become reframed as places linked purely with the life of Jesus.

Paradoxically, the narrative both rejects the earthly city (as a city of the Jews and Ṣalāḥ al-Dīn) and accepts it at the same time, through its continuous linkage with the life of Jesus. This opinion further reflects Christian attitudes in this period toward the preferred status of the heavenly Jerusalem over the earthly. In its consideration of the earthly city under the hands of Ṣalāḥ al-Dīn, the *IP* attempts to reject Jerusalem as a place linked with the Islamic or Judaic traditions. In turn, the narrative then reinterprets the physical space of Jerusalem as one linked solely to the life of Jesus (and Christians). In its attempts to both reject and accept the place of the earthly Jerusalem, the text further reveals the following contradiction: the understanding of the earthly city (or the Temple Mount) as inferior to the heavenly, but the necessity of visiting the earthly city, which is viewed as the only means to its heavenly counterpart.

The (Un)contested City: Richard I and the Pilgrim's Progress to Jerusalem

Whereas the opening sections of the *IP* focus on former events within the city of Jerusalem—notably, through descriptions of the Frankish conquest of the city and the more contemporary victories of Ṣalāḥ al-Dīn—the introduction of the English king Richard I about a quarter of the way into book 1 catalyzes both a temporal shift in the narrative from past to present and also redirects the focus from the earthly Jerusalem to the heavenly one. In contrast to Ṣalāḥ al-Dīn, whose successes were *terrenae*, the *IP* presents Richard to be the initial and exemplary pilgrim, whose journey to Jerusalem metaphorically reflects contemporary Christian beliefs about the heavenly city of the afterlife. Although the *IP*'s account of Richard's journey to Jerusalem is rich in the information it provides—that is, about Richard's life, his relationship with Philip II of France, and the events taking place in the Levant in the late twelfth century—this section focuses primarily on Richard's preparation for his journey to Jerusalem and the three aborted attempts that were made to visit the city. Through the analysis of these segments in the *IP*, the concluding section of this chapter demonstrates that the continuous abandonment of both visiting and conquering Jerusalem reflect an understanding in the narrative that the possession of the earthly city was not a significant goal of Richard's journey (as opposed to the narratives of the First Crusade). Jerusalem's contested status is not lamentable, and what becomes problematic for Christian believers is, paradoxically, only to reach Jerusalem as a means of securing their places in the heavenly city of the afterlife. The justifications provided by both Richard and his army to delay their attack on Jerusalem further demonstrate contemporary Christian beliefs following the Third Crusade, which saw the earthly city solely as a destination of pilgrimage where the *imitatio Christi* could be fully realized.

After the Archbishop of Tyre announces the destruction of the Holy Land (*IP*, 31–32) Richard, the Count of Poitou, is introduced:

> Richard, the great-hearted count of Poitou, was the first to receive the sign of the cross to avenge the Cross's injury. He preceded everyone in this action, inviting everyone to follow his example. . . . The Lord, judging this man's constancy as worthy of reward, chose him first to incite all the others. And when all the other princes had either died or retreated, He retained him as executor of His affairs.
>
> Primus omnium magnanimus Pictaviae comes Ricardus ob ulciscendam crucis injuriam cruce insignitur, et omnes praecedit facto, quos invitat exemplo. . . . Hanc viri constantiam Dominus remunerandam judicans, quem primum aliorum omnium incentorem elegit, eum caeteris principibus vel defunctis vel regressis negotii Sui executorem reservavit. (32)[18]

Akin to the figure of Ṣalāḥ al-Dīn, whom the *IP* describes as being chosen as a tool through which God could punish the unfaithful Christian population (5–6), here again the *IP* claims that it was Richard who was chosen by God as an example to incite "aliorum"—presumably, other Christians. Richard, described as "primum omnium magnanimous" (32), is further celebrated as being retained by God as an executor of his affairs, when all the other princes had died or retreated. Ṣalāḥ al-Dīn, the individual chosen by God to take over the physical city of Jerusalem, is in multiple ways presented as a foil for Richard, and Richard, whom God prefers and facilitates his wishes through, is portrayed as the exemplary individual whose focus is not to conquer the city of Christ but to lead others to it.

Following the reference to Richard's position as the leader of the journey to Jerusalem comes a statement about his status: "Although the count took the cross, he embarked on the pilgrim journey only after he was made king on his father's death" (Hic licet comes crucem accepit, iter tamen peregrinationis post mortem patris rex factus arripuit; 32).[19] Although Nicholson claims that this statement appears to provide a link between book 1 and the events in book 2, the reflection on Richard's position as a monarch once again

18. Ambroise, *Estoire*, lines 59–64, also presents Richard as the first to take the cross: "Richard, the valiant count of Poitiers, did not wish to fail God at the time of His need and His call. So he took the Cross for the love of Him. He was the first of the great men of the lands from which we came [to do so]." (Li cuens de Peitiers li vaillanz, /Richarz, n'i volt estre faillanz, /Al besoing Deu e sa clamor, /Si se croissa por sue amor. /Premiers fu de toz les hauz homes /Des terres dont nos de ça sumes.)

19. See Nicholson, trans., *The Chronicle of the Third Crusade*, 5; Stubbs, ed., *Itinerarium peregrinorum*, lxxi–lxxii; and Mayer, *Das Itinerarium peregrinorum*, 7–45.

generates another level of contrast between him and Ṣalāḥ al-Dīn. As was noted in the previous section, the *IP* mentions specifically Ṣalāḥ al-Dīn's lack of noble birth (8) and expresses the opinion, among others, that his conquests are undeserved because of his inferior status (10–11). Ṣalāḥ al-Dīn's position as a Muslim leader is also seen as inferior (a position that Ṣalāḥ al-Dīn himself acknowledges in the text), since the *IP* claims that he appeared to Prince Enfrid of Turon (Humfrey II of Toron, or Tībnin) as a candidate for knighthood and received a knight's belt from him in accordance with the rite of the Franks.[20]

Just as Richard's position as king is specifically referenced in his introduction in book 1, in book 2 his preparation toward Jerusalem is prefaced by a brief section on the death of Henry II, Richard's procession at Westminster, and his anointment as king (142–43).[21] According to the *IP*, after putting the kingdom of England in order and celebrating Christmas at Normandy, Richard hastily prepares for his pilgrimage to Jerusalem:

> For his intention to set out on his pilgrimage and discharge his vow troubled him constantly. He judged that a delay would be dangerous while the debt was still outstanding.
>
> Sollicitabat enim eum sine intermissione arripiendae suae peregrinationis intentio, votique solutio, moram aestimans periculosam, dum superesset debitum inchoandum. (145–46)

Richard's introduction in the *IP* both sets up a contrast between a preceding view of the city of Jerusalem (represented through the figure of Ṣalāḥ al-Dīn and the vision of Jerusalem as a heavenly city) now channeled through Richard as the exemplary pilgrim. This conceptualization of the physical city as a means to the heavenly becomes further explained during Richard's exploits in the Holy Land. His journey to Jerusalem, however, becomes delayed and abandoned on multiple occasions. The continuous evasion of the city of

20. Another legend claims that Ṣalāḥ al-Dīn visited Hugh of Tiberias. See Suzanne Duparc-Quioc, *Le Cycle de la Croisade* (Paris: Champion, 1955), 131.

21. Henry II died on July 6, 1189 CE, and Richard was crowned king on September 3 of the same year. According to Roger of Howden, *Chronica Magistri Rogeri de Houedene*, vol. 3, ed. W. Stubbs (London: Longmans, 1867), 8, Richard started preparing his fleet for a crusade even before he was crowned king. This section in the *IP* also makes reference to the killing of Jews in London on the day of Richard's coronation.

Jerusalem further indicates the narrative's position toward the earthly city as a prefiguration to the heavenly, and one that Richard and his army do not seem particularly concerned about conquering.

At the end of book 4, Richard conquers Cyprus (181–209), arrives and takes over Acre (210–39), and is victorious at Arsūf (262–75), destroying many of Ṣalāḥ al-Dīn's fortresses. Richard's army is described as rejoicing, for they believe the time has come to now make their way to Jerusalem (305). The Templars advise Richard not to go to Jerusalem at this juncture. The first reason is based on military strategy: if Richard's army puts all its efforts into the battle, it will become locked between Ṣalāḥ al-Dīn's forces on one side and the Turkish army on the other (305). In its place, the account offers a secondary and more significant reason to abandon the move toward Jerusalem:

> Secondly, suppose everything went as they wished, and they captured the city of Jerusalem? Even this did not seem to be an advantage unless they at once assigned the toughest men to guard the city, and they asserted that this would not be easy to do so, especially because they realized that the common people were very eager to complete their pilgrimage so that they could go back home without delay, because they were absolutely worn out with the stress of the journey.
>
> tum et si omnia succederent ad votum, et obtinerent civitatem Jerusalem, nec hoc etiam expedire visum est, nisi statim viri robustissimi deputarentur qui custodirent civitatem; quod quidem autumabant non de facili posse compleri, praesertim cum plebem perpendissent avidissimam ad peregrinationem consummandam, ut inde sine mora repatriarent singuli, turbationis rerum jam ultra modum pertaesi. (305–6)[22]

This second reason is the text's claim that the earthly city of Jerusalem is not these pilgrims' patria, or homeland, as suggested through the verb "repatriarent" in this passage. This attitude expressed in the *IP* stands in direct contrast to those present in the accounts of Pope Urban II's speeches at Clermont in which, after their conquest of Jerusalem, the Franks saw Jerusalem not only as their homeland but also as a place that, after their journey, they desired to inhabit.[23]

22. Ambroise, *Estoire*, lines 7673–7716.

23. Guibert of Nogent, *Gesta Dei per Francos*, in RHC Occ. 4:207, 221, 232, 241; Baldric of Dol, *Gesta Dei per Francos*, in RHC Occ. 4:14; Robert the Monk, *Historia Jherosolimitana*, in RHC Occ. 3:881–82.

At the beginning of book 5 the *IP* once again expresses its belief that the earthly city is one to visit but not inhabit as, after abandoning their mission to Jerusalem for a second time, Richard and his pilgrims advance toward the rebuilding of Ascalon. Though the army is in despair about this decision, the *IP* claims that if it had been better informed about the poor state of those in Jerusalem, due to the severe cold and stormy weather, the army would have taken some comfort in its decision to refrain from entering the city (308):

> Without doubt, the long-desired city of Jerusalem could have been easily captured. Yet it could not have been held by our people for long, because when the pilgrimage was completed the people would have gone home and there would not have been anyone left who could defend it.
>
> et procul dubio de facili civitas illa diu desiderata Jerusalem expugnaretur. Sed diu a nostris retineri non posset, quia peracta peregrinatione populo repatriante, non superesset gens quae eam defendere valeret. (309)[24]

Although the narrative confidently expresses that the poor state of the Turks (presumably the Seljuqs) would have been advantageous for Richard's army, once again the text asserts the opinion that the difficulty would not have been in conquering the city but in finding Christians to inhabit it once it had been acquired.[25] Consistently, the method by which the *IP* expresses its regard for the earthly Jerusalem is one that not only supports the abandonment of the task of conquering the physical city but also advises that holding Jerusalem would lead to more peril for those unwilling to remain there to inhabit it.

24. According to Ambroise, it was Richard who searched and convinced the army to regroup and head on to Ramla, since the men were so distressed about not being able to go to Jerusalem: "Had it not been for the king of England who had them looked for and searched for everywhere so that he brought them all back, many would have been left there that day. All turned from there in their divisions. On the day we turned back the journey took us to Ramla."

"Sin e fust le rei dë Engletere, / Qui fust par tot cerchier e quere, / Tanz que toz les en aporterent / Tuit d'iloc bataille tornerent. / E fumes a Rames la jornee / Le jor de cele returnee." Ambroise, *Estoire*, lines 7821–27).

25. Earlier, the *IP* expresses the opinions that when the Turks in Jerusalem heard that Richard was coming they were so terrified that even Ṣalāḥ al-Dīn fled from the city (370). Ambroise claims that Ṣalāḥ al-Dīn found out from a spy that the army was not coming, as God did not wish it at that time (*Estoire*, lines 9881–84). Bahā' al-Dīn states that there was no panic in Jerusalem and steps were being taken for its defense (*al-Nawādir al-Sulṭāniyya*, 341).

Figure 6. Psalter map of the world (after 1262 CE) with the heavenly Jerusalem, and the earthly Jerusalem found at the center of the map. © The British Library Board, Additional 28681, fol. 9.

Although Richard initially deserts the path to Jerusalem based on the Templars' advice at the beginning of book 4, it is now, for the third time, Richard who counsels his army of the disadvantages of making their way to Jerusalem, giving many reasons against the idea. The initial cause is a fear of a blockade from Ṣalāḥ al-Dīn from the plain of Ramula. Second, because of the limited size of his army for both the siege and rescue, and also having a particular concern for those bringing food supplies, Richard is further unsupportive of his men heading toward Jerusalem. Third, Richard believes the attack to be a rash enterprise and one that he will be blamed for in the future. Finally, because they are "foreigners" and know nothing about the region (379–81), Richard claims that visiting Jerusalem would be an unwise move. With this rationale, he refers the matter to a council, which recommends breaking off the pilgrimage to Jerusalem and making preparations to besiege Egypt or "Babylonia" (381–82).

Richard's Lamentation: The Heavenly Jerusalem Realized

During his army's stay at Joppa, Richard is given a piece of the True Cross from the Syrian Bishop of St. George (376–77). This offering both exalts the pilgrims accompanying Richard and also results in their lack of motivation:

> So for some time the army rejoiced over the Holy Cross and adored it. Then the ordinary common people began to complain. "Lord God, what shall we do now? Surely, we don't still have to go to Jerusalem? What more is left for us to do? Do we have to go on until the pilgrimage is complete?"
>
> Igitur cum sanctam illam crucem diutius in excercitu adorassent, super illa non modicum gavisi, plebs et vulgus ignobile conquesti sunt dicentes, "Domine Deus, quid ergo erit nobis? Numquid adhuc in Jerusalem eundum est? quid ultra faciemus? an ad itineris illius consummationem durabimus.? (379)[26]

The outlook expressed by the "plebs et vulgus ignobile" suggests that the obtainment of the True Cross is not only equivalent to but perhaps more significant than the obtainment of the city of Jerusalem. Moreover, the earthly

26. Ambrose, *Estoire*, lines 10,137–211.

Jerusalem is expendable in the sense that when the True Cross is obtained even outside the physical city, there is no reason to enter it. Here it is the obtainment of a piece of the Holy Cross, a physical remnant of the humanity of Jesus, that becomes equated with the pilgrimage to Jerusalem. The "plebs" experience satisfaction in their pilgrimage with the obtainment of a piece of this relic, further inquiring, "quid ergo erit nobis?" Although some of the people express a desire not to continue their pilgrimage to Jerusalem, Richard urges them to go on. After the Battle of Joppa (410–24), Richard falls ill from exhaustion (425), but is able to obtain a three-year truce with Ṣalāḥ al-Dīn (426–27).[27] The terms include the destruction of Ascalon, the restoration of Jappa to the Christians, and safe and free access for the Christians to the Holy Sepulcher:

> He sanctioned an inviolable peace between the Christians and Saracens. Both should have safe and free passage everywhere, and access to the Lord's Holy Sepulchre without any exactions.
>
> Confirmandam etiam sanxit inviolandam pacem inter Christicolas et Saracenos, salvumque utorumque libere per omnia esse meatum, et ad Sanctum Dominicum Sepulcrum absque cujuscunque pensionis exactione accessum. (429)[28]

Securing safe passage, Richard and his followers make their way to Jerusalem. The people are organized into three parties, each placed under the control of one of these individual commanders: Andrew de Chavigny, Ralph Teissun, and Hubert Walter, the bishop of Salisbury (*IP*, 432–433; *Estoire*, 11,872–970). Upon their arrival at Jerusalem, these pilgrims are described as experiencing exceptional joy, kneeling on the ground and rendering thanks to God (*IP*, 435–436; *Estoire*, 12,014–100). As they enter the city, the pilgrims visit and kiss the Holy Sepulcher and the True Cross (the one that was in the possession of Ṣalāḥ al-Dīn and was left behind in the city). They then proceed to Mount Calvary, where Jesus was crucified, and then to the church sited on Mount Zion. They then make a series of visits to holy sites in Jerusalem,

27. Ambrose, *Estoire*, lines 11,680–690; 11,727–800.

28. Bahā' al-Dīn also claims that Ṣalāḥ al-Dīn wanted a truce because his army was tired from the war (*al-Nawādir al-Sulṭāniyya*, 383, 387) and accounts for the same terms as present in the *IP*.

> From there we proceeded to the right of Mount Cavalry, where the Lord was crucified, where the stone on which the Lord's cross was fixed in Golgotha cracked open. When we had kissed this place, we proceeded to the Church sited on Mount Sion. On the left side is the place from which Mary the Blessed Mother of God passed from this world to the Father. Having kissed this place with tears, we hurried on and went to see the sacrosanct table on which Christ deigned to eat bread. . . . We hurried on from there as far as the Sepulchre of Mary the Blessed Mother of God in the middle of the vale of Josaphat [Jehoshaphat], next to the pool of Siloam, which we kissed devotedly and with contrite heart. From there, not altogether safely, we went up into that vaulted room in which it is said that our Lord and Redeemer was held for the night, awaiting his crucifixion on the morrow. We poured out pious tears there and placed affectionate kisses on the place . . . Leaving Jerusalem we reached Acre.
>
> Inde perreximus ad dextram in Montem Calvariae quo crucifixus est Dominus, ubi lapis increpuit quo infixa fuerat crux Dominica in Golgotha. Quem locum cum fuissemus osculati, perreximus in Ecclesiam sitam in Monte Syon, in cujus parte sinistra locus apparuit a quo Beata Dei Genitrix Maria transivit ab hoc mundo ad Patrem. Illi loco fixis cum lacrymis osculis, cursitantes pervenimus ad videndam sacrosanctam mensam illam, in qua dignatus est Christus panem comedere. . . . Illinc properavimus usque ad sepulcrum Beatae Dei Genitricis Mariae, in Josaphat valle, medio, juxta Siloe osculandam devote et corde contrito. Deinde non omnino securi, in ipsam illam testudinem accessimus, in qua dicebatur Dominus et Redemptor noster nocte comprehensus, crucifigendus in crastino. Illic fusis piis lacrymis et affectuosius illi loco fixis osculis. . . . Postea recendentes ab Jerusalem pervenimus Achonem. (*IP*, 436; *Estoire*, 12,014–12,100).

The description of the pilgrim's progression through the city of Jerusalem reflect a conceptualization of the city that differs from those present in the narratives of the preceding chapters. It was particular monuments in the city that were lamented within these texts—the Dome of the Rock, the Church of the Holy Sepulcher, and Mount Zion, respectively. These edifices functioned as metonyms for the earthly city and were deliberated on within these accounts as places that had to be reconquered from enemy hands. In the *IP* it is not the physical monuments but how these monuments house the memory of the life of Jesus that stand as a dominant symbol for the earthly Jerusalem. The desire to obtain the earthly city is also one not equated with domination over the physical city but instead with the performance and imitation of Jesus's life on earth. Through the act of pilgrimage and replicating the life of Jesus within Jerusalem, these pilgrims then metaphorically "conquer" the earthly city. The goal is therefore not to remain or occupy the Holy Land but to tread on the land where God sent his son to the earth.[29] The *IP* further acknowledges how these men were now saved (i.e., that their souls would enter heaven) as a result of their pilgrimage.

Yet the description of the pilgrims' final arrival to Jerusalem in the *IP* does not include a direct reference to whether or not Richard also took part in the visit.[30] In the *IP*, Richard is the monarch who facilitates the journey of these pilgrims to Jerusalem, since the pilgrims never enter the city until Richard has signed a truce with Ṣalāḥ al-Dīn. Upon his departure, the "people" (perhaps the local population, or those remaining behind), break out in lamentation:

> O Land of Jerusalem, now abandoned by all aid! What a great defender you have lost! Who will protect you from the attackers if the truce is broken, now that King Richard is going away?
>
> O terra sancta, Deo te commendo, Qui pia Sua gratia mihi tantum vivendi tribuat spatium, ut in beneplacito Suo tibi quandoque succurrere. (442)

At the beginning of the text a link is established between the *terrenae* and the figure of Ṣalāḥ al-Dīn. The conquest of Jerusalem, both by the Franks and Ṣalāḥ al-Dīn, is presented in the *IP* as one of the past and a reflection of a prior understanding of the significance of the earthly city. Yet, as noted in this passage, it is Richard who has now been connected to the *terra* (land). Whereas the description of the conquest of Ṣalāḥ al-Dīn had been posited within the Hebrew model of lamentation, which the narrative attempted to shift away from through the figure of Richard, here Richard's departure is cause for lamentation.

This lamentation compares to other lamentations discussed in this book in that the trajectory of lament seems to shift from a genre originally

29. Saint Anselm of Canterbury, *Cur Deus Homo*, in PL 158, cols. 359–432.

30. Ambroise does make a reference to Richard's presence (*Estoire*, lines 12,221–222) and seems to have been in the second party since in this section the narrative shifts to the first person. This section and those following are increasingly different from that of the *IP*. See Nicholson, trans., *The Chronicle of the Third Crusade*, xxn103, 381.

dominated by women to a monotheistic world that sees male rulers as protectors of the city. As discussed in the introduction, Mesopotamian laments envisioned destructions of cities when their gods and goddesses abandoned these spaces as protectors. Each of these lamentations composed around the loss of Jerusalem in the medieval period equate the position of the monotheistic God as protector with a male monarch or ruler: the Zengid powers, specifically Ṣalāḥ ad-Dīn; Pope Urban II and the Frankish army; Prince Levon II of Cilicia; and Richard I of England. Here too Richard is seen as a form of salvation for the physical city, despite the fact that throughout its narrative, the *IP* continuously attempts to position the heavenly Jerusalem as more significant than a Jewish and Muslim (earthly) Jerusalem.

The attempts to distance the narrative from past conceptualization of the earthly Jerusalem reveals itself to be unsuccessful at the end of the *IP*. Richard's personage, as a leader of pilgrims to the heavenly city, has now shifted to one that presents him as the savior of the earthly Jerusalem. Richard as protector also establishes the belief that pilgrimage alone is still worldly. For these pilgrims, the earthly Jerusalem is not the true patria of the Christian, and thus Richard's journey to the city was perhaps not based on religious fervor but grounded in military conquest. Through this paradox the *IP* exposes the very internal contradiction in Christian attitudes toward Jerusalem, which both reject the position of the earthly city (as understood in the Hebrew tradition) and at the same time envisage the earthly Jerusalem as exclusively Christian.[31]

The description of Richard's journey to the city of Jerusalem can bring us to some conclusions. The role of the earthly Jerusalem in the *IP* is linked simultaneously to both the figure of Ṣalāḥ al-Dīn and of Jesus. As a destina-

31. Although who the author of the *Itinerarium Peregrinorum* has proved difficult to answer, William Stubbs, H. G. Bohn, and Hans Eberhard Mayer offer the following possibilities, respectively: Geoffrey of Vinsauf, who composed a book of poetry dedicated to Pope Innocent III (1198–1216); Guido Adduanensis, the continuer of the *Libellus*; or Richard de Templo, prior of the Holy Trinity in London, who seems to be the most accepted possibility. See Stubbs, *Itinerarium peregrinorum*, xli–xlii, lxxix; H. G. Bohn, "Preface," in *Chronicles of the Crusades*, ed. H. G. Bohn (London: Bell, 1903), iii–v; and Mayer, *Das Itinerarium peregrinorum*, 105–6. See also Nicholson, trans., *The Chronicle of the Third Crusade*, 6–15. Though book 1 is believed to have circulated separately from the rest and the work has been arguably composed by various authors, it is possible that the beginning of the *IP* reflects the figure of Richard as seen by his contemporaries and the end of the account as seen of later decades. As a monastic, perhaps the author of the *IP* also attempted to disavow the importance of performing the act of pilgrimage—an attitude that had developed within the laity and the nobility following the First Crusade.

tion of pilgrimage, pilgrims view the earthly city as place where the Passion of Christ could be actualized, and as a gateway to the heavenly city (though this collapses after they acquire the True Cross). European crusaders as pilgrims are presented as neither displaying a deep yearning for the acquisition of the physical city of Jerusalem nor a nostalgia for its past conquest. The pilgrims accompanying these crusaders offer no desire to remain behind or inhabit the city once they are there. The True Cross and its obtainment seem to be more significant than the physical city itself. The lament for the city and the liberation of Jerusalem from the hands of the Muslim powers present in Pope Urban II's speeches at Clermont is one that is not present in the *IP*. Christian claims to the city, and their justifications for its reconquest, are also almost entirely absent, perhaps because of the failed efforts of both Richard and the Third Crusade. The *IP*, therefore, seems to reflect the growing change in Christian views toward Jerusalem following the Third Crusade, which revert to the predominant attitude set before its conquest of 1099 CE: that the heavenly Jerusalem was far superior to the earthly one.[32]

In my readings of city lamentations composed over the loss of Jerusalem in the medieval Mediterranean, I hope to have shown that the taxonomies and orientalizing tropes that for so long dominated the perspective of this period inhibited the exposure of the complex interpenetration of various ethnoreligious cultures, whose intercultural exchange collectively gave rise to an established genre of lamenting the loss of cities—and specifically Jerusalem. In this book, I have examined city lamentations as active reformulations of the literary and political vision of ancient city laments, particularly those of the Hebrew Bible. These literary works shift between voices of the past and prophecies of the future, conjuring images of the loss of the city as reflections

32. There are some contemporary examples that coincide with the *IP*'s attitude toward the earthly Jerusalem. The first is a passage attributed to Abelard that compares a visit to Jerusalem to the receiving of the Eucharist, drawing a likeness between the journey of pilgrimage and the Passion of Christ; see *Commentarius Cantabrigiensis in epistolas Pauli e schola Petri Abaelardi. In epistolam ad Habraeos*, ed. A. Landgraf (Notre Dame, IN: Publications in Medieval Studies at the University of Notre Dame, 1945), 747. The second is a marching song composed between the years 1096 and 1099 CE titled "Iherusalem mirabilis," which dwells on the Crucifixion; see "Iherusalem maribalis," in *Analecta hymnica medii aevi*, vol. 55b, ed. Guido Maria Dreves (Leipzig: Reisland, 1922), no. 96. The third is the treatise composed by Bernard of Clairvaux; see Bernardus Claraevallensis [Bernard of Clairvaux], *De Laude Novae Militiae*, in *Opera*, vol. 3, ed. J. Leclercq (Rome: Editiones. Cistercienses, 1963), 215, 217, 224.

of their own contemporary sociopolitical circumstances. In their imaginations of Jerusalem, the authors examined in this book remap the city as their own, and in doing so geographically and textually re-create their own Jerusalem(s). For Ibn al-Abīwardī, lamenting Jerusalem is a place where the text can call for a pan-Islamic brotherhood and connect the Abbasids to a sacred city. For Pope Urban II, the Church of the Holy Sepulcher and a new Latin Christian topography (as described in Fulcher of Chartres's account) solidifies and propagates a call for crusade and the obtainment of a Jerusalem that is sacred for the Latin faith. For Grigor Tłay, lamenting Jerusalem is the vehicle through which the prominent position of Prince Levon II can be exhibited and the possibility of an Armenian kingdom of Cilicia achieved. In order to promote his political endeavors, Grigor imagines an Armenian Jerusalem, one with a strong alliance to Rome.

Lamentations in the ancient world were political, and they are the same in the medieval Mediterranean world. They allow each of the ethnoreligious traditions to negotiate its position with its own monotheistic God. The contested nature of Jerusalem further allows each of these traditions to create its own topography of the city. Through lamentation these traditions express their hopes for the future of Jerusalem and their own respective empires, mediating also their place within the foreign. The range of cultures in this study—Armenian, Arabo-Islamic, and the Latin West—reflect further how the ritual of lament transcends physical and imaginary boundaries, limitations often imposed by contemporaneous politics that sought to focus on difference, on driving a wedge between cultures that had influenced one another for centuries. That these cultures simultaneously engage in contact and conflict reverberates through these poems of lament, which perhaps no longer mourn a city but instead the memory of one. Using the multicultural and multiconfessional Mediterranean as a framework for analysis enlightens us to how different cultural visions of Jerusalem function similarly. These laments pulsate between nostalgia and the potential impossibility of return, between an "unreal city" and the Jerusalem the works map as their own. Perhaps what these medieval Mediterranean lamentations have come to show us is that the only way a lost city can ever truly be recovered is through mourning and memory—in lamentation. To speak of Jerusalem, to have Jerusalem live anew, one must first lament Jerusalem.

Selected Bibliography

Primary Sources

Abū al-Muẓaffar Ibn al-Abīwardī. *Dīwān al-Abīwardī Abī al-Muẓaffar Muḥammad ibn Aḥmad ibn Isḥaq al-Matūfī sanat.* Damascus: Majma' al-Lughah al-'Arabīyah bi-Dimashq, 1974–75.

[Aelius Aristides.] *Aelii Aristidis Smyrnaei quae supersunt Omnia*, ed. Keil, Bruno 1898. Reprinted, Whitefish, MT: Kessinger, 2010.

Agat'angełos. *History of the Armenians.* Edited and translated by Robert W. Thomson. New York: State University of New York Press, 1976.

al-Athīr, 'Izz al-Dīn Ibn. *al-Kāmil fī al-Tārīkh.* Vol. 10, edited by C. J. Tornberg. Beirut: Dār Ṣādir, 1967.

——. *The Chronicle of Ibn al-Athīr for the Crusading Period, from al-Kamil fi'l-Ta'rikh.* Vol. 1, translated by D. S. Richards. Aldershot, England: Ashgate, 2006.

Albert of Aachen. *Historia Ierosolimitana: History of the Journey to Jerusalem.* Edited and translated by Susan B. Edgington. Oxford: Oxford University Press, 2007.

Alishan, Ł. *Sisuan: Hamagrut'iwn Haykakan Kilikioy ew Lewon Mecagorc.* Venice: St. Łazar, 1885.

Ambroise, *The History of the Holy War: Ambroise's Estoire de la Guerre Sainte.* 2 vols. Edited and translated by Marianne Ailes and Malcolm Barber. Woodbridge, England: Boydell, 2003.

[Ananias of Širak.] *The Geography of Ananias of Širak: Ašxarhac'oyc', the Long and the Short Recensions.* Translated by Robert H. Hewsen. Wiesbaden: Reichert, 1992.

Augustine. *Confessions.* Loeb Classical Library, vols. 26–27. Cambridge, MA: Harvard University Press, 1979.

——. *De Civitate Dei.* Edited by G. P. Goold. Cambridge, MA: Harvard University Press, 1957.

Avdalbegyan, M. T'. *Xač'atur Keč'arec'i.* Erevan: Armenian SAH GA, 1958.

'Azimi, al-. "La chronique abrégée d'al-'Azīmī'." Edited by Claude Cahen. *Journal Asiatique* 230 (1938): 353–448.

Baudri de Bourgeuil [Baldric of Dol]. *Historia Hierosolymitanae.* In RHC Occ. 4.

——. *Poèmes: Baudri de Bourgueil.* Edited by Jean-Yves Tilliette. Paris: Les Belles Lettres, 1998.

Bernardus Claraevallensis [Bernard of Clairvaux]. *De Laude Novae Militiae.* In *Opera*, vol. 3, edited by J. Leclercq. Rome: Editiones Cistercienses, 1963.

Biṭrīq, Ibn al-. *al- Ta'rīkh al-Majmū' 'alā al-Taḥqīq wa-al-Taṣdīq.* Beirut: Maṭba'at al-Abā' al-Yasū'īyīn, 1909.

The Chronicle of the Third Crusade: The Itinerarium Peregrinorum et Gesta Regis Ricardi. Translated by Helen J. Nicholson. Aldershot, England: Ashgate, 1997.

Dawādārī, Ibn al-. *Die Chronik des Ibn al-Dawādārī.* Vol. 6, edited by S. Munaggid. Cairo; Weisbaden: In Kommission bei Harrassowtiz, 1961.

Eusebius. *De Vita Constantini.* In PG 20. Translated by J. H. Bernard in PPTS 1.

——. *Eusebius: The Ecclesiastical History.* 2 vols. Edited by H. J. Lawlor. Cambridge, MA: Harvard University Press, 1980.

Fulcher de Chartres [Fulcher of Chartres]. *Gesta Francorum Iherusalem Peregrinantium.* In RHC Occ. 3.

——. *A History of the Expedition to Jerusalem 1095–1127*, translated by Frances Rita Ryan, edited by Harold S. Fink. Knoxville: University of Tennessee Press, 1969.

Gesta Francorum: The Deeds of the Franks and Other Pilgrims to Jerusalem. Edited and translated by Rosalind Hill. Oxford: Oxford University Press, 2002.

Gilo of Paris. *The Historia Vie Hierosolimitanae of Gilo of Paris.* Edited and translated by C. W. Grocock and J. E. Siberry. Oxford: Oxford University Press, 1997.

Grigor Tłay. *Grigor Tłay: Banastełcutiwnner ev Poemner.* Edited by A. Š. Mnac'akanyan. Erevan: Armenian SAH GA, 1972.

Guibert of Nogent. *Gesta Dei per Francos.* In RHC Occ. 4.

——. *The Deeds of God through the Franks: A Translation of Guibert de Nogent's Gesta Dei per Francos.* Edited and translated by Robert Levine. Woodbridge, England: Boydell and Brewer, 1997.

——. *Guibert de Nogent's Autobiographie.* Edited and translated by Edmond-René Labande, Paris: Société d'Éditions "Les Belles Lettres," 1981.

Guillaume de Tyr [William of Tyre]. *Le Continuation de Guillaume de Tyr.* In RHC Occ. 4.

Hieronymus. *Commentariorum in Isaiam libri XII–XVIII.* In *Esaiam paruula adbreviatio*, CCSL 73A.

Homer. *Odyssey.* Translated by Robert Fagles. London: Penguin, 1996.

Ibn ʿAlawī, Al-Sayyid Muḥammad. *The Hadith of Israʾ and Miʿraj/The Immense Merits of Al-Sham.* Translated by Gibril Fouad Haddad. Fenton, Michigan: Islamic Supreme Council of America, 1999.

Ibn Qutaybah, ʿAbd Allāh ibn Muslim. *Kitāb al-Shiʿr wa-l-Shuʿarāʾ.* Edited by M. J. de Goeje. Leiden: Brill, 1904.

Ibn Saʿd. *Kitāb al-ṭabaqāt al-ḳabīr.* Edited by ʿAlī Muḥammad ʿUmar. Cairo: Maktabat al-Khānjī, 2001.

Ibn Taghrībirdī. *Annals, Entitled ʿan-Nujūm az-ẓāhira fi muluḳ Miṣr wal-Qāhiraʾ.* Vol. 5, edited and translated by William Popper. Berkeley: University of California Press, 1954.

———. *Nujūm al-ẓāhira.* Vol. 5. Cairo: Maṭbaʿat dār al-kutub, 1939.

Isfahānī, ʿImād ad-Dīn al-. *al-Fat al-qussī fī l-fat al-qudsī.* Documents relatifs a l'histoire des Croisades 10. Paris: Académie des Inscriptions, 1972.

Isḥāq, Muḥammad Ibn. *Sīrat Rasūl Allāh.* Cairo: Maktabat wa Maṭbas Inscriptions, 1972.

[Isidore of Seville.] *Isidori Hispalensis episcopi: Etymologiarum sive originum.* Vol. 14, edited by W. M. Lindsay. Oxford: Clarendon, 1911.

Itinerarium peregrinorum et gesta regis Ricardi. Edited by William Stubbs. London: Longman, 1864.

Itinerarium Peregrinorum et Gesta Regis Ricardi: Untersuchungen uber einige englische chronisten des zwölften und des beginnenden dreizehnten jahrhunderts. Edited by Hans Lamprecht. Torgau, Germany: Nitschke, 1937.

Kathīr, Ismāʿīl ibn. *al-Bidāya wa al-Nihāya fī al-Tāʾrīḳh.* 14 vols. Edited by Aḥmad Abū Mulḥim. Cairo: Matbaʿat al-Saʿāda, 1935.

Kesarecʿi, Ewsebios. *Patmutyun Eḳelecʿwoy.* Edited by Abraham Charian. Venice: St. Łazar, 1877.

Khaṭīb, Lisān al-Dīn Ibn al-. *Aʿmāl al-aʿlām.* 2nd. ed. Edited by E. Lévi Provençal. Beirut: Dār al-makshūf, 1956.

Khayyāṭ, Ibn al-. *Dīwān.* Damascus: Al-majmaʿ al-ʿArabī, 1958.

Khuraymī, al-. Abū Yaʿqūb Isḥāq. *Dīwān al-Khuraymī.* Edited by ʿAlī Jawād al-Ṭāhir and Muḥammad Jabbār al-Muʿaybid. Beirut: Dār al-Kitāb al-Jadīd, 1971.

La Chanson de Roland: Old French and English Translation. Edited and translated by Gerard J. Brault. University Park: Pennsylvania State University Press, 1984.

L'Estoire de Eracles empereur et la conqueste de la Terre d'Outremer. In RHC Occ. 2.

Mattʿeos Uṙhayecʿi [Matthew of Edessa]. Mambrē Mēlik'-Adamian and Nersēs Tēr Mikʿayēlian, eds. *Žamanaḳagrutʿiwn.* Vałaršapat, Armenia: Great House of Echmiadzin, 1898.

Maqrīzī, al-. *Ittiʿāẓ al-ḥunafāʾ.* Edited by J. al-Shayyal. Cairo: Dār al-Fikr al-ʿArabī, 1948.

Masʿūdī, ʿAli al-. *Murūj al-Dhahab wa-Maʿādin al-Jawhar.* Vol. 3. Beirut: al-Jāmiʿah al-Lubnānīyah, 1966–79.

[Matthew of Edessa.] *Patmutʿiwn.* In RHC Doc. Arm. 1.

Muqaddasī, al-. *Aḥsan al-Taqāsīm fī Ma'rifat al-Aqālīm*. Edited by M. J. de Goeje. Leiden: Brill, 1866.

——. *Aḥsan at-Taqāsīm fi Ma'rifat al-Aqālīm: La meilleure repartition pour la connaissance des provinces*. Translated by André Miquel. Damascus: Institut français de Damas, 1963.

Nersēs Šnorhali. *Ołb Edesioy*. With text and commentary by Manik Mkrtč'yan. Erevan: Armenian SAH GA, 1973.

[Niketas Choniates.] *Nicetae Choniatae Historia*. Edited by Immanuel B. Bekker. Bonn: Weber, 1835.

Orderic Vitalis. *General Introduction*, edited by Marjorie Chibnall. Vol. 1 of *The Ecclesiastical History of Orderic Vitalis*. Oxford: Oxford University Press, 1969.

Otto of Freising. *Ausgewählte Quellen zur Deutschen Geschichte des Mittelalters*. Edited by A. Schmidt. Berlin: Rütten & Loening Verlag, 1957.

Plato, *Republic*. 2 vols. Edited and translated by Chris Emlyn-Jones and William Preddy. Loeb Classical Library 237 and 276. Cambridge, MA: Harvard University Press, 2013.

Radulfo Cadomensi [Ralph of Caen]. *Gesta Tancredi in Expeditione Hierosolymitana*. In RHC Occ. 5.

Raimundi de Aguilers [Raymond of Aguilers]. *Historia Francorum qui ceperunt Iherusalem*. In RHC Occ. 5.

Robertus Monachus [Robert the Monk]. *Historia Jherosolimitana*. In RHC Occ. 3.

——. *Robert the Monk's History of the First Crusade: Historia Iherosolimitana*. Translated by Carol Sweetenham. Aldershot, England: Ashgate, 2005.

Roger of Howden, *Chronica Magistri Rogeri de Houedene*, 3 vols ed. W. Stubbs (London: Longmans, 1867).

Untersuchungen uber einige englische chronisten des zwölften und des beginnenden dreizehnten jahrhunderts. Edited by Hans Lamprecht. Torgau, Germany: Nitschke, 1937.

Sacrorum Conciliorum nova et amplissima collectio, cujus Johannes Dominicus Mansi et post ipsius morten Florentius et Venetianus editores ab anno 1758 A.D. annum 1798 priores triginta unum tomos ediderunt, nunc autem continuatat et absoluta. Edited by J. D. Mansi. Paris: H. Welter, 1903.

Shaddād, Bahā' al-Dīn Ibn. *al-Nawādir al-Sulṭānīyya wa-l-Maḥāsin al-Yūsufiyya*. In RHC Or. 3.

——. *The Rare and Excellent History of Saladin, or al-Nawādir al-Sulṭāniyya wa'l-Maḥāsin al-Yūsufiyya*. Translated by. D. S. Richards (Aldershot, England: Ashgate, 2001).

Sulamī, Ṭāhir al-. *The Book of the Jihad of 'Ali ibn Tahir al-Sulami*. Edited and translated by Niall Christie. Farnham, England: Ashgate, 2015.

Tabarānī, Sulaymān Ibn Aḥmad. *Al Mu'jam al-Kabīr*. Beirut: Dār Iḥyā' al Turāth al-'Arabī, 1984.

Ṭabarī, Jarīr al-. *The History of al-Ṭabarī*. 40 vols. Translated by W. Montgomery Watt and M. V. McDonald. Albany: State University of New York Press, 1985–99.

——. *Ta'rīkh al-rusul wa'l-mulūk*. 15 vols. Edited by M. J. de Goeje. Leiden: Brill, 1879–1901.

Tudebode, Peter. *Historia de Hierosolimitano Itinere*. Edited and translated by John H. Hill, and Laurita L. Hill. Philadelphia: American Philosophical Society, 1974.

——. *Historia de Hierosolymitano Itinere.* In RHC Occ. 5.
Vardan Arewelec'i, *Havakumn Patmutiwn.* In RHC Doc. Arm. 1.
——. "The Historical Compilation of Vardan Arewelec'i." Translated by Robert W. Thomson. *Dumbarton Oaks Papers* 43 (1989): 125–226.
Willermo, Tyrensi Archiepiscopo [William of Tyre]. *Historia rerum in partibus transmarinis gestarum.* In RHC Occ. 3.
William of Malmesbury. *Gesta Regum Anglorum.* Vol. 2. Edited and translated by R. A. B. Mynors, R. M. Thomson, and M. Winterbottom. Oxford: Oxford University Press, 1998.

Secondary Sources

Akbari, Suzanne Conklin. *Idols in the East: European Representations of Islam and the Orient, 1100–1450.* Ithaca, NY: Cornell University Press, 2009.
Akbari, Suzanne Conklin, and Karla Mallette, eds. *A Sea of Languages: Rethinking the Arabic Role in Medieval Literary History.* Toronto: University of Toronto Press, 2013.
Albrektson, Bertil, *Studies in Text and Theology of the Book of Lamentations.* Studia Theologica Lundensia 21. Lund, Sweden: Gleerup, 1963.
Alexander, Philip S. "Geography and the Bible (Early Jewish Geography)." In *D–G*, edited by David Noel Freedman, 977–88. Vol. 2 of *Anchor Bible Dictionary.* Garden City, NY: Anchor, 1992.
——. "Jerusalem as the Omphalos of the World. On the History of a Geographical Concept." In *Jerusalem: Its Sanctity and Centrality to Judaism, Christianity, and Islam*, edited by L. I. Levine, 104–19. New York: Continuum, 1999.
——. "Notes on the *Imago Mundi* in the Book of Jubilees." *Journal of Jewish Studies* 33 (1982): 197–213.
——. *The Targum of Lamentations.* The Aramaic Bible 17B. Collegeville, MN: Liturgical Press, 2007.
Alexiou, Margaret. *The Ritual Lament in the Greek Tradition.* Cambridge: Cambridge University Press, 1974.
Alishan, Ł. *Léon le Magnifique.* Edited by G. Baian. Venice: St. Łazar, 1888.
Alphandéry, Paul, and Alphonse Dupront, *La Chrétienté et l'idée de Croisade.* Paris: A. Michel, 1954.
Amelang, James S. "Mourning becomes Eclectic: Ritual Lament and the Problem of Continuity." *Past and Present* 187 (2005): 3–31.
Amikam, Elad. *Medieval Jerusalem and Islamic Worship: Holy Places, Ceremonies, Pilgrimage.* Leiden: Brill, 1995.
Anapatakan. *Hamaṙod patmutiwn hay-latinakan haraberuteanc' skizbēn minč'ev 1382.* Beirut: Stanalu hamar dimel Aram Panossian, 1981.
Andrée, Alexander. *Gilbertus Universalis: Glossa Ordinaria in Lamentationes Ieremie Prophete, Prothemata et Liber I.* Acta Universitatis Stockholmiensis Studia Latina Stockholmiensia 52. Stockholm: Almquist och Wiksell, 2005.
Anisī, ʿAbd al-Bāsiṭ al-, ed. *Dīwān al-Abīwardī Abī al-Muẓaffar Muḥammad ibn Aḥmad ibn Isḥaq al-Matūfī.* Vol. 2. Damascus: Majmaʿ al-Lughah al-ʿArabīyah bi-Dimashq, 1975.

Antreassian, Assadour. *Jerusalem and the Armenians.* Jerusalem: St. James, 1968.

Arnoud, Dominique. *Le Rire et les Larmes dans la Littérature Grecque d'Homère à Platon.* Paris: Belles Lettres, 1990.

Asbridge, Thomas. *First Crusade: A New History.* New York: Oxford University Press, 2004.

Astren, Fred. "Depaganizing Death: Aspects of Mourning in Rabbinic Judaism and Early Islam." In *Bible and Qur'an: Essays in Scriptural Intertextuality*, edited by John C. Reeves, 183–99. Atlanta: American Academy of Religion, 2003.

Azarya, Victor. *The Armenian Quarter of Jerusalem: Urban Life behind Monastery Walls.* Berkeley: University of California Press, 1984.

Balgy, Alexander. *Historia doctrinae catholicae inter Armenos.* Vienna: Typis Congregationis Mechitaristicae, 1878.

Barber, Malcolm. *Crusaders and Heretics, 12th–14th centuries.* Aldershot, England: Variorum, 1995.

Barbour, Jennie. *The Story of Israel in the Book of Qohelet: Ecclesiastes as Cultural Memory.* Oxford: Oxford University Press, 2013.

Barker, Andrew, ed. *The Musician and His Art.* Vol. 1 of *Greek Musical Writings.* Cambridge: Cambridge University Press, 1987.

Barthélemey, Dominique. *Les davancirs d'Aquila.* Vetus Testamentum Supplements 10. Leiden: Brill, 1963.

Beledian, Krikor. *Erkxosut'iwn Narekac'ii hed.* Erevan, Armenia: Sargis Khachents, 2008.

Bishop, Edmund. *Liturgica Historica: Papers on the Liturgy and Religious Life of the Western Church.* Oxford: Clarendon, 1962.

Blake, E. O. "The Formation of the 'Crusade Idea,'" *Journal of Ecclesiastical History* 21 (1970): 11–31.

Boas, Adrian J. *Jerusalem in the Time of the Crusades: Society, Landscape, and Art in the Holy City under Frankish Rule.* London: Routledge, 2001.

Bobzin, Hartmut. "Jerusalem aus muslimischer Perspektive während der Kreuzfahrerzeit." In *Jerusalem im Hoch und Spätmittelalter: Konflikte und Konfliktbewältigung, Vorstellungen und Vergegenwärtigungen*, edited by Dieter Bauer, Klaus Herbers, and Nikolas Jaspert, 203–18. Frankfurt: Campus Verlag, 2001.

Bordonove, Georges. *Les Croisades et le Royaume de Jérusalem.* Paris: Pygmalion, 1992.

Bormans, Maurice. "Jérusalem dans la tradition réligieuse musulmane." *Islamochristiana* 7 (1981): 1–18.

Bowen, Nancy R. "The Daughters of Your People: Female Prophets in Ezekiel 13:17–23." *Journal of Biblical Literature* 118 (1999): 417–33.

Boyarin, Daniel. *Carnal Israel: Reading Sex in Talmudic Culture.* Berkeley: University of California Press, 1993.

———. *A Radical Jew: Paul and the Politics of Identity.* Berkeley: University of California Press, 1997.

———. "'This We Know to Be the Carnal Israel': Circumcision and the Erotic Life of God and Israel." *Critical Inquiry* 18 (1992): 474–505.

Boym, Svetlana. *The Future of Nostalgia.* New York: Basic Books, 2001.

Bredero, Adriaan H. "Jérusalem dans l'Occident medieval." In *Mélanges offerts à René Crozet à l'occasion de son 70e anniversaire par ses amis, ses collégues, ses élèves et les membres cu C.E.S.C.M.*, vol. 1, edited by Pierre Gallais, 259–71. Poitiers, France: Société d'Études Médiévales, 1966.

Brener-Idan, Athalya, ed. *A Feminist Companion to Exodus to Deuteronomy.* Sheffield, England: Sheffield Academic Press, 1994.

Broshi, M. "Excavations on the House of Caiaphas, Mount Zion." In *Jerusalem Revealed: Archeology in the Holy City 1968–1974*, edited by Yigael Yadin, 57–60. Jerusalem: Israel Exploration Society, 1976.

Brundage, James A. *The Crusades: A Documentary Survey.* Milwaukee, WI: Marquette University Press, 1962.

——. "'Cruce Signari': The Rite for Taking the Cross in England." *Traditio* 22 (1966): 289–310.

Brunner, Karl, ed. *Der Mittelenglische versroman über Richard Löwenherz: Kritische ausgabe nach allen handscriften mit einleitung, anmerkungen und deutscher übersetzung.* Vienna: Braumüller, 1913.

Bull, M. J. "The Capetian Monarchy and the Early Crusade Movement: Hugh of Vermandois and Louis VII." *Nottingham Medieval Studies* 40 (1996): 25–46.

Burman, Thomas E. *Reading the Qur'an in Latin Christendom, 1140–1560.* Philadelphia: University of Pennsylvania Press, 2007.

Burstein, Eitan. "Quelques remarques à propos du vocabulaire de Guibert de Nogent." *Cahiers de civilisation médiévale* 21 (1978): 247–63.

Busse, Heribert. "Jerusalem and Mecca, the Temple and the Kaaba: An Account of Their Interrelation in Islamic times." In *The Holy Land in History and Thought*, edited by Moshe Sharon, 236–46. Leiden: Brill, 1988.

Cahen, Claude. "Points de vue sur la 'Révolution ʿabbāside.'" *Revue Historique* 230 (1963): 295–338.

Cain, Andrew. *The Letters of Jerome: Asceticism, Biblical Exegesis, and the Construction of Christian Authority in Late Antiquity.* Oxford: Oxford University Press, 2009.

Calkin, Siobhain Bly. *Saracens and the Making of English Identity: The Auchinleck Manuscript.* New York: Routledge, 2005.

Catlos, Brian A. *Muslims of Medieval Latin Christendom, c. 1050–1614.* Cambridge: Cambridge University Press, 2015.

Christie, Niall. "Jerusalem in the Kitāb al-Jihad of ʿAli ibn Tahir al-Sulami." *Medieval Encounters* 13, no. 2 (2007): 209–21.

Ciholas, Paul. *Omphalos and the Cross: Pagans and Christians in Search of a Divine Center.* Macon, GA: Mercer University Press, 2003.

Civil, Miguel. "The Sumerian Writing System: Some Problems." *Orientalia*, n.s., 42 (1973): 21–34.

Cohen, Jeremy. *Living Letters of the Law: Ideas of the Jew in Medieval Christianity.* Berkeley: University of California Press, 1999.

——. "The Muslim Connection, or, On the Changing Role of the Jew in High Medieval Theology." In *From Witness to Witchcraft: Jews and Judaism in Medieval Christian Thought*, edited by Jeremy Cohen, 141–62. Wiesbaden: Harrasowitz, 1996.

Commentarius Cantabrigiensis in epistolas Pauli e schola Petri Abaelardi. In epistolam ad Habraeos. Edited by A. Landgraf. Notre Dame, IN: Publications in Medieval Studies at the University of Notre Dame, 1945.

The Commentary on the Qur'ān, by Abū Ja'far Muḥammad b. Jarīr al-Ṭabarī; Being an Abridged Translation of Jāmi' al-bayān 'an ta'wīl āy al-Qur'ān. Translated by J. Cooper, edited by W. F. Madelung and A. Jones. Oxford: Oxford University Press, 1987.

Constable, Olivie Remie, ed. *Medieval Iberia: Readings from Christian, Muslim, and Jewish Sources.* Philadelphia: University of Pennsylvania Press, 1997.

Cooperson, Michael, and Shawkat M. Toorawa, eds. *Arabic Literary Culture 500–925.* Detroit: Gale, 2005.

Coppa, Frank J., ed. *The Great Popes through History: An Encyclopedia.* Vol. 1. Westport, CT: Greenwood, 2002.

Cowdrey, H. E. J. "Pope Urban II's Preaching of the First Crusade." *History* 55 (1970): 177–88.

——. *Popes and Church Reform in the 11th Century.* Aldershot, England: Ashgate, 2000.

Cowe, Peter. "Medieval Armenian Literary and Cultural Trends (Twelfth–Seventeenth Centuries)." In *The Dynastic Periods: From Antiquity to the Fourteenth Century*, edited by Richard Hovannisian, 293–325. Vol. 1 of *The Armenian People from Ancient to Modern Times.* New York: St. Martin's, 1977.

Crone, Patricia, and Michael Crook. *Hagarism: The Making of the Islamic World.* Cambridge: Cambridge University Press, 1977.

Dajani-Shakeel, Hadia. "Al-Quds: Jerusalem in the Consciousness of the Counter-Crusade in the Meeting of Two Worlds." *Studies in Medieval Culture* 21 (1986): 201–21.

——. "Jihād in Twelfth-Century Arabic Poetry: A Moral and Religious Force to Counter the Crusades." *Muslim World* 66, no.2 (1976): 96–113.

Daniel, Elton L. *The Political and Social History of Khurasan under Abbasid Rule.* Chicago: Bibliotheca Islamica, 1979.

Daniel, Norman. *Heroes and Saracens: An Interpretation of the Chansons de Geste.* Edinburgh: Edinburgh University Press, 1994.

Davidson, Olga M. "Women's Lamentations as Protest in the 'Ṣāhnāma." In *Women in the Medieval Islamic World*, edited by Gavin R. G. Hambly, 131–46. New York: St. Martin's, 1998.

Dīn, Shaykh Muḥammad Mahdī Shams al-. *The Rising of al-Ḥusayn: Its Impact on the Consciousness of Muslim Society.* Translated by I. K. A. Howard. New York: Methuen, 1985.

Dorey, T. A., ed. *Latin Biography.* New York: Routledge, 1967.

Dobbs-Allsopp, F. W. "Lamentations from Sundry Angles: A Retrospective." In *Lamentations in Ancient and Contemporary Cultural Contexts*, edited by Nancy C. Lee and Carleen Mandolfo, 14–25. Atlanta: Society of Biblical Literature, 2008.

——. *Weep, O Daughter of Zion: A Study of the City-Lament Genre in the Hebrew Bible.* Rome: Editrice Pontificio Istituto Biblico, 1993.

Delaruelle, Étienne. "Essai sur la formation de l'idée de Croisade." *Bulletin de littérature ecclésiastique* 42 (1941): 27–31.

Duparc-Quioc, Suzanne. *Le Cycle de la Croisade.* Paris: Champion, 1955.

———. "Les manuscrits de la Conquête de Jérusalem." *Romania* 65 (1939): 183–203.
Dussaud, René. *Topographie historique de la Syrie antique et médiévale.* Paris: Geuthner, 1927.
Edbury, Peter W., ed. *The Conquest of Jerusalem and the Third Crusade.* Aldershot, England: Ashgate, 1998.
———. *Crusade and Settlement.* Cardiff, Wales: University College Cardiff Press, 1985.
Elad, Amikam. *Medieval Jerusalem and Islamic Worship: Holy Places, Ceremonies, Pilgrimage.* Leiden: Brill, 1995.
El Cheikh, Nadia Maria. "The Gendering of Death in *Kitab al-ʿIqd al-Farid.*" *Al-Qantara* 31 (2010): 411–36.
———. *Women, Islam, and Abbasid Identity.* Cambridge, MA: Harvard University Press, 2015.
Elinson, Alexander. *Looking Back at al-Andalus: The Poetics of Loss and Nostalgia in Medieval Arabic and Hebrew Literature.* Brill Studies in Middle Eastern Literatures 34. Leiden: Brill, 2009.
———. "Loss Written in Stone: Ibn Shuhayd's *Ritha*ʾ for Cordoba and Its Place in the Arabic Elegiac Tradition." In *Transforming Loss into Beauty: Essays on Arabic Literature and Culture in Honor of Magsa al-Nowaihi*, edited by Marlé Hammond and Dana Sajdi, 79–114. Cairo: American University of Cairo Press, 2008.
———. "Tears Shed over the Poetic Past: The Prosification of the *Rithā*ʾ *al-Mudun* in al-Saraquṣṭī's *Maqāma Qayrawāniyya.*" *Journal of Arabic Literature* 36, no. 1 (2005): 1–27.
Endress, Gerhard. *Islam: An Historical Introduction.* 2nd ed. New York: Columbia University Press, 2002.
Englisch, Brigitte. *Ordo orbis terrae: Die Weltsicht in den Mappae mundi des frühen und hohen Mittelalters.* Berlin: Akademie Verlag, 2002.
The Epic of Gilgamesh. Translated by Andrew George. London: Penguin, 1999.
Erdmann, Carl. *Die Entstehung des Kreuzzugsgedankens.* Stuttgart: Kohlhammer, 1955.
Ferris, Paul Wayne, Jr. *The Genre of the Communal Lament in the Bible and the Ancient Near East.* Atlanta: Scholars Press, 1992.
Fishbein, Michael, trans. *The War between Brothers.* Vol. 31 of *The History of al-Ṭabarī.* Albany: State University of New York Press, 1985.
Flanagan, James W. "Mapping the Biblical World: Perceptions of Space in Ancient Southwestern Asia." In *Mappa Mundi: Mapping Culture/Mapping the World*, edited by Jacqueline Murray, 1–18. Windsor, ON: Humanities Research Group at the University of Windsor, 2001.
Flori, Jean. *Richard Cœur de Lion: le roi-chevalier.* Paris: Payot et Rivages, 1999.
Folda, Jaroslav. *The Art of the Crusaders in the Holy Land, 1099–1187.* Cambridge: Cambridge University Press, 1995.
———. *Crusader Art in the Holy Land: From the Third Crusade to the Fall of Acre, 1187–1291.* Cambridge: Cambridge University Press, 2005.
Foley, Helene. *Female Acts in Greek Tragedy.* Princeton, NJ: Princeton University Press, 2001.
———. "The Politics of Lamentation." In *Tragedy, Comedy, and the Polis: Papers from the Greek Drama Conference*, edited by A. Sommerstein, S. Halliwell, J. Henderson, and B. Zimmerman, 101–43. Bari, Italy: Levante Editori, 1993.

Fowler, Alistair. *Kinds of Literature: Introduction to the Theory of Genre and Mode.* Cambridge, MA: Harvard University Press, 1982.

France, John. *The Crusades and Their Expansion of Latin Christendom, 1000–1714.* Abingdon, England: Routledge, 2005.

——. "The Use of the Anonymous *Gesta Francorum* in the Early Twelfth-Century Sources of the First Crusade." In *From Clermont to Jerusalem: The Crusades and Crusader Societies 1095–1500*, edited by Alan V. Murray, 29–42. Turnhout, Belgium: Brepols, 1998.

France, John, and William G. Zajak, eds. *The Crusades and Their Sources: Essays Presented to Bernard Hamilton.* Aldershot, England: Ashgate, 1998.

Franco, Carlo. "Aelius Aristides and Rhodes: Concord and Consolation." In *Aelius Aristides: Between Greece, Rome, and the Gods*, edited by William Harris and Brooke Holmes, 217–50. Leiden: Brill, 2008.

Frazee, Charles A. "The Christian Church in Cilician Armenia: Its Relations with Rome and Constantinople to 1198." *Church History* 45, no. 2 (1976): 166–84.

Frolow, H. *La relique de la Vraie Croix. Recherches sur le développement d'un culte.* Paris: Institut d'Études Byzantines, 1961.

Frymer-Kensky, Tivka. *In the Wake of the Goddess: Women, Culture, and the Biblical Transformation of the Pagan Myth.* New York: Ballantine, 1992.

Gabrieli, Francesco. *Arab Historians of the Crusades.* Berkeley: University of California Press, 1969.

Galambush, Julie. *Jerusalem in the Book of Ezekiel: The City as Yahweh's Wife.* Atlanta: Scholars Press, 1992.

Galichian, Rouben. *Historical Maps of Armenia: the Cartographic Heritage.* London: Taurus, 2004.

Garsoïan, Nina. *L'église arménienne et le grand schisme d'orient.* Leuven, Belgium: Peeters, 1999.

Garulo, Teresa. "La nostalgia de al-Andalus. Génesis de un tema literario." *Qurtuba* 3 (1998): 47–63.

Gervers, Michael. *Tolerance and Intolerance: Social Conflict in the Age of the Crusades.* Syracuse, NY: Syracuse University Press, 2001.

Ghazarian, Jacob G. *Armenian Kingdom of Cilicia during the Crusades: Integration of Cilician Armenia with the Latins, 1080–1393.* Richmond, England: Curzon, 2000.

Gilchrist, John. "The First Crusade and the Idea of Crusading by Jonathan Riley-Smith" (review) *Speculum* 63, no. 3 (1988): 14–17.

Goitein, S. D. *Studies in Islamic History and Institutions.* Leiden: Brill, 1968.

Gottschalk, Hans L. *Al-Malik al-Kāmil von Egypten und seine Zeit.* Wiesbaden: Otto Harrassowitz, 1958.

Grabar, Oleg. "The Umayyad Dome of the Rock in Jerusalem." *Ars Orientalis* 3 (1959): 33–62.

Gregory the Great. *Morals on the Book of Job.* Vols. 1–3. Library of Fathers of the Holy Catholic Church. Oxford: Parker, 1844–50.

Grigor Tłay. *Grigor Tłay: Panastełzutyunner ev Boemner*, edited by A. Š. Mnac'akanyan. Erevan: Armenian SAH GA, 1972.

Grunebaum, Gustave E. von "Aspects of Arabic Urban Literature Mostly in the Ninth and Tenth Centuries." *Al-Andalus* 20 (1955): 259–81.

———. "The Sacred Character of Islamic Cities." In *Islam and Medieval Hellenism: Social and Cultural Perspectives*, edited by Dunning S. Wilson, 25–37. London: Variorum Reprints, 1976.

Guénée, Bernard. *Histoire et culture historique dans l'Occident médiéval.* Paris: Aubler Montaigne, 1980.

Guibert de Nogent. *Gesta Dei per Francos. Geste de Dieu par les francs. Histoire de la première croisade.* Edited and translated by Monique-Cécile Garand. Turnhout, Belgium: Brepols, 1998.

Guillaume, A., trans. *The Life of Muhammad: A Translation of Ishaq's "Sirat Rasul Allah."* Oxford: Oxford University Press, 1955.

Hacikyan, Agop J., Gabriel Basmajian, Edward S. Franchuk, and Nourhan Ouzounian, eds. and trans. *From the Sixth to the Eighteenth Century.* Vol. 2 of *The Heritage of Armenian Literature.* Detroit: Wayne State University Press, 2002.

Hagenmeyer, Heinrich. *Historia hierosolymitana (1095–1127); mit Erläuterungen und einem Anhange herausgegeben.* Heidelberg: Winters, 1913.

———. *Epistulae et chartae ad historiam primi belli sacri spectantes quae supersunt aevo aequales ac genvinae. Die Kreuzzugsbriefe aus den Jahren 1088–1100.* Innsbruck: Verlag der Wagnershen Universitäts-Buchhandlung, 1901.

Halevi, Leor. "Wailing for the Dead: The Role of Women in Early Islamic Funerals." *Past and Present* 183 (2004): 3–39.

Hallo, William W. *Origins: The Ancient Near Eastern Background of Some Modern Western Institutions.* Leiden: Brill, 1996.

Hamdar, Abir. "Jihad of Words: Gender and Contemporary Karbala Narratives." *Yearbook of English Studies* 39, nos. 1–2 (2009): 84–100.

Harley, J. B., and David Woodward, eds. *Cartography in Prehistoric, Ancient, and Medieval Europe and the Mediterranean.* Vol. 1 of *The History of Cartography.* Chicago: University of Chicago Press, 1987.

Harris, Rivkah. *Gender and Aging in Mesopotamia: The Gilgamesh Epic and Other Ancient Literature.* Norman: University of Oklahoma Press, 1992.

Hayes, Dawn Marie. *Body and Sacred Place in Medieval Europe (1100–1389).* New York: Routledge, 2003.

Heffernan, Thomas J., and E. Ann Matter, eds. *The Liturgy of the Medieval Church.* 2nd ed. Kalamazoo, MI: Medieval Institute Publications, 2005.

Hehl, Ernst-Dieter. *Kirche und Krieg im 12 Jahrhundert.* Stuttgart: Hiersemann, 1980.

Henderson, John. *The Medieval World of Isidore of Seville: Truth from Words.* Cambridge: Cambridge University Press, 2007.

Heng, Geraldine. *Empire of Magic: Medieval Romance and the Politics of Cultural Fantasy.* New York: Columbia University Press, 2003.

———. *The Invention of Race in the European Middle Ages.* Cambridge: Cambridge University Press, 2018.

Heskett, Randall. *Reading the Book of Isaiah: Destruction and Lament in the Holy Cities.* New York: Palgrave Macmillan, 2011.

Hewsen, Robert H. *Armenia: A Historical Atlas.* Chicago: University of Chicago Press, 2001.

——. "The Geography of Armenia." In *The Dynastic Periods: From Antiquity to the Fourteenth Century*, edited by Richard G. Hovannisian, 1–17. Vol. 1 of *The Armenians from Ancient to Modern Times.* New York: St. Martin's, 1997.

Hillenbrand, Carole. *Crusades: Islamic Perspectives.* New York: Routledge, 2000.

——. "The First Crusade: the Muslim Perspective." In *The First Crusade: Origins and Impact*, edited by Jonathan Phillips, 130–41. Manchester, England: Manchester University Press, 1997.

——. *A Muslim Principality in Crusader Times: The Early Artuqid State.* Istanbul: Netherlands Historisch-Archaeologisch Instituut te Istanbul, 1990.

——. *Turkish Myth and Muslim Symbol: The Battle of Manzikert.* Edinburgh: Edinburgh University Press, 2007.

Hindley, Geoffrey. *The Crusades: A History of Armed Pilgrimage and Holy War.* London: Constable, 2003.

——. *The Crusades: Islam and Christianity in the Struggle for World Supremacy.* New York: Carroll and Graf, 2004.

Hintlian, Kevork. *History of Armenians in the Holy Land.* Jerusalem: St. James, 1976.

Holst-Warhaft, Gail. *Dangerous Voices: Women's Laments and Greek Literature.* London: Routledge, 1992.

Holt, P. M. *The Age of the Crusades: The Near East from the Eleventh Century to 1517.* London: Longman, 1986.

——. *The Crusader States and Their Neighbours: 1098–1291.* London: Pearson, 2004.

Honko, Lauri, and Vilmos Voigt, eds. *Genre, Structure, and Reproduction in Oral Literature.* Budapest: Akadémiai Kiadó, 1980.

Horden, Peregrine, and Sharon Kinoshita, eds. *A Companion to Mediterranean History.* Malden, MA: Blackwell, 2014.

Horden, Peregrine, and Nicholas Purcell, *The Corrupting Sea: The Study of Mediterranean History.* Malden, MA: Blackwell, 2000.

Housley, Norman. *Contesting the Crusades.* Malden, MA: Blackwell, 2006.

Huart, Clément. *A History of Arabic Literature.* New York: Appleton, 1903.

Hughes, Richard A. *Lament, Death, and Destiny.* Studies in Biblical Literature 68. New York: Lang, 2004.

Hunt, E. D. *Holy Land Pilgrimage in the Later Roman Empire.* Oxford: Oxford University Press, 1982.

Husain, Adnan A. and K. E. Fleming, eds. *A Faithful Sea: The Religious Cultures of the Mediterranean, 1200–1700.* Oxford: Oneworld, 2007.

Husain, Adnan, and Margaret Aziza Pappano, "The One Kingdom Solution?: Diplomacy, Marriage, and Sovereignty in the Third Crusade." In *Cosmopolitanism and the Middle Ages*, edited by John M. Ganim and Shayne Aaron Legassie, 121–40. New York: Palgrave Macmillan, 2013.

Ḥuwwar, Muḥammad Ibrāhīm. *al-Ḥanīn ilā al-waṭan fī al-adab al-ʿarabī ḥattā nihāyat al-ʿaṣr al-umawī.* Cairo: Dār nahḍat Miṣr liṭ-ṭabʿ wa-al-nashr, 1973.

Hyder, Syed Akbar. *Reliving Karbala: Martyrdom in South Asian Memory.* Oxford: Oxford University Press, 2008.

Inglisian, V. "Chalkedon und die armenische Kirche." In *Das Konzil von Chalkedon*, vol. 2, edited by A. Grillmeier and H. Bacht, 361–417. Würzburg, West Germany: Echter Verlag, 1953.

Jacobi, Renate. *Studien zur Poetik der altarabischen Qaṣide.* Wiesbaden: Steiner, 1971.

Join-Lambert, Michel. *Jerusalem.* London: Elek, 1958.

Jubb, Margaret. *The Legend of Saladin in Western Literature and Historiography.* Studies in Comparative Literature 34. Lewiston, NY: Mellen, 2000.

Katzir, Y. "The Patriarch of Jerusalem, Primate of the Latin Kingdom." In *Crusade and Settlement*, edited by Peter W. Edbury, 169–75. Cardiff, Wales: University College Cardiff Press, 1985.

——. "The Vicissitudes of the True Cross of the Crusaders." In *The Crusaders in Their Kingdom: 1095–1291*, edited by B. Z. Kezar, 243–253. Jerusalem: Yad Izhak Ben-Zvi, 1987.

Kedar, Benjamin Z. *The Franks in the Levant: 11th to 14th Centuries.* Aldershot, England: Ashgate, 1993.

——. *The Horns of Ḥaṭṭīn.* Jerusalem: Yad Izhak Ben-Zvi, 1992; London: Variorum, 1992.

——. "Intellectual Activities in a Holy City: Jerusalem in the Twelfth Century." In *Sacred Space: Shrine, City, Land*, edited by Benjamin Z. Kedar and R. J. Zwi Werblowsky, 127–39. New York: New York University Press, 1998.

——. "The Jerusalem Massacre of July 1099 in the Western Historiography of the Crusades." In *Crusades*, vol. 3, edited by Benjamin Z. Kedar, Jonathan Riley-Smith, Helen Nicholson, and Michael Evans, 15–75. New York: Routledge, 2004.

Kennedy, Hugh. *The Prophet and the Age of the Caliphates.* London: Longman, 2004.

Kēōkʿčian, Vahram. *Hay Erusałemə dareru mēǰēn.* Jerusalem: Armenian Convent Printing Press, 1965.

Khallikān, Aḥmad Ibn. *Wafayāt al-Aʿyān wa-anbāʾ abnāʾ al-zamān/Ibn Khallikān's Biographical Dictionary.* Vol. 3, translated by MacGuckin de Slane. Paris: Oriental Translation Fund of Great Britain and Ireland, 1868.

Kinoshita, Sharon. *Medieval Boundaries: Rethinking Difference in Old French Literature.* Philadelphia: University of Pennsylvania Press, 2013.

——. "Medieval Mediterranean Literature." *PMLA* 124, no. 2 (2009): 600–608.

Klosterman, Erich. *Die griechischen christlichen Schriftsteller der ersten Jahrhunderte.* Vol. 6. Leipzig: Heinriche, 1901.

Konrad, R. "Das himmlische und das irdische Jerusalem im mittelalterlichen Denken." In *Speculum historiale, Festschrift J. Spörl*, edited by C. Bauer, 523–40. Munich, 1965.

Kötting, Bernhard. *Peregrinatio religiosa: Wallfahrten in der Antike und das Pilgerwesen in der alten Kirche.* Münster, West Germany: Regensberg, 1950.

Kramer, Samuel Noah. *Lamentation over the Destruction of Ur.* Assyriological Studies 12. Chicago: Oriental Institute of the University of Chicago, 1940.

——. "The Weeping Goddess: Sumerian Prototypes of the *Mater Dolorosa.*" *Biblical Archaeologist* 46, no. 2 (1983): 69–80.

Krecher, J. "Zum Emesal-Dialekt des Sumerischen." In *Dietz, Adam Falkenstein zum 17: September 1966*, edited by E. Otto, 87–110. Wiesbaden: Heidelberger Studien zum alten Orient, 1967.

Krey, A. C. *The First Crusade: Accounts of Eyewitnesses and Participants.* Princeton, NJ: Princeton University Press, 1921.

———. "A Neglected Passage in the *Gesta* and Its Bearing on the Literature of the First Crusade." In *The Crusades and Other Historical Essays; Presented to D. C. Munro by His Former Students*, edited by Louis John Paetow, 57–78. New York: Ayer, 1928.

Kselman, John S. "Sinai and Zion in Psalm 93." In *David and Zion: Biblical Studies in Honor of J. J. M. Roberts*, edited by Bernard F. Batto and Kathryn L. Roberts, 69–76. Winona Lake, IN: Eisenbrauns, 2004.

Kühnel, Bianca. *Crusader Art of the Twelfth Century: A Geographical, an Historical, or an Art Historical Notion?* Berlin: Mann Verlag, 1994.

Lambros, Spyridon. *Μιχαήλ 'Ακομινάτου τοῦ Χωνιάτου τά σωζόμενα.* 1879–80. Reprint, Groningen, Netherlands: Bouma's Beckhuis N. V., 1968.

Lane-Poole, S. *A History of Egypt in the Middle Ages.* 2nd. ed. London: Methuen, 1914.

Langdon, Stephen. *Babylonian Liturgies.* Paris: Geuthner, 1913.

———. *Sumerian and Babylonian Psalms.* Paris: Geuthner, 1909.

Lapidus, Ira M. *A History of Islamic Societies.* Cambridge: Cambridge University Press, 2002.

Lassner, Jacob. *The Shaping of 'Abbāsid Rule.* Princeton, NJ: Princeton University Press, 1980.

Lászlo, Juhász. "Planctus destructionis regni Hungariae per Tartaros." In *Scriptores Rerum Hungaricarum*, vol. 2, edited by Imre Szentpétery, 589–98. Budapest: Academia Litter. Hungarica, 1937.

Lazarus-Yafeh, Hava. "The Sanctity of Jerusalem in Islam." In *Jerusalem*, edited by John M. Oesterreicher and Anne Sinai, 216–18. New York: Day, 1974.

Lee, Nancy C. "The Singers of Lamentations: (A)scribing (De)claiming Poets and Prophets." In *Lamentations in Ancient and Contemporary Cultural Contexts*, edited by Nancy C. Lee and Carleen Mandolfo, 33–46. Atlanta: Society of Biblical Literature, 2008.

———. *The Singers of Lamentations: Cities under Siege, from Ur to Jerusalem to Sarajevo.* Leiden: Brill, 2002.

Lefebvre, Henri. *La présence et l'absence: contribution à la théorie des représentations.* Paris: Casterman, 1980.

———. *La production de l'espace.* Paris: Anthropos, 2000.

Le Goff, Jacques. "Warriors and Conquering Bourgeois: The Image of the City in Twelfth-Century French Literature." In *The Medieval Imagination*, translated by Arthur Goldhammer, 151–76. Chicago: University of Chicago Press, 1988.

Lehtonen, Tuomas M. S., and Kurt Villads Jensen, eds. *Medieval History Writing and Crusading Ideology.* Helsinki: Finnish Literature Society, 2005.

Le Strange, Guy. *Palestine under the Moslems.* London, 1890.

Levenson, J. D. *Sinai and Zion: An Entry into the Jewish Bible.* San Francisco: Harper and Row, 1985.

Levine, Lee L., ed. *Jerusalem: Its Sanctity and Centrality to Judaism, Christianity, and Islam.* New York: Continuum, 1999.

Ligato, Guiseppe. "The Political Meanings of the Relic of the Holy Cross among the Crusaders and in the Latin Kingdom of Jerusalem: An Example of 1185." In *Autour de la Première Croisade*, edited by Michel Balard, 315–30. Paris: Publications de la Sorbonne, 1996.

Lloyd, Simon. *English Society and the Crusades, 1216–1307.* Oxford: Oxford University Press, 1988.

Lock, Peter. *The Routledge Companion to the Crusades.* London: Routledge, 2006.

Loraux, Nicole. *Mothers in Mourning.* Translated by Corinne Pache. Ithaca, NY: Cornell University Press, 1998.

——. *The Mourning Voice: An Essay on Greek Tragedy.* Ithaca, NY: Cornell University Press, 2002.

Maalouf, Amin. *The Crusades through Arab Eyes.* New York: Schocken, 1984.

MacEvitt, Christopher. *The Crusades and the Christian World of the East: Rough Tolerance.* Philadelphia: University of Pennsylvania Press, 2007.

Mālik. *Al-Muwatta of Imam Malik ibn Anas: The First Formulation of Islamic Law.* Translated by Aisha Abdurrahman Bewley. London: Madinah, 1989.

Mallette, Karla. *European Modernity and the Arab Mediterranean.* Philadelphia: University of Pennsylvania Press, 2010.

——. *The Kingdom of Sicily, 1100–1250: A Literary History.* Philadelphia: University of Pennsylvania Press, 2005.

Manion, Lee. *Narrating the Crusades: Loss and Recovery in Medieval and Early Modern English Literature.* Cambridge: Cambridge University Press, 2014.

Marcombe, David. *Leper Knights: The Order of St. Lazarus of Jerusalem in England, c. 1150–1544.* New York: Boydell, 2003.

Markowski, Michael. "*Crucesignatus*: Its Origins and Early Usage." *Journal of Medieval History* 10 (1984): 157–65.

May, Herbert G. "Cosmological Reference in the Qumran Doctrine of the Two Spirits and the Old Testament Imagery." *Journal of Biblical Literature* 82 (1963): 1–14.

Mayer, Hans Eberhard. *Das Itinerarium peregrinorum: eine zeitgenössische englische Chronik zum dritten Kreuzzug in ursprünglicher Gestalt.* Stuttgart: Hiersemann, 1962.

McClung, William Alexander. *The Architecture of Paradise: Survivals of Eden and Jerusalem.* Berkeley: University of California Press, 1983.

McClure, Laura. *Spoken Like a Women: Speech and Gender in Athenian Drama.* Princeton, NJ: Princeton University Press, 1999.

McDonald, Nicola. *Pulp Fictions of Medieval England: Essays in Popular Romance.* Manchester, England: Manchester University Press, 2004.

Meisami, Julie Scott. "Between Arabia and al-Andalus: Nostalgia as an Arabic Poetic Genre." In *Poetica medieval tra Oriente e Occidente.* Rome: Carroci editore, 2003.

Melville, Charles, and Ahmad Ubaydli, eds. *Arabic Sources (711–1501).* Vol. 3 of *Christians and Moors in Spain.* Warminster, England: Aris and Phillips, 1992.

Metlitzki, Dorothee. *The Matter of Araby in Medieval England.* New Haven, CT: Yale University Press, 1977.

Michalowski, Piotr. "Orality and Literacy and Early Mesopotamian Literature." In *Mesopotamian Epic Literature: Oral or Aural?*, edited by Marianne E. Vogelzang and Herman L. J. Vanstiphout, 227–45. Lewiston, NY: Mellen, 1992.

Monroe, James T. *Hispano-Arabic Poetry.* Berkeley: University of California Press, 1974.

Morrow, William. *Protest against God: The Eclipse of a Biblical Tradition*. Hebrew Bible Monographs 4. Sheffield, England: Sheffield Phoenix, 2006.

——. "The Revival of Lament in Medieval *Piyyuṭîm*." In *Lamentations in Ancient and Contemporary Contexts*, edited by Nancy C. Lee and Carleen Mandolfo, 139–50. Atlanta: Society of Biblical Literature, 2008.

Muḥammad, ʿAbd al-Raḥmān Ḥusayn. *Rithāʾ al-mudun wa-al-mamālik al-zāʾila*. Cairo: Maṭbaʿat al-Jabalāwī, 1983.

Munro, Dana Carleton. "The Speech of Pope Urban II at Claremont, 1095." *American Historical Review* 11, no. 2 (1906): 231–42.

Murray, Alan V. "'Mighty against the Enemies of Christ': The Relic of the True Cross in the Armies of the Kingdom of Jerusalem." In *The Crusades and Their Sources: Essays Presented to Bernard Hamilton*, edited by John France and William G. Zajak, 217–328. Aldershot, England: Ashgate, 1998.

Murray, Penelope. "Tragedy, Women, and the Family in Plato's *Republic*." In *Plato and the Poets*, edited by Pierre Destrée and Fritz-Gregor Herrmann, 175–93. Leiden: Brill, 2011.

Nichols, Stephen G. "Poetic Places and Imaginary Spaces: Anthropology of Space in Crusader Literature." In *Rereading Allegory: Essays in Memory of Daniel Poirion*, edited by Sahar Amer and Noah D. Guynn, 111–33. Yale French Studies 95. New Haven, CT: Yale University Press, 1999.

——. "Urgent Voices: The Vengeance of Images in Medieval Poetry." In *France and the Holy Land: Frankish Culture at the End of the Crusades*, edited by Daniel H. Weiss and Lisa Mahoney, 22–42. Baltimore: Johns Hopkins University Press, 2004.

Nicholson, Helen J. "The Military Orders and the Kings of England in the Twelfth and Thirteenth Centuries." In *From Clermont to Jerusalem: The Crusades and the Crusader Societies, 1095–1500*, edited by Alan V. Murray, 203–18. Turnhout, Belgium: Brepols, 1998.

——. "Women on the Third Crusade." *Journal of Medieval History* 23, no. 4 (1997): 335–49.

Nicholson, Reynold A. *A Literary History of the Arabs*. Cambridge: Cambridge University Press, 1956.

Norgate, Kate. "The 'Itinerarium Peregrinorum' and the 'Song of Ambrose.'" *English Historical Review* 25, no. 99 (1910): 523–47.

Nowaihi, Magda al-. "Elegy and the Confrontation of Death in Arabic Poetry." In *Transforming Loss into Beauty: Essays on Arabic Literature and Culture in Honor of Magda al-Nowaihi*, edited by Marlé Hammond and Dana Sajdi, 3–20. Cairo: American University of Cairo Press, 2008.

Oesterreicher, John M., and Anne Sinai, eds. *Jerusalem*. New York: Day, 1974.

O'Shea, Stephen. *Sea of Faith: Islam and Christianity in the Medieval Mediterranean World*. New York: Walker, 2006.

Ousterhout, Robert, ed. *The Blessings of Pilgrimage*. Urbana: University of Illinois Press, 1990.

Ovhanessian, Armen. *Cilician Armenians and the Crusades*. Detroit: Armenian Cultural Association, 1958.

Parry, Robin A., and Heath A. Thomas, eds. *Great Is Thy Faithfulness? Reading Lamentations as Sacred Scripture.* Eugene, OR: Wipf and Stock, 2011.

Pennington, Kenneth. "The Rite for Taking the Cross in the Twelfth Century." *Traditio* 30 (1974): 429–35.

Petter, Donna Lee. *The Book of Ezekiel and Mesopotamian City Laments.* Orbis Biblicus et Orientalis 246. Göttingen: Vandenhoeck und Ruprecht, 2011.

Petuchowski, Jakob J. *Theology and Poetry: Studies in the Medieval Piyyut.* London: Routledge and Kegan Paul, 1978.

Phillips, Jonathan. *The First Crusade: Origins and Impact.* New York: St. Martin's, 1997.

Pinault, David. "Shia Lamentation Rituals and Reinterpretations of the Doctrine of Intercession: Two Cases from Modern India." *History of Religions* 38, no. 3 (1999): 285–305.

Poiron, Daniel, ed. *Jérusalem, Rome, Constantinople: l'image at le mythe de la ville.* Paris: Presses de l'Université de Paris–Sorbonne, 1986.

Prawer, Joshua. "The Armenians in Jerusalem under the Crusaders." In *Armenian and Biblical Studies*, edited by Michael E. Stone, 222–36. Jerusalem: St. James, 1976.

———. *Histoire du royaume latin de Jérusalem.* 2 vols. Paris: Éditions du Centre National de la Recherche Scientifique, 1969–70.

———. *History of the Jews in the Latin Kingdom of Jerusalem.* Oxford: Oxford University Press, 1998.

———. "Jerusalem in the Christian and Jewish Perspectives of the Early Middle Ages." In *Settimane di studio del centro Italiano di studi sull'alto medioevo. XXVI. Gli Ebrei nell' Alto Medioevo.* Spoleto: Centro italiano di studi sull'alto medioevo, 1980.

———. "The Jerusalem the Crusaders Captured: A Contribution to Medieval Topography of the City." In *Crusade and Settlement: Papers Read at the First Conference of the Society for the Study of the Crusades and the Latin East and Presented to R. C. Smail*, edited by Peter W. Edbury. Cardiff, Wales: University College Cardiff Press, 1985.

———. The Latin Kingdom of Jerusalem: European Colonialism in the Middle Ages. London: Weidenfeld and Nicolson, 1972.

Prawer, Joshua, and Haggai Ben-Shammai, eds. *The History of Jerusalem: The Early Muslim Period, 638–1099.* Jerusalem: Yad Izhak Ben-Zvi, 1996.

Prawer, Joshua, Benjamin Zeev Kedar, Hans Eberhard Mayer, and Raymond Charles Smail, eds. *Outremer: Studies in the History of the Crusading Kingdom of Jerusalem Presented to Joshua Prawer.* Jerusalem: Yad Izhak Ben-Zvi, 1982.

Regan, Geoffrey. *Lionhearts: Saladin and Richard I.* London: Constable, 1998.

———. *Saladin and the Fall of Jerusalem.* London: Croom Helm, 1987.

Riley-Smith, Jonathan, ed. *Atlas of the Crusades.* New York: Facts on File, 1991.

———. *The Crusades: A Short History.* London: Athlone, 1987.

———. *Crusades, Christianity, and Islam.* New York: Columbia University Press, 2008.

———. *Crusades: Idea and Reality, 1095–1274.* London: Arnold, 1981.

———. *The First Crusade and the Idea of Crusading.* Philadelphia: University of Pennsylvania Press, 1986.

———, ed. *Oxford Illustrated History of the Crusades.* Oxford: Oxford University Press, 1997.

———. *What Were the Crusades?* New York: Palgrave Macmillan, 2002.

Robinson, Chase. *'Abd al-Malik*. Oxford: Oxford University Press, 2005.
——. *Islamic Historiography*. Cambridge: Cambridge University Press, 2003.
Rocco, Samuel. *Herod's Judea: A Mediterranean State in the Classical World*. Tübingen, Germany: Mohr Siebeck, 2008.
Rousset, Paul. *Les Origines et les caractères de la première Croisade*. Neuchâtel, Switzerland: La Baconniére, 1945.
Runciman, Steven. *A History of the Crusades*. 3 vols. Cambridge: Cambridge University Press, 1987.
Sackur, Ernst, ed. *Sybillinische Texte und Forschungen*. Halle an der Salle, West Germany: Niemeyer, 1963.
Said, Edward. *Orientalism*. New York: Random House, 1979.
Samet, Nili. *The Lamentation over the Destruction of Ur: A Revised Edition*. Ramat-Gan, Israel: Eisenbrauns, 2010.
Sanjian, Avedis K. *The Armenian Communities in Syria under Ottoman Dominion*. Cambridge, MA: Harvard University Press, 1965.
——. "Step'anos Orbelian's 'Elegy on the Holy Cathedral of Etchmiadzin': Critical Text and Translation." In *Armenian and Biblical Studies*, edited by Michael E. Stone, 237–82. Jerusalem: St. James, 1976.
Sarkissian, Karekin I. *The Council of Chalcedon and the Armenian Church*. Antelius, Lebanon: Armenian Church Prelacy, 1964.
Sawalanianc', Tigran. *Patmutyun Erusałēmi*. Vol. 1. Jerusalem: n.p., 1931.
Schein, Sylvia. "Between Mount Moriah and the Holy Sepulchre. The Changing Traditions of the Temple Mount in the Central Middle Ages." *Traditio* 40 (1984): 175–95.
——. *Gateway to the Heavenly City: Crusader Jerusalem and the Catholic West (1099–1187)*. Aldershot, England: Ashgate, 2005.
Schoell, R., and G. Kroll, eds. *Novellae*. Vol. 3 of *Corpus Iuris Civilis*. Berlin: Apud Weidmannos, 1895.
Segal, C. *Euripides and the Poetics of Sorrow*. Durham, NC: Duke University Press, 1993.
Shaban, M. A. *The 'Abbāsid Revolution*. Cambridge: Cambridge University Press, 1970.
Shubbar, Jawād. *Adab al-Ṭaff*. Beirut: Mu'assasat al-A'lamī lil-maṭbū'āt, 1969.
Sicard, Damien. *La liturgie de la mort dans l'église Latine: des origines à la Réforme Carolingienne*. Münster, West Germany: Aschendorff, 1978.
Sinclair, Andrew. *Jerusalem: The Endless Crusade*. New York: Century, 1995.
Sinjilawi, Ibrahim al-. "The Lament for Fallen Cities: A Study of the Development of the Elegiac Genre in Classical Arabic Poetry." PhD diss., University of Chicago, 1983.
Sivan, Emmanuel. "The Beginnings of the Faḍā'il al-Quds literature." *Israel Oriental Studies* 1 (1971): 263–71.
——. "Islam and the Crusaders: Antagonism, Polemics, Dialogue." In *Religionsgespräche in Mittelalter*, edited by Bernard Lewis and Friedrich Niewöhner, 207–15. Wolfenbüttel, Germany: Wolfenbütteler Mittelalter-Studein, 1992.
——. La génèse de la contre-croisade: "Un traité Damasquin du début du XIIe siècle." *Journal Asiatique* 254 (1966): 206–22.
——. "Le caractère de Jérusalem dans l'Islam aux XIIe-XIIIe siècles." *Studia Islamica* 27 (1976): 149–82.
——. *L'Islam et la Croisade*. Paris: Librairie d'Amérique et d'Orient, 1968.

Smail, R. C. *Crusading Warfare, 1097–1193.* Cambridge: Cambridge University Press, 1956.

Son, Kiwoong. *Zion Symbolism in Hebrews.* Waynesboro, GA: Paternoster, 2005.

Stetkevych, Jaroslav. *The Zephyrs of Najd: The Poetics of Nostalgia in Classical Arabic Nasib.* Chicago: University of Chicago Press, 1993.

Stetkevych, Suzanne Pinckney. "Abbasid Panegyric and the Poetics of Political Allegiance: Two Poems of al-Mutanabbī on Kāfūr." In *Qasida Poetry in Islamic Asia and Africa*, edited by Stefan Sperl and Christopher Shackle, 35–63. Leiden: Brill, 1996.

——. "Archetype and Attribution in Early Arabic Poetry: al-Shanfara and the Lamiyyat al-Arab, *International Journal of Middle East Studies* 18, no. 3 (1986): 361–90.

——. *The Formation of the Classical Islamic World.* Early Islamic Poetry and Poetics 37. Burlington, VT: Ashgate, 2009.

——. "From *Jāhiliyyah* to *Badīʿiyyah*: Orality, Literacy, and the Transformation of Rhetoric in Arabic Poetry." *Oral Tradition* 25, no. 1 (2010): 211–30.

——. *The Mute Immortals Speak: Pre-Islamic Poetry and the Poetics of Ritual.* Ithaca, NY: Cornell University Press, 2010.

Stowe, David W. "History, Memory, and Forgetting in Psalm 137." In *The Bible in the Public Square: Its Enduring Influence in American Life*, edited by Mark A. Chancey, Carol Meyers, and Eric M. Meyers, 137–58. Society of Biblical Literature 27. Atlanta: SBL Press, 2014.

Sumption, Jonathan. *Pilgrimage: An Image of Medieval Religion.* London: Faber and Faber, 1975.

Suter, Ann, ed. "Lament in Euripides' *Trojan Women.*" *Mnemosyne*, ser. 4, 56, no. 1 (2003): 1–28.

——. *Lament: Studies in the Ancient Mediterranean and Beyond.* New York: Cambridge University Press, 2008.

Suter, Ann, Mary R. Bachvarova, and Dorota Dutsch, eds. *The Fall of Cities in the Mediterranean: Commemoration in Literature, Folk-Song, and Liturgy.* Cambridge: Cambridge University Press, 2016.

Tan, Kim Huat. *The Zion Traditions and the Aims of Jesus.* Cambridge: Cambridge University Press, 1997.

Thomson, Rodney M. *William of Malmesbury.* Woodbridge, England: Boydell, 1987.

Thomson, Robert W. *A Bibliography of Classical Armenian Literature to 1500 AD.* Corpus Christianorum. Turnhout, Belgium: Brepols, 1995.

——. "Supplement to the *Bibliography of Classical Armenian Literature to 1500 AD:* Publications 1993–2005." *Le Muséon* 120 (2007): 198–99.

Thorp, Nigel R., ed. *La Chanson de Jérusalem.* Vol. 6 of *La Chanson de Jérusalem: The Old French Crusade Cycle.* Tuscaloosa: University of Alabama Press, 1992.

Tolan, John V. *Islam in the Medieval European Imagination.* New York: Columbia University Press, 2002.

——. *Medieval Christian Perceptions of Islam.* New York: Garland, 1996.

Trigg, Joseph W. *Origen.* London: Routledge, 1998.

Trotter, D. A. *Medieval French Literature and the Crusades.* Geneva: Librairie Droz, 1988.

Turner, Harold W. *From Temple to Meeting House: The Phenomenology and Theology of Places of Worship.* Amsterdam: Mouton, 1979.

Turner, Victor, and Edith Turner. *Image and Pilgrimage in Christian Culture: Anthropological Perspective.* New York: Columbia University Press, 1978.

Tyerman, Christopher. *England and the Crusades, 1095–1588.* Chicago: University of Chicago Press, 1998.

——. *Fighting Christendom: Holy War and the Crusades.* Oxford: Oxford University Press, 2004.

——. *God's War: A New History of the Crusades.* Boston: Harvard University Press, 2006.

——. *The Invention of the Crusades.* Basingstoke, Hampshire : Macmillan Press, 1998.

——. "What the Crusades Meant to Europe." In *The Medieval World*, eds. Peter Linehan and Janet L. Nelson, 131–46. New York: Routledge, 2001.

Tyrer, John Walton. *Historical Survey of Holy Weeks, Its Services and Ceremonial.* London: Oxford University Press, 1932.

Van Ess, Josef. *Anfänge muslimischer Theologie: Zwei antiqadaritische Traktate aus dem ersten Jahrhundert der Higra.* Beirut: Orient-Institut der Deutschen Morgenländischen Gesellschaft, 1977.

——. *The Flowering of Muslim Theology.* Translated by Jane Marie Todd. Cambridge, MA: Harvard University Press, 2006.

——. *Zwischen Hadit und Theologie: Studien zum Entstehen prädestinatianischer Überlieferung.* Berlin: De Gruyter, 1974.

Van Lint, Theo Maarten. "Grigor Narekac'i's *Tal Yarut'ean*: The Throne Vision of Ezekiel in Armenian Art and Literature." In *Apocryphes arménians: Transmission, traduction, creation, iconographie. Actes du colloque international sur la literature apocryphe en langue arménienne, Genève, 18–20 septembre 1997*, edited by Valentina Calzolari Bouvier, Jean-Daniel Kaestli, and Bernard Outtier, 105–27. Lausanne: Éditions du Zèbre, 1999.

——. "The Poem of Lamentation over the Capture of Jerusalem Written in 1189 by Grigor Tłay Catholicos of All Armenians." In *The Armenians in Jerusalem and the Holy Land*, edited by Michael E. Stone, Roberta R. Ervine, and Nira Stone, 121–43. Hebrew University Armenian Studies 4. Leuven, Belgium: Peeters, 2002.

——. "Seeking Meaning in Catastrophe: Nersēs Šnorhali's *Lament on Edessa.*" In *East and West in the Crusader States: Context—Contacts—Confrontations*, edited by Krijnie Ciggaar and Herman Teule, 49–105. Leuven, Belgium: Peeters, 1999.

Van Oort, Johannes. *Jeruzalem en Babylon: een onderzoek van Augustinus' De stad van God en de bronnen van zijn leer der twee steden.* The Hague: Boekencentrum, 1986.

Van Wees, H. "A Brief History of Tears: Gender Differentiation in Archaic Greece." In *When Men Were Men: Masculinity, Power and Identity in Classical Antiquity*, edited by Lin Foxhall and John Salmon, 10–53. London: Routledge, 1998.

Villey, Michel. *La Croisade: Essai sur la formation d'une théorie juridique.* Paris: Vrin, 1942.

Vincent, Hugues, and F.-M. Abel. *Jérusalem Nouvelle.* Paris: Gabalda, 1914.

Walker, P. W. L. *Holy City, Holy Places? Christian Attitudes to the Holy Land in the Fourth Century.* Oxford: Clarendon, 1990.

Watt, W. M. *Muhammad at Medina.* Oxford: Oxford University Press, 1956.

Weiss, Daniel H., and Lisa Mahoney, eds. *France and the Holy Land: Frankish Culture at the End of the Crusades.* Baltimore: Johns Hopkins University Press, 2004.

Weit, Gaston. *Baghdad: Metropolis of the Abbasid Caliphate.* Translated by Seymour Feiler. Norman: University of Oklahoma Press, 1971.

Werlblowsky, R. J. Zwi. "Introduction: Mindscape and Landscape." In *Sacred Space: Shrine, City, Land,* edited by Benjamin Z. Kedar and R. J. Zwi Werblowsky, 9–17. New York: New York University Press, 1998.

Wesnick, A. J. "The Ideas of the Western Semites concerning the Navel of the Earth," in *Verhandelingen der Koninklijke Akademie van Wetenschappen te Amsterdam: Afdeeling Letterkunde,* n.s. 17, no. 1. Amsterdam: Müller, 1916.

Wheeler, Brannon M. "'The Land in Which You Have Lived': Inheritance of the Promised Land in Classical Islamic Exegesis." In *Studies in Jewish Civilization: Visions of Israel from Biblical to Modern Times,* vol. 11, edited by Leonard J. Greenspoon and Ronald A. Simkins, 48–83. Omaha, NE: Creighton University Press, 2001.

Wilkinson, John. *Jerusalem Pilgrims: Before the Crusades.* Jerusalem: Ariel, 1977.

Wilson, Dunning S., ed. *Islam and Medieval Hellenism: Social and Cultural Perspectives.* London: Variorum Reprints, 1976.

Winkler, Alexandre. *Le tropisme de Jérusalem dans la prose et la poésie: (XIIe–XIVe siécle); essai sur la littérature des croisades.* Paris: Champion, 2006.

Wirth, Eugen. *Syrien: eine geographische Landeskunde.* Darmstadt, West Germany: Wissenschaftliche Buchgesellschaft, 1971.

Witzel, H.-J. "Le problème de l'auteur des Gesta Francorum et aliorum Hierosolymitanorum." *Moyen Âge* 61 (1955): 319–28.

Wolska, Wanda. *La Topographie chrétienne de Cosmas Indicopleustès: Théologie et science au VIe siècle.* Bibliothèque Byzantine, Etudes 3. Paris: Éditions du Cerf, 1962.

Wood, John C. *When Men Are Women: Manhood among Gabra Nomads of East Africa.* Madison: University of Wisconsin Press, 1999.

Xač'atryan, Poghos. *Hay mijnadaryan patmakan ołber.* Erevan: Armenian SAH GA, 1972.

Yeager, Suzanne. *Jerusalem in Medieval Narrative.* Cambridge: Cambridge University Press, 2011.

Zambaur, E. de. *Manuel de Généalogie et de Chronologie pour l'Histoire de l'Islam.* Hanover, Germany: Lafaire, 1927.

Zayyāt, ʿAbd Allāh Muḥammad al-. *Rithāʾ al-mudun fī al-shiʿr al-Andalusī.* Benghazi: Jāmiʿat Qāryūnus, 1990.

Zeitlin, Froma. *Playing the Other: Gender and Society in Classical Greek Literature.* Chicago: University of Chicago Press, 1996.

Zimmern, Heinrich. *Babylonische hymnen und gebete.* Leipzig J. C. Hinrichs, 1911.

Index